Mastering and Using
Microsoft Excel 5.0
Windows 3.1

H. Albert Napier
Philip J. Judd

CTI

A DIVISION OF COURSE TECHNOLOGY
ONE MAIN STREET, CAMBRIDGE, MA 02142

an International Thomson Publishing company I(T)P

Cambridge • Albany • Bonn • Boston • Cincinnati • London • Madrid • Melbourne
Mexico City • New York • Paris • San Francisco • Singapore • Tokyo • Toronto • Washington

Mastering and Using Microsoft Excel 5.0, Windows 3.1 is published by CTI.

Managing Editor	Wendy Gordon
Production Manager	Patty Stephan
Production Editor	Jean Bermingham
Copy Editor	Carmen Wheatcroft
Text Designer	Gex, Inc.
Cover Designer	Stuart Cuttriss, Cuttriss and Hambleton

© 1996 by CTI.
A Division of Course Technology – I(T)P

For more information contact:

Course Technology
One Main Street
Cambridge, MA 02142

International Thomson Editores
Campos Eliseos 385, Piso 7
Col. Polanco
11560 Mexico D.F. Mexico

International Thomson Publishing Europe
Berkshire House 168-173
High Holborn
London WCIV 7AA
England

International Thomson Publishing GmbH
Kônigswinterer Strasse 418
53227 Bonn
Germany

Thomas Nelson Australia
102 Dodds Street
South Melbourne, 3205
Victoria, Australia

International Thomson Publishing Asia
211 Henderson Road
#05-10 Henderson Building
Singapore 0315

Nelson Canada
1120 Birchmount Road
Scarborough, Ontario
Canada M1K 5G4

International Thomson Publishing Japan
Hirakawacho Kyowa Building, 3F
2-2-1 Hirakawacho
Chiyoda-ku, Tokyo 102
Japan

All rights reserved. This publication is protected by federal copyright law. No part of this publication may be reproduced, stored in a retrieval system, or transmitted in any form or by any means, electronic, mechanical, photocopying, recording, or otherwise, or be used to make a derivative work (such as translation or adaptation), without prior permission in writing from Course Technology.

Trademarks
Course Technology and the open book logo are registered trademarks of Course Technology.
I(T)P The ITP logo is a trademark under license.
Custom Edition is a registered trademark of International Thomson Publishing, Inc.
Microsoft and Windows are registered trademarks of Microsoft Corporation.

Some of the product names and company names used in this book have been used for identification purposes only and may be trademarks or registered trademarks of their respective manufacturers and sellers.

Disclaimer
CTI reserves the right to revise this publication and make changes from time to time in its content without notice.

ISBN 0-7600-4091-5

Printed in the United States of America

10 9 8 7 6 5 4 3 2 1

Contents

Preface: vi

Microsoft Office Professional O1

Chapter One: Getting Started with Microsoft Office Professional O3
Chapter Overview O3
What is Microsoft Office Professional? O4
How Microsoft Office Can Help You in Your Work O4
Hardware and Software Requirements O8
Starting Microsoft Office Professional Applications O8
Identifying Common Elements of Microsoft Applications O11
Exiting Microsoft Applications O14
Organizational Plan for the Book O14
Exercises O15

Chapter Two: Quick Start for Office O17
Chapter Overview O17
Completing a Project with Office Applications O18
Copying Information from Excel to Word O22
Copying Information from Excel to PowerPoint O26
Utilizing the Help Feature O28
Exercises O30

Chapter Three: Using the Microsoft Office Manager Toolbar O33
Chapter Overview O33
Identifying the Microsoft Office Manager Toolbar Buttons O34
Accessing the Microsoft Office Manager Menu O34
Customizing the Microsoft Office Manager Toolbar O35
Modifying the Appearance and Location of the Microsoft Office Manager Toolbar O37
Changing the Contents of the Microsoft Office Manager Menu O39
Exercises O40

Microsoft Excel 5.0 E1

Chapter One: Quick Start for Excel E3
Chapter Overview E3
Identifying Components of the Excel Window E4
Moving Around the Workbook Window E6

Creating a Worksheet E8
Editing a Worksheet E10
Saving a Workbook E11
Printing a Worksheet E12
Closing a Workbook E12
Opening a New Workbook E13
Opening an Existing Workbook E14
Exiting Excel E15
Exercises E15

Chapter Two: Organizing Workbooks and Designing Worksheets Properly E17

Chapter Overview E17
Designing Workbook and Worksheet Layout E18
Designing Worksheets within a Workbook E18
Documenting a Workbook E19
Naming a Sheet Tab E22
Exercises E23

Chapter Three: Creating Worksheets E25

Chapter Overview E25
Entering Worksheet Titles, Column Titles, and Row Titles E26
Expanding the Width of a Column E31
Entering Data and Formulas and Copying Information in a Worksheet E33
Selecting a Format for the Data E41
Correcting Rounding Errors E44
Enhancing the Appearance of a Worksheet E46
Using Absolute Cell References E53
Splitting a Window into Panes E55
Changing the Assumptions to Complete a "What-If" Analysis E57
Using the Spelling Feature E57
Exercises E59

Chapter Four: Printing Features E63

Chapter Overview E63
Using Print Preview and the Print Feature E64
Inserting Page Breaks E70
Creating and Using Range Names E72
Exercises E73

Chapter Five: Creating and Printing Charts E75

Chapter Overview E75
Identifying Parts of a Chart E76
Creating a Column Chart on a New Sheet E78
Creating an Embedded Chart E81
Printing an Embedded Chart E83
Printing an Embedded Chart and Worksheet E84
Deleting an Embedded Chart from a Worksheet E85
Sizing and Moving an Embedded Chart E85
Changing the Location of a Legend E86
Removing and Changing Axes Scales E87
Changing the Fonts of Chart Text E90
Changing Colors and Hatch Patterns E91
Inserting and Removing Gridlines E93
Adding Unattached Text and Graphic Objects to a Chart E94
Exercises E97

Chapter Six: Creating and Using Multiple Worksheets and Workbooks E99

Chapter Overview E99
Grouping Worksheets E100
Entering Data and Formulas in Multiple Worksheets E101
Formatting Multiple Worksheets E103
Inserting and Formatting a Summary Sheet E103
Creating Formulas with 3-D References E104
Printing Multiple Worksheets E105
Linking Workbooks Together E106
Exercises E108

Chapter Seven: Introduction to Lists, Sorting, and Filtering   E109
- Chapter Overview   E109
- Identifying Basic Terms and Guidelines   E110
- Entering Data in a List   E110
- Sorting Data in a List   E114
- Editing Data in a List   E116
- Finding Data Using the Form Command   E117
- Using AutoFilter to Filter Data in a List   E118
- Using Advanced Filter   E125
- Using the Subtotals Command   E128
- Exercises   E130

Chapter Eight: Introduction to Macros   E133
- Chapter Overview   E133
- Creating a Macro   E134
- Executing a Macro   E137
- Editing a Macro   E138
- Recording Additional Steps Into an Existing Macro   E138
- Creating a Macro in the Personal Macro Workbook   E140
- Removing a Macro from the Personal Macro Workbook   E143
- Using a Shortcut Key to Execute a Macro   E144
- Exercises   E146

Chapter Nine: Integrating Word and Excel Data   E149
- Chapter Overview   E149
- Inserting a Copy of Excel Worksheet Data into a Word Document   E150
- Embedding Excel Worksheet Data in a Word Document   E154
- Linking Excel Worksheet Data to a Word Document   E161
- Linking an Excel Chart to a Word Document   E163
- Exercises   E167

Business Simulation

Index   I1

Preface

Today there are tens of millions of people using personal computers in their work and recreational activities. Many individuals are making use of word processing, spreadsheet, presentation, database management, and electronic mail software applications. Microsoft Corporation has created Microsoft Office Professional, which includes all these software applications. This book introduces the student to Microsoft Office and then focuses specifically on the Microsoft Excel 5.0 software. This book has been developed to:

- Acquaint the student with spreadsheet software.
- Provide the student with a working knowledge of Microsoft Excel 5.0.
- Provide the student with an excellent reference source to advance his or her knowledge of Excel.

Hardware and Software Requirements

To use the versions of Office and Excel covered in this book, you must have an IBM or compatible personal computer. It is recommended that your computer have an 80386 or higher processor, and that it have at least 6 MB of RAM and 62 MB of hard disk space for a complete installation of all packages.

Authors' Experience

The authors have worked with personal computers since PCs came to the market in the late 1970s. In addition, the authors have more than 42 years of combined teaching and computer consulting experience.

Market Needs-Based Approach

More than 70,000 people have attended personal computer training classes through Napier & Judd, Inc. Attendees have been from Fortune 500 companies, Big Six accounting firms, government organizations, and small- and mid-size companies.

By providing PC software training services for organizations, Napier and Judd are able to ascertain employer software knowledge prerequisites. Napier and Judd books thus provide students with the knowledge and skills necessary for today's marketplace.

Distinguishing Features

Quick Start Approach

In Chapter 1 of the Office unit, the student learns the basics of getting started with Microsoft Office Professional and the common elements of the Office applications.

Chapter 2 of this unit provides a quick start for using Microsoft Office and its applications. After completing Chapter 2, the student can 1) open the various software applications, 2) copy data and a chart from an Excel workbook to a Word document, and 3) copy a chart from an Excel workbook to an existing PowerPoint presentation slide.

In the Excel unit, the first chapter provides a quick start for the important "create-edit-print" cycle. After finishing the quick start, the student can 1) open the software application, 2) create a document associated with the application, 3) edit the document, 4) save the document, 5) preview and print the document, 6) close the document, 7) open and edit an existing document, and 8) exit the software application.

Learning through Examples

The book is designed for students to learn through examples rather than learning a series of features or commands. The materials are built around a series of example problems. The student learns commands for one example, then the commands are reinforced in others. New features are covered in subsequent examples.

Business Simulation

A full-color module follows the Excel unit, allowing students to practice the techniques they have learned through hands-on business examples. In the module, students assume the role of an entry-level employee in a business environment. In addition to practicing working with Word, Excel, and PowerPoint, students are taught how to perform searches on the World Wide Web using the program Netscape Navigator.

Step-by-Step Instructions and Screen Illustrations

All examples in this text include step-by-step instructions. Screen illustrations are used extensively to help students learn the features of Microsoft Excel. The authors have found this approach very useful for both novice and more advanced users.

Extensive Exercises

At the end of each chapter, realistic exercises provide comprehensive coverage of the topics introduced in the chapter.

Level of Instruction

This book is designed to familiarize the student with various beginning, intermediate, and advanced topics in Microsoft Excel. The book assumes the student has little or no spreadsheet background, but does have knowledge of the Windows environment.

This book is characterized by its continuity, simplicity, and practicality. This book does not replace the Microsoft Excel *User's Guide* that accompanies Microsoft Excel. Used in conjunction with the *User's Guide*, this book will provide the student with a complete understanding of the capabilities of Microsoft Excel.

Organization/Flexibility

The book is divided into two units. The first unit includes chapters on Microsoft Office. Chapter 1 shows the student how to get started with Microsoft Office. The difference between Microsoft Office and Microsoft Office Professional is specified. An example of using Microsoft Office applications together is covered. The processes for starting and exiting the various applications are illustrated. Common elements of Microsoft applications are presented.

Chapter 2 provides students with a quick start for Microsoft Office. A method for copying information among the various applications is examined. The Help feature is considered. The Microsoft Office Manager (MOM) Toolbar is investigated in Chapter 3. Various methods for working with the MOM toolbar as well as customizing it are presented.

The second unit includes the chapters on Excel. Chapter 1 provides a quick start for using Excel. The components of the Excel window are detailed and methods for moving through the Excel worksheet window are demonstrated.

When you create worksheets, it is important to use good design principles. Chapter 2 explains how to organize a workbook and design a worksheet properly.

Chapter 3 contains a step-by-step process for creating and enhancing a worksheet. Operations included are entering worksheet titles, column titles, and row titles; widening columns; entering assumptions; entering numbers and formulas; copying information; selecting a format for the data; entering underlines and double underlines; inserting blank rows; changing the font appearance; using drag-and-drop to move or copy cell contents; applying shading to selected cells; placing a box border around selected cells; copying formats; using absolute cell references; splitting a window into panes; performing a "what-if" analysis; and using the Spelling feature.

It is often necessary to print a worksheet. Chapter 4 includes information on using Print Preview and the Print feature. The process for inserting page breaks is illustrated. Methods for creating and using range names are presented.

Chapter 5 includes a step-by-step process for creating and printing a chart. Operations included are identifying parts of a chart; creating a column chart on a new sheet; creating an embedded chart; printing an embedded chart and worksheet; deleting an embedded chart from a worksheet; sizing and moving an embedded chart; changing the location of a legend; removing and changing axes scales; changing the fonts of chart text; changing colors and hatch patterns; inserting and removing gridlines; and adding unattached text and graphic objects to a chart.

Chapter 6 includes a discussion of the use of multiple worksheets in a workbook and the use of multiple workbooks. Topics incorporated are grouping of worksheets; entering data and formulas in multiple worksheets; formatting multiple worksheets; creating formulas with 3-D references; and linking workbooks together.

While Excel does not provide all the capabilities of a database management application like Access, many database-like operations can be applied to data listed in a worksheet. Chapter 7 includes topics on identifying basic terms and guidelines; entering data in a list; sorting data in a list; editing data in a list; finding data in a list using the Form command; using AutoFilter to filter data in a list; using Advanced Filter; and using the Subtotals command.

In many situations, the same steps are applied to the development of a worksheet each time it is used. In Excel, a macro can be developed that instructs the computer to repeat the steps automatically rather than have the user enter the set of steps each time. Macros are introduced in Chapter 8. Topics covered include creating a macro; executing a macro; editing a macro; recording additional steps into an existing macro; creating a macro in the Personal Macro Workbook; removing a macro from the Personal Macro Workbook; and using a shortcut key to execute a macro.

One of the major reasons for using Microsoft Office and its applications is to share information among the applications. Chapter 9 includes examples of integrating Word and Excel data. The processes for copying, embedding, and linking Excel worksheet data into a Word document are illustrated. A method for linking an Excel chart to a Word document is presented.

CourseTools

The teaching materials available with this book are known as CourseTools and are offered separately or together in the Instructor's Resource Kit and may be ordered through the instructions printed on the inside covers of this book.

Student Files Disks

Student Files Disks contain all of the data files that students will use while working through this book. Adopters of this text are granted the right to post the Student Files Disks on any stand-alone computer or network used by students who have purchased a copy of this book.

Course Test Manager

Course Test Manager is cutting-edge Windows-based software that helps instructors design and administer pretests, practice tests, and actual examinations. The full-featured program provides random test generation of practice tests, immediate online feedback, and generation of detailed study guides for questions that are incorrectly answered. Online pretests help instructors assess student skills and plan instruction. Also, students can take tests at the computer, and tests can be automatically graded and can generate statistical information for the instructor on individual and group performance. Instructors can also use Course Test Manager to produce printed tests.

Instructor's Manual

The Instructor's Manual is written by the authors and has been quality-assurance tested. The Instructor's Manual provides additional information and exercises for classroom use. A disk containing solutions to all end-of-chapter exercises found in the book accompanies the Instructor's Manual. Also included are transparency pages for selected figures.

Microsoft Office Professional

1 Getting Started with Microsoft Office Professional

2 Quick Start for Office

3 Using the Microsoft Office Manager Toolbar

Getting Started with Microsoft Office Professional

1

Objectives

In this chapter you will learn to:
- Describe Microsoft Office and Microsoft Office Professional
- Determine how Microsoft Office can help you in your work
- Determine the hardware and software requirements
- Start Microsoft Office Professional applications
- Identify common elements of Microsoft applications
- Exit Microsoft Office Professional applications

Chapter Overview

This book assumes that you have little or no knowledge of Microsoft Office or the applications that are utilized with Microsoft Office. It does assume, though, that you have worked with personal computers and are familiar with Microsoft Windows. Chapter 1 introduces you to the capabilities of Microsoft Office and how the product can assist in your work. This chapter illustrates the use of Microsoft Office. The process for initiating the use of Microsoft Office and its related applications is shown. The computer hardware and software requirements for using Microsoft Office applications are explained. Finally, the chapter specifies the process for exiting the various applications.

What Is Microsoft Office Professional?

Microsoft Office 4.2 is a software suite that contains several other applications. If you have Microsoft Office, the software packages included are:

Microsoft Word for Windows Version 6.0

Microsoft Excel for Windows Version 5.0

Microsoft PowerPoint for Windows Version 4.0

Microsoft Mail 3.2 Workstation (License is included, but software is not.)

If you have Microsoft Office Professional 4.3, you have the packages mentioned above as well as the following additional application:

Microsoft Access 2.0 for Windows

This book assumes that you have Microsoft Office Professional. If you do not have Microsoft Access for Windows, you may wish to omit the unit about Microsoft Access.

Word provides you with word processing capabilities. **Word processing** is the preparation and production of documents using automated equipment. Today, most word processing activities are completed with personal computers and word processing software. Using personal computers, you can complete word processing tasks as well as a host of other duties, including desktop publishing.

Excel is a spreadsheet software that allows you to create worksheets and charts as well as complete operations such as sorting data. With Excel, you can create financial budgets for an organization or yourself, reports, and a variety of other forms. Spreadsheets may also be referred to as *worksheets*.

PowerPoint is an application used to create materials, called slides, for presentations. These slides can contain text, graphs, organization charts, and other objects. The slides are placed in a presentation file that you can use to print transparencies for an overhead projector. The slides can also be viewed directly on your computer monitor or on a screen using a projector connected to your computer.

Access provides you with database management capabilities. The software allows you to store and retrieve information in databases. The software permits you to query the database and determine answers to specific questions about the data within the database. For example, you could determine which customers in a particular state had sales in excess of a particular value during the month of June.

Mail allows you to send information electronically rather than by the postal service, a courier, or other type of delivery service. Such a software package also lets you leave messages for individuals whenever you cannot reach them by telephone. This type of software is particularly useful for people in different geographic locations.

> **FYI**
>
> Rather than include the text *Microsoft* and *for Windows* each time the name of an application is used, the text will refer to the respective software package as *Office*, *Word*, *Excel*, *PowerPoint*, *Access*, or *Mail*.

How Microsoft Office Can Help You In Your Work

Office consists of a set of software applications that work together very well. The software packages have similar features and are easily integrated with each other. The menu bars, dialog boxes, and toolbars have a similar appearance. In many situations, the tools (buttons) on the various toolbars appear exactly the same and perform identical operations.

The primary purpose for using Office and its related software applications is to share information among the various software applications. For example, you may want to include a portion of an Excel worksheet or chart in a Word document or use an outline created in a Word document as the starting point for a PowerPoint presentation.

Another example of integration is to use Access to store a mailing list for a company's employees. You could use Access to create a list of employees in a specific department. Word can use this list in a merge procedure that creates individual letters for the persons appearing on the department mailing list. With Mail, you can then electronically distribute the documents to the appropriate personnel.

Information can be shared between applications by **copying** data from a source application and **pasting** it into a destination application.

Whenever you need the applications to share data that is dynamic, you can choose to link the data between applications. When you **link** data from a source application to a destination application, the data reside only in the source application. The destination application contains only a representation of the data, which is updated automatically whenever the data in the source application are changed.

You can also edit linked data from the destination application. For example, suppose you have linked data from an Excel worksheet to a Word document and are working in the Word document. With a linked object, you simply double-click the linked data to open the Excel application and workbook. You can then make changes to the data in Excel and the Word document will automatically be updated.

If you **embed** data from a source application into a destination application, you are actually placing a *copy* of the data in the destination application. All editing is done in the destination application and there is no link to the source application. You can double-click the embedded object to display the source application menu and toolbars to be used in editing the object.

Example of Using Office Applications Together

Suppose you work in the Sales department of a lumber company. A weekly progress report is prepared that presents a summary of the week's sales activities. The progress report contains text information on various activities, worksheet information, and charts. The report is distributed to several people.

Figure 1-1 contains the first page of the document. This document was created using Word. Note the sales data for each day. This numeric information was created in Excel.

The Excel worksheet appears in Figure 1-2. The values in the worksheet have been copied from the Excel worksheet to the Word document.

At some point, the manager responsible for the progress report will need to make a presentation related to the weekly data. Charts are particularly useful in presentations to illustrate financial results. PowerPoint allows you to make slides for such a presentation. You can create charts within PowerPoint or link a chart in Excel to a PowerPoint slide. Figure 1-3 contains a PowerPoint slide that includes a chart. The chart was prepared in Excel using the values in Figure 1-2. The chart created in Excel was copied to the PowerPoint slide.

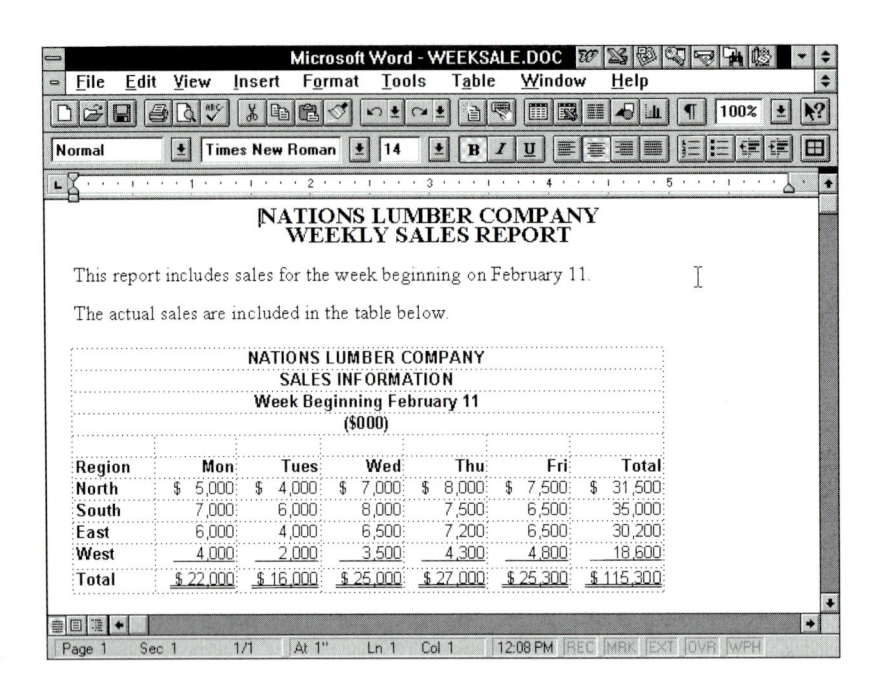

Figure 1-1

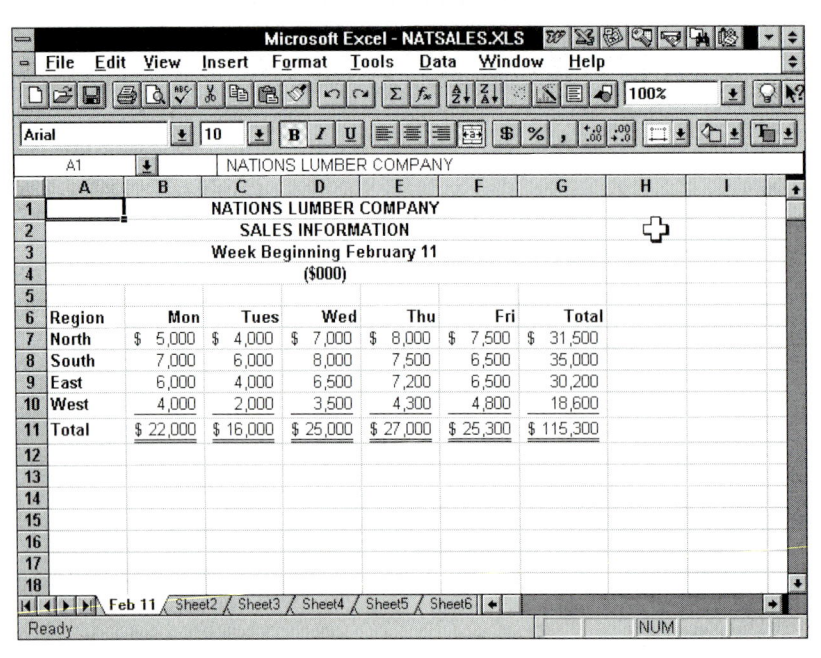

Figure 1-2

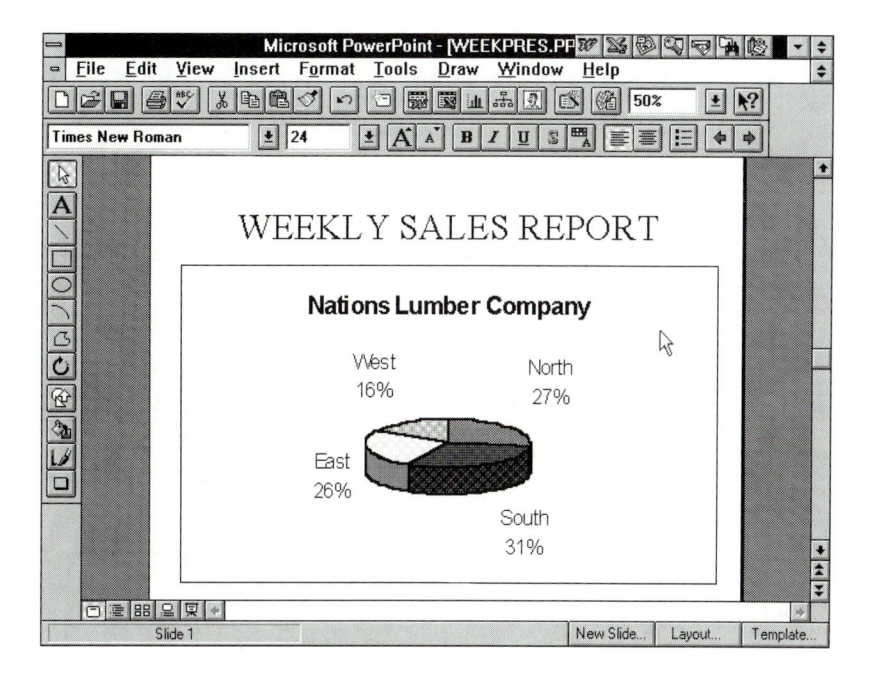

Getting Started with Microsoft Office Professional

Figure 1-3

As noted earlier, the weekly sales report is distributed to several individuals. Rather than prepare several separate documents to be mailed to several individuals, you can create a single document and then merge the names of addressees to create several documents. To accomplish this task, you need a mailing list of the names of those people who will receive the report. You can create and save such a list of individuals in Word or Access. Figure 1-4 contains a database from Access that includes a mailing list. Through a standard process, you can merge the mailing list with a Word document and create the letters for all individuals receiving the report.

Figure 1-4

As you progress through this book, you will learn how to use the individual applications Word, Excel, PowerPoint, and Access. You will also learn to integrate the applications using various techniques.

Hardware and Software Requirements

To use the versions of Office, Word, Excel, PowerPoint, and Access covered in this book, you must have an IBM or compatible personal computer. It is recommended that your computer have an 80386 or higher processor, and that it have at least 6 MB of RAM and 62 MB of hard disk space for a complete installation of all packages.

When you purchase Office and the related applications, you receive a set of disks on which the software is stored. You will install the software from the diskettes onto the hard disk of your computer. Then you will access the programs on the hard disk. For instructions on how to install Office and the other software on a hard disk, see the *User's Guide* that comes with the software.

Supplies

When using a personal computer, you will need several items. First, you should have access to the Office, Word, Excel, PowerPoint, Access, and Mail *User's Guides* that come with the software.

You will also need to have some floppy diskettes on which to store documents. Make sure you have the proper type of diskettes for the computer you are using. You can purchase diskettes at office supply stores and campus bookstores. You may also want a diskette storage box to protect your diskettes when you are not using them.

If the diskettes you purchase are not already formatted, you will need to format them before you can save any documents. Refer to your Windows *User's Guide* for the procedures on formatting diskettes.

Starting Microsoft Office Professional Applications

> **FYI**
>
> You may sometimes use the keyboard to use Windows features. When the keyboard is used to issue a command, this text illustrates keyboard strokes as follows:
>
> ⏎ ENTER
>
> If you are asked to press one key and, while holding the key down, to press another key, the instruction will appear as:
>
> SHIFT + F7

Before you attempt to access Office and the applications and place them in the memory of your computer, first check all connections.

Turn on   the computer

You access Office and the applications through Windows. If Windows does not automatically start when you turn on the computer, you must initiate Windows before running Office and the applications. If Windows loads automatically, you may proceed to page 9 without following the instructions below.

Assuming that Windows is installed in the WINDOWS directory on the C: drive, use the following steps to load the software into your computer:

Type   WIN

Press   ⏎ ENTER

The Windows software is loaded into the memory of your computer. The Microsoft Office Manager (MOM) toolbar appears at the top of the screen. Your screen should look similar to Figure 1-5.

> **FYI**
>
> For mouse instructions, we will call the left mouse button the mouse button. The right mouse button will be referred to as the alternate mouse button. When using a mouse, click means to press a mouse button and then release it. Drag means to press and hold the mouse button down and then move the mouse. Double-click means to press a mouse button twice very rapidly.

Getting Started with Microsoft Office Professional

Figure 1-5

If the MOM toolbar does not appear on your screen, double-click the Microsoft Office group icon in the Program Manager. Then double-click the Microsoft Office program icon. The Microsoft Office copyright screen appears on your monitor. In a few seconds, the top part of your screen should look similar to Figure 1-5. Note: Cue Cards may appear the first few times you use the Office Manager. The Cue Cards feature offers help about how to use Microsoft Office Manager features. If the Cue Cards dialog box appears on the screen, you can close the feature by double-clicking the Control-menu box in the Cue Cards dialog box. Chapter 3 discusses the Cue Cards feature.

The Microsoft Office Manager Toolbar

The Microsoft Office Manager (MOM) toolbar appears in the top-right corner of your screen. In the remainder of this book, the Microsoft Office Manager toolbar is sometimes called the **MOM toolbar**. A series of buttons appears on the MOM toolbar. The buttons represent the various applications that are installed. If the mouse pointer is positioned on one of the application buttons, a ToolTip appears to identify the application name. Initially, the MOM toolbar should look similar to Figure 1-6. You will learn how to customize the MOM toolbar in Chapter 3.

Figure 1-6

In this book, it is assumed that the MOM toolbar includes buttons for:

Button	Application
	Microsoft Word
	Microsoft Excel
	Microsoft PowerPoint
	Microsoft Access
	Microsoft Mail
	Find File
	Microsoft Office

You can access the various applications by clicking on the appropriate button on the MOM toolbar. Another method for opening one of the software packages is to use the MOM toolbar menu.

To display the MOM toolbar menu:

Click   the Microsoft Office button on the MOM toolbar

Your screen should look like Figure 1-7.

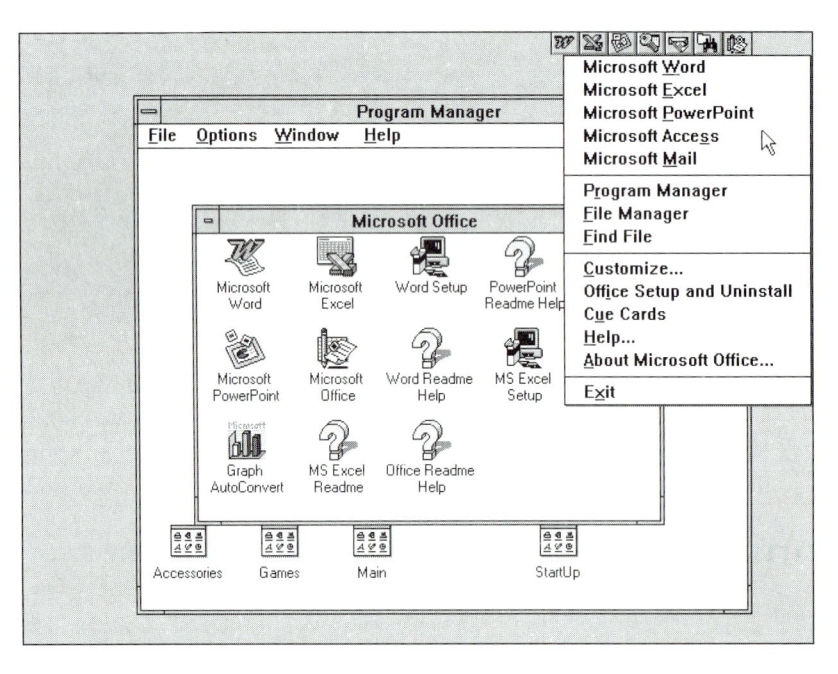

Figure 1-7

To access one of the applications or other options on the menu, click the appropriate item.

To close the MOM toolbar menu:

Click   the Microsoft Office button on the MOM toolbar

Getting Started with Microsoft Office Professional

Accessing the Microsoft Word Application

In this section, you will initiate the use of Word and Excel.

To start using Word:

Click the Microsoft Word button on the MOM toolbar

The Word software is placed into the memory of your computer and the initial Word window appears. A **window** is a rectangular area on your screen in which you can view a software application such as Word or an application document. The Tip of the Day dialog box may appear.

> In the remaining chapters of this book, if the Tip of the Day dialog box appears, click the OK command button to remove it.

To remove the Tip of the Day dialog box if it appears:

Click the OK command button

Your screen should look like Figure 1-8.

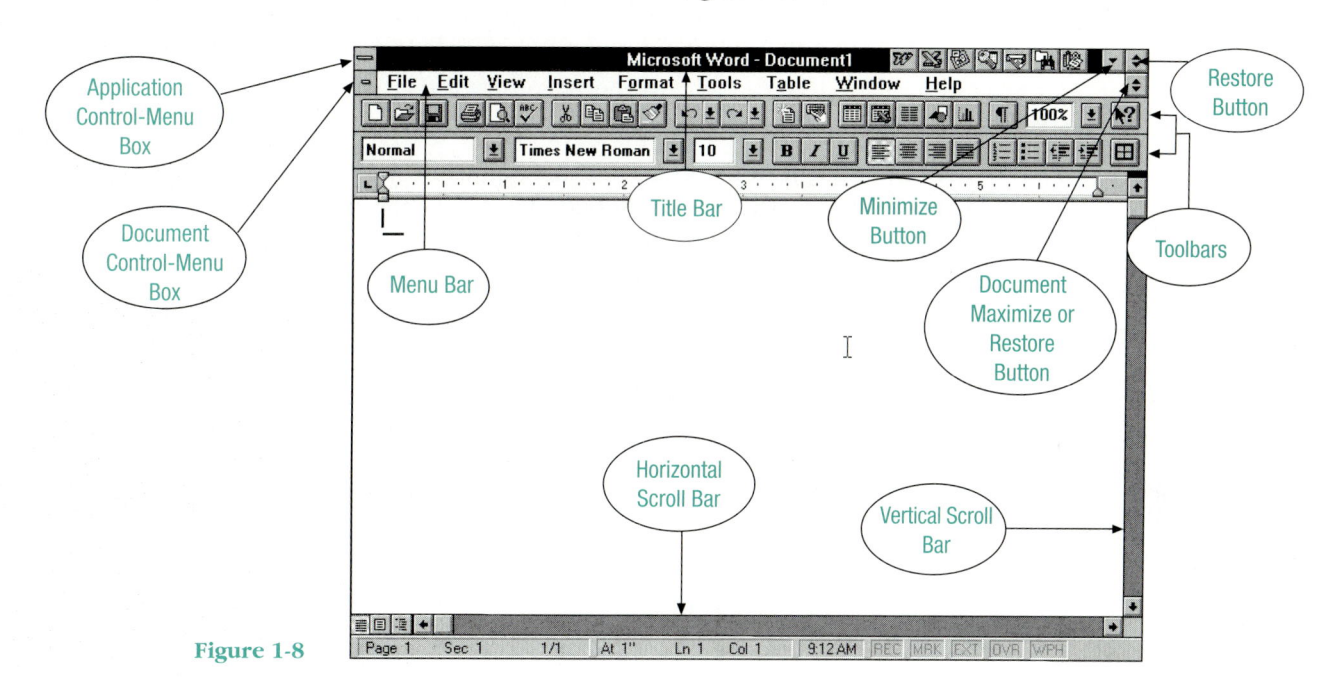

Figure 1-8

Identifying Common Elements of Microsoft Applications

Figure 1-8 notes several common elements of all Microsoft applications. These elements are described below.

Title Bar

The **title bar** appears at the top of the Microsoft application window. It includes the application Control-menu box, the software product name, the filename, the Minimize button, and the Maximize or Restore button.

Application Control-Menu Box

The **application Control-menu box**, located in the top-left corner of the screen, is used to display the Control menu. Every window has a Control menu. The Control menu typically contains commands such as Restore, Move, Size, Minimize, Maximize, Close, and Switch To. In some Control menus, all of the commands may not be available and will be shown in a lighter color than other commands. You can access the Control-menu box by moving the mouse pointer to the Control-menu box and clicking the mouse button or by holding down the ALT key and then pressing the SPACEBAR key.

Document Control-Menu Box

The **document Control-menu box**, located below the application Control-menu box, contains the Restore, Move, Size, Minimize, Maximize, Close, and Next Window menu commands. Access the document Control-menu box by moving the mouse pointer to the document Control-menu box and clicking the mouse button or by holding down the ALT key and pressing the hyphen (-) key.

Minimize Button

The **Minimize button** appears near the top-right corner of the window and resembles an upside-down triangle. Use this button to reduce the application window to an icon. When you move the mouse pointer to the Minimize button and click the mouse button, the application window changes to an icon.

Maximize Button

The application **Maximize button** sometimes appears in the top-right corner of the window and looks like an up-pointing triangle. Use it to maximize or enlarge the size of the window on your screen. If the window is already maximized, the Maximize button is not visible. The Restore button (described below) appears in its place.

Restore Button

The application **Restore button** usually appears in the top-right area of the window. It looks like double triangles. Use the top Restore button to change the size of the application window to a medium size on your screen. Use the bottom Restore button to change the document window to a medium size on your screen.

Document Maximize or Restore Button

The **document Maximize** or **Restore button** is located below the application Maximize or Restore button. Use it to maximize the size of the document window on your screen. If the document window is already maximized, the Restore button changes the document window to a smaller size. You can use this button by moving the mouse pointer to the document Maximize or Restore button and clicking the mouse button.

Menu Bar

The **menu bar**, located at the top of the screen below the title bar, contains menus, including File, Edit, View, Insert, Format, Tools, Table, Window, and Help. Some menu items vary between applications. The use of the menu bar and menus are covered in more detail in Chapter 2.

Toolbars

The **toolbars**, located below the menu bar, contain a set of icons called buttons. Most Microsoft Office applications initially display the Standard toolbar and the Formatting toolbar. The buttons on the toolbars represent commonly used commands. The buttons allow you to quickly perform tasks by clicking on the button. In addition to the Standard and Formatting toolbars, there are several other toolbars available in the various applications.

ToolTips

When the mouse pointer rests on a toolbar button, a **ToolTip** appears identifying the name of the button.

Vertical Scroll Bar

The **vertical scroll bar** appears on the right side of the document area. This scroll bar includes scroll arrows and a scroll box. The vertical scroll bar is used to view various parts of the document. Methods for using the vertical scroll bar are discussed in the application sections of this book.

Horizontal Scroll Bar

The **horizontal scroll bar** appears near the bottom of the document area. This scroll bar includes scroll arrows and a scroll box. The horizontal scroll bar is used to view various parts of the document. Methods for using the horizontal scroll bar are discussed in the application sections of this book.

Screen elements that are specific to Microsoft Word are discussed in Chapter 1 of the Word unit.

Accessing the Microsoft Excel Application

To access the Excel software:

Click the Microsoft Excel button on the MOM toolbar

The Excel software is placed into the memory of your computer, and the initial Excel window appears. Your screen should look like Figure 1-9. Notice that the elements described in Figure 1-8 are visible in Figure 1-9. The elements that are specific to Microsoft Excel are discussed in Chapter 1 of the Excel unit.

Word is still active. You can access Word using the MOM toolbar. Note: If the MOM toolbar is not visible on the screen, use the Task List (CTRL+ESC) to switch to the Microsoft Office Manager.

To view the Word window again:

Click the Microsoft Word button on the MOM toolbar

The Word application window appears. Your screen should look like Figure 1-8 again.

You can open other applications along with Word and Excel. However, if you do that, your machine's memory will eventually limit the number of open programs.

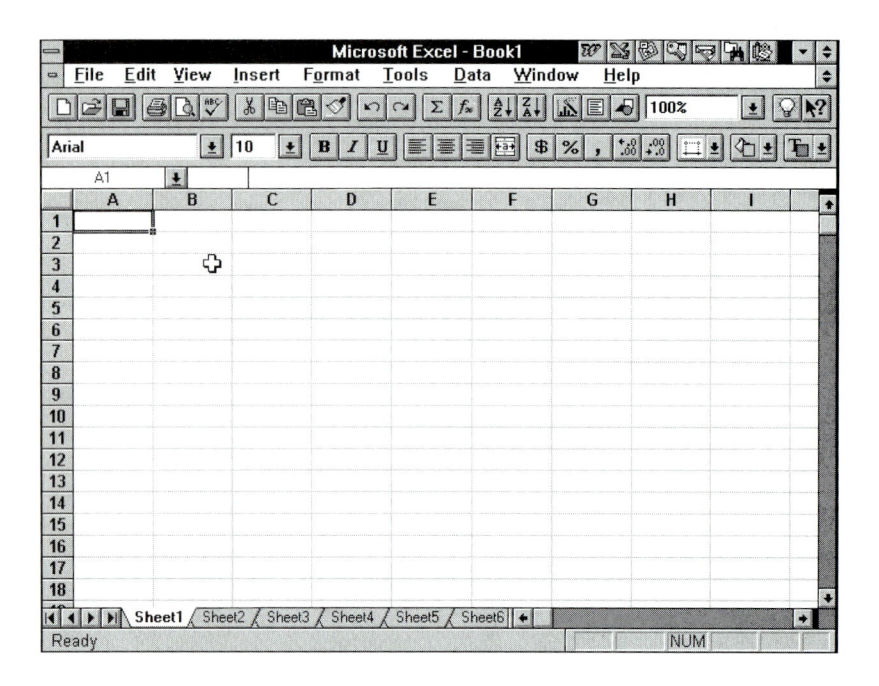

Figure 1-9

> Please note that while it is grammatically correct to place punctuation inside a quote mark, you will see several examples in this book in which the punctuation appears outside the quote mark.
>
> The punctuation appears outside the quote mark when the punctuation is not part of the specified text. The authors do not want misunderstanding about whether the punctuation is part of the specific text or merely the end of a phrase or sentence.

Exiting Microsoft Applications

At this point, you need to exit the open applications and Office.

Since the last application you initiated was Word, you will exit this software first.

To exit Word:

Double-click   the Word application Control-menu box

To exit Excel:

Double-click   the Excel application Control-menu box

Organizational Plan for the Book

This chapter covered some basics about Microsoft Office and how to access the software applications associated with Office. Chapter 2 introduces the process for integrating the use of the Office application software to complete a project. The MOM toolbar is discussed in more detail in Chapter 3. The next four units of the book cover, in the following order, the Word, Excel, PowerPoint, and Access software applications.

After the discussions of Word and Excel are completed, Chapter 9 of the Excel unit discusses various methods of integrating information included in documents created using the application software. Similar chapters are included at the end of the PowerPoint and Access units.

Getting Started with Microsoft Office Professional

Exercise 1

INSTRUCTIONS: Define or explain the following:

1. Click _____

2. Window _____

3. MOM toolbar _____

4. Drag _____

5. Restore button _____

6. Title bar _____

7. Document Maximize or Restore button _____

8. Double-click _____

9. Toolbars _____

10. Horizontal scroll bar _____

11. Application Control-menu box _____

12. Menu bar _____

13. ToolTips _____

14. Vertical scroll bar _____

15. Document Control-menu box _____

16. Minimize button _____

17. Maximize button _____

18. Word processing _____

Exercise 2

INSTRUCTIONS: Circle T if the statement is true and F if the statement is false.

T   F   1. Office consists of a set of software applications that work together very well.
T   F   2. Microsoft Office Professional 4.3 includes only Word, Excel, and PowerPoint.
T   F   3. Excel is an application used to create materials, called slides, for presentations.
T   F   4. Word processing is the preparation and production of documents using automated equipment.
T   F   5. The primary purpose for using Office and its related software applications is to share information between the various software applications.
T   F   6. The Microsoft Office Manager toolbar is sometimes called the MOM toolbar.
T   F   7. The title bar appears at the bottom of a Microsoft application window.
T   F   8. The Maximize button is used to reduce the application window to an icon.
T   F   9. When the mouse pointer rests on a toolbar button, a ToolTip appears identifying the name of the button.
T   F   10. The Minimize button is used to maximize or enlarge the size of the window on your screen.

Exercise 3

INSTRUCTIONS: Identify the common elements of all Microsoft applications in the figure below.

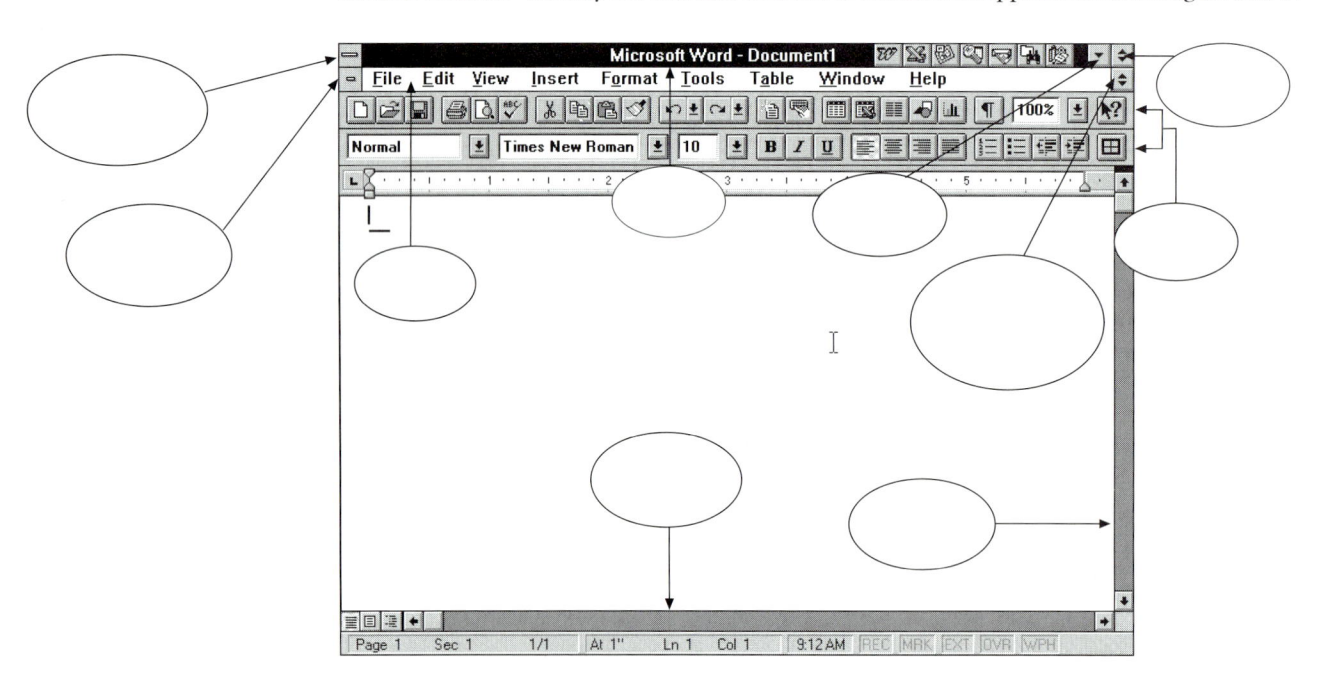

Exercise 4

INSTRUCTIONS: Access the Word application using the MOM toolbar. Exit the Word application.

Exercise 5

INSTRUCTIONS: Access the Excel application using the MOM toolbar. Exit the Excel application.

Quick Start for Office

2

Objectives

In this chapter you will learn to:

→ Complete a project with Office applications
→ Copy information from Excel to Word
→ Copy information from Excel to PowerPoint
→ Utilize the Help feature

Chapter Overview

To complete a project in an office environment, you may need several software applications. For example, you may need to use word processing, worksheet, presentation, database, and e-mail software in the process. This chapter demonstrates the use of some of these types of packages to prepare a weekly sales report.

Completing a Project with Office Applications

Suppose you are a sales analyst for Nations Lumber Company. Each week, you are required to prepare a sales report that includes a brief description of activities for the last week. You need to include a table of numbers from a worksheet that contains weekly sales. The worksheet also includes a chart showing each day's sales as a percentage of the weekly total. You need to place the chart in a presentation that the sales manager will use at a later date. When you have completed the document, you must send it to a group of individuals in the sales department. The names and addresses of these individuals are contained in a database.

The example in this chapter is simple. It has been prepared to provide an overview of how to use Office, Word, Excel, and PowerPoint together.

When you have completed the exercises in this chapter, the document will look like Figure 2-1.

NATIONS LUMBER COMPANY
WEEKLY SALES REPORT

This report include sales for the week beginning on February 11.

The actual sales are included in the table below.

NATIONS LUMBER COMPANY
SALES INFORMATION
Week Beginning February 11
($000)

Region	Mon	Tues	Wed	Thu	Fri	Total
North	$ 5,000	$ 4,000	$ 7,000	$ 8,000	$ 7,500	$ 31,500
South	7,000	6,000	8,000	7,500	6,500	35,000
East	6,000	4,000	6,500	7,200	6,500	30,200
West	4,000	2,000	3,500	4,300	4,800	18,600
Total	$ 22,000	$ 16,000	$ 25,000	$ 27,000	$ 25,300	$ 115,300

The sales for each region as a percent of total weekly sales is indicated in the following chart.

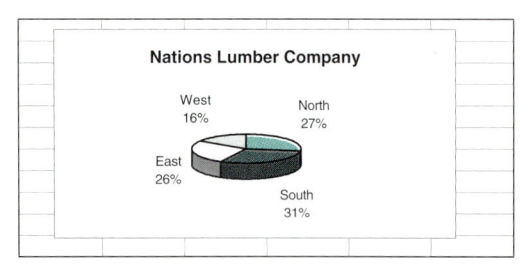

Nations Lumber Company

- West 16%
- North 27%
- East 26%
- South 31%

The next sales report will be sent next Monday.

This report was prepared by Student Name.

Figure 2-1

Quick Start for Office

Make sure that the MOM toolbar appears on your screen and that no other software package is active. Also, ensure that you put the student diskette in your computer's disk drive.

To initiate the use of Word:

Click the Microsoft Word button on the MOM toolbar

Word is active and a blank document appears on your screen. You will open a file that exists on the floppy diskette found at the back of this book. The name of the file is SALESRPT.DOC. You use it each time you prepare a sales report.

When working with Windows applications, there are usually multiple ways to accomplish a task. The *menu method* and the *toolbar method* are two common ways to access commands.

For example, to open a file, you can either:

- Choose the **O**pen command on the **F**ile menu, or
- Click the Open button on the Standard toolbar.

> The ▤ symbol will be used to identify the menu method for accessing commands. The ᐂ symbol will be used to identify the toolbar method for accessing commands.

> If you wish to use the keyboard to select a command from the menu, press the ALT key and the underlined letter of the menu item. This book boldfaces the underlined character in each command sequence. In most cases, you can mix the use of the mouse and the keyboard methods.

To open the SALESRPT.DOC document using the menu method:

Choose **F**ile on the menu bar

The commands on the File menu are displayed. An ellipsis (...) beside a command indicates that a dialog box appears if the command is selected. Commands shown in a lighter color are not available at this time.

Choose the **O**pen command

The Open dialog box appears. Your screen should look similar to Figure 2-2.

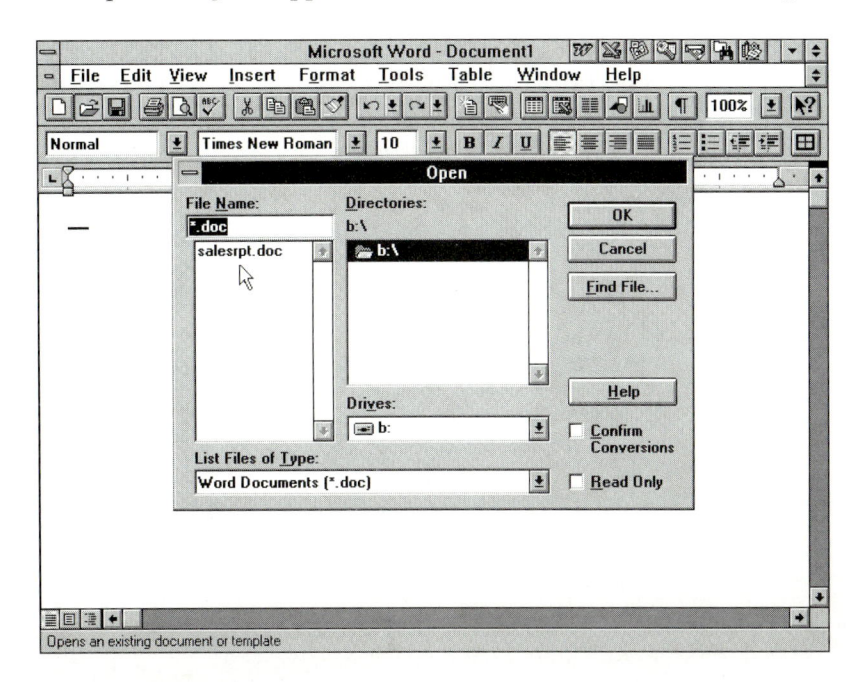

Figure 2-2

A **dialog box** provides options within a command. Notice that the current drive and directory appear to the right of the File **N**ame text box.

Dialog boxes often contain option buttons, check boxes, list boxes, text boxes, and command buttons. These and other elements of a dialog box are described below.

Option buttons are round buttons. Whenever these round buttons appear in a group box within a dialog box, only one can be active. You can choose the appropriate option button by clicking on the option button or by holding down the ALT key and pressing the underlined letter associated with that option.

Check boxes are small square boxes in which you can check or place an X. In Figure 2-2, check boxes appear in the lower-right corner. If a check box contains an X, then that feature is on, or active. If the check box is blank, then that feature is off, or inactive. To activate a check box, click on the box to insert an X or hold down the ALT key and press the underlined letter associated with that check box to insert an X. To turn off the feature, repeat the procedure to remove the X.

List boxes provide a list of names from which you can make a choice. Sometimes you cannot see the entire list. If this is the case, a scroll bar appears next to the list for you to view the remaining options. To choose an item from a list box using the mouse, click on the item in the list box. When using the keyboard, hold down the ALT key and press the underlined letter associated with the list box, then press the pointer-movement keys to choose the proper item.

Text boxes allow you to type an option in them. For example, in Figure 2-2 the File **N**ame text box lets you type a name for the desired file. To choose a text box, double-click inside the text box area or hold down the ALT key and press the underlined letter associated with the text box.

Command buttons are rectangular buttons. Common command buttons are the OK and Cancel buttons, both of which are shown in Figure 2-2. To choose a command button, click the command button with the mouse or hold down the ALT key and press the underlined letter of the command button. If the desired command button has a darkened outline, pressing the ENTER key also accepts the choice. If the desired command button does not have an underlined letter and does not have a darkened outline, you can press the TAB key several times until the desired command button has a darkened outline.

Spin boxes are small squares containing up and down triangles. Spin boxes appear to the right of some numeric text boxes, such as those for line spacing and margins. Click the up or down triangle to increase or decrease the number, respectively.

> Another alternative for moving between various items in a dialog box is to press the TAB key.

> Notice that you can set up your Microsoft applications to save files on a different disk or directory other than the one established during installation. In this book, it is assumed that the student is using the diskette provided with this book. If another drive or directory is utilized, you will need to indicate the appropriate path. As you use this book, save a document to a file only when you are instructed to do so.

Click	SALESRPT.DOC in the File **N**ame text box
Click	the OK command button

Quick Start for Office

> An alternate method of opening a file is to double-click on the filename in the File **N**ame list box of the Open dialog box.

The SALESRPT.DOC document appears and your screen should look like Figure 2-3.

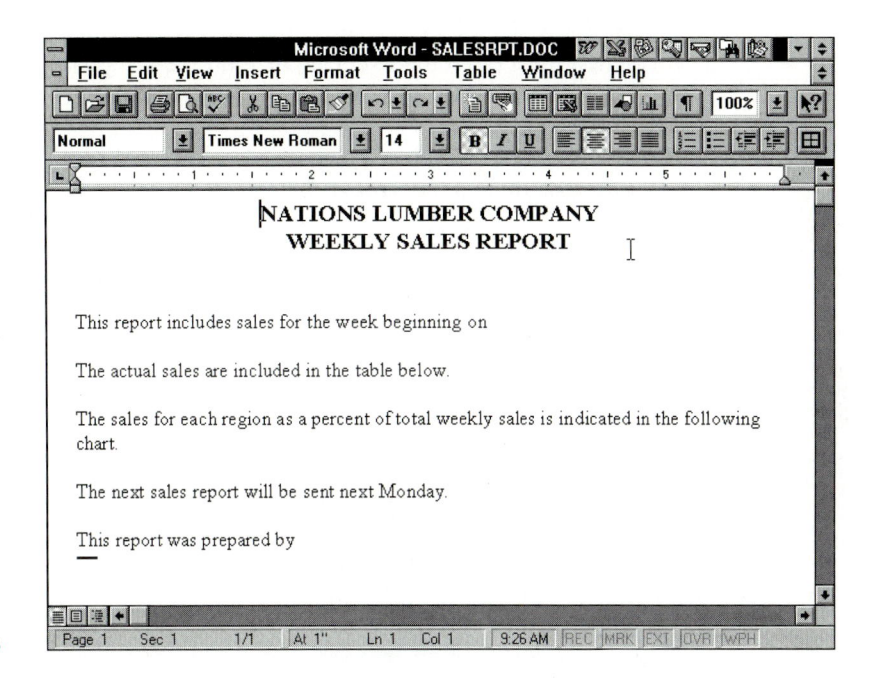

Figure 2-3

When the mouse pointer is positioned in the document area, its shape changes to an I-beam.

To enter the weekly report date:

Move	the I-beam to the end of the first sentence
Click	the mouse button
Press	SPACEBAR
Type	February 11.

Be sure to include the period after the date. The top part of your screen should look like Figure 2-4.

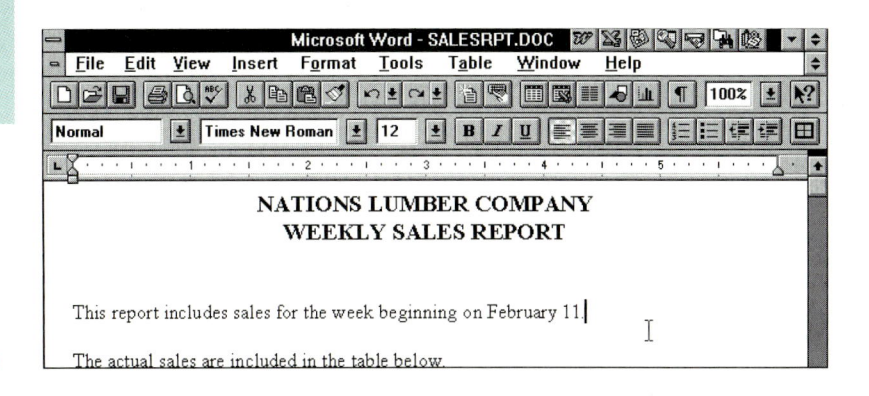

Figure 2-4

> **FYI**
>
> The filename appearing on the title bar for some figures in this book may refer to the figure number or it may indicate a different document number. In most cases, your filename will be different.

Copying Information from Excel to Word

At this point, you need to place the weekly sales information in the sales report. The data are stored in an Excel worksheet.

You first must open the Excel application. To start using Excel:

Click the Microsoft Excel button on the MOM toolbar

The Excel application is now open. The data for the sales report are stored on your floppy diskette in a file named NATSALES.XLS.

To open the NATSALES.XLS file using the Open button on the Standard toolbar:

Click the Open button on the Standard toolbar

The Open dialog box appears. The top part of your screen should look similar to Figure 2-5. Notice the similarities between the Word Open dialog box and the Excel Open dialog box.

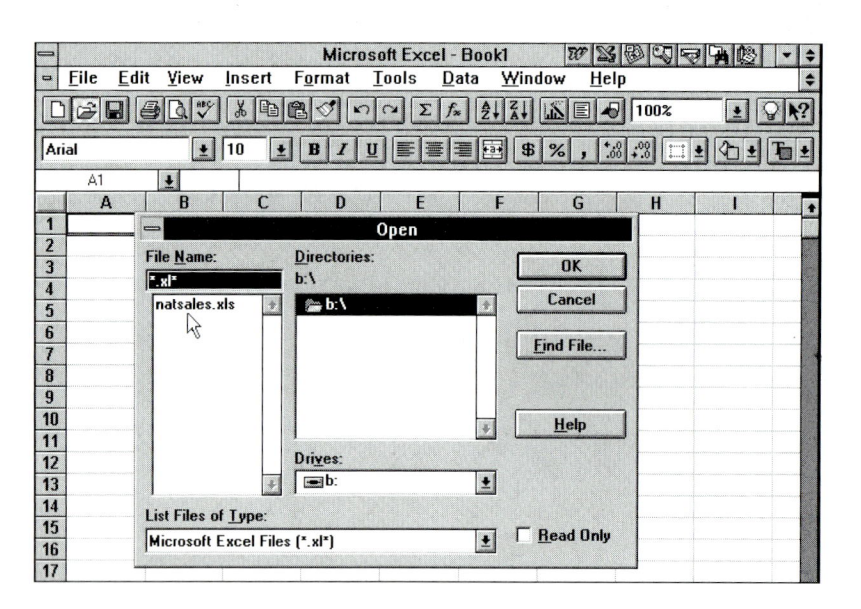

Figure 2-5

To continue:

Click NATSALES.XLS in the File **N**ame text box

Click the OK command button

The NATSALES.XLS workbook appears and your screen should look like Figure 2-6.

With Microsoft applications, you can use the Clipboard to copy and paste information from one document to another. In this example, you will copy the data appearing in the NATSALES.XLS Excel worksheet and paste it into the SALESRPT.DOC Word document. Before you copy the data, you must first select them.

Quick Start for Office

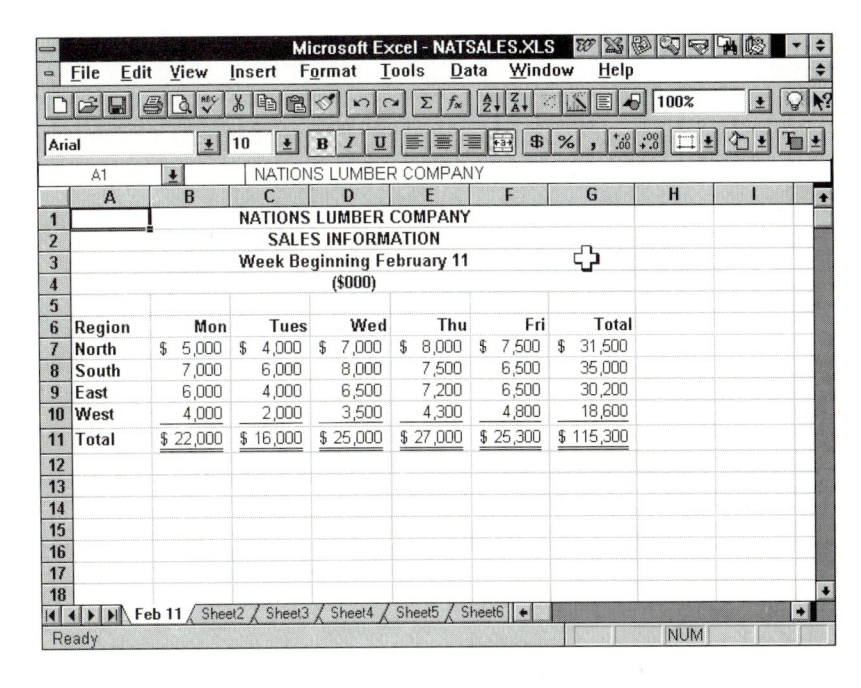

Figure 2-6

[Screenshot of Microsoft Excel - NATSALES.XLS showing the Nations Lumber Company sales information worksheet with data for Mon-Fri across North, South, East, West regions]

To select the desired cells:

Click	on cell A1 in the NATSALES.XLS worksheet (if necessary)
Move	the mouse pointer to the interior of cell A1 (the mouse appears as a white cross)
Drag	to the right and down until cells A1 through G11 are selected

The highlighted cells are called a *range*. Cell A1 is the anchor, or beginning cell, of the range. It does not change color when it is selected. Ranges are discussed in greater detail in the Excel section of this book.

When you wish to copy information, you can use the menu or a button on the Standard toolbar.

- You can choose the **Copy** command on the **Edit** menu.
- You can click the Copy button on the Standard toolbar.

To copy the worksheet to the Clipboard using the menu method:

Choose	Edit
Choose	Copy

When you wish to paste the copied information, you can use the menu or a button on the Standard toolbar.

- You can choose the **Paste** command on the **Edit** menu.
- You can click the Paste button on the Standard toolbar.

To paste the worksheet into the Word document using the menu method:

Click	the Word [W] button on the MOM toolbar
Move	the I-beam to the blank line below the second sentence
Click	the mouse button

Mastering and Using Microsoft Office Professional

Press　　　　　ENTER　to insert one blank line

Choose　　　　Edit

Choose　　　　Paste

The worksheet appears in the document.

Your screen should look like Figure 2-7.

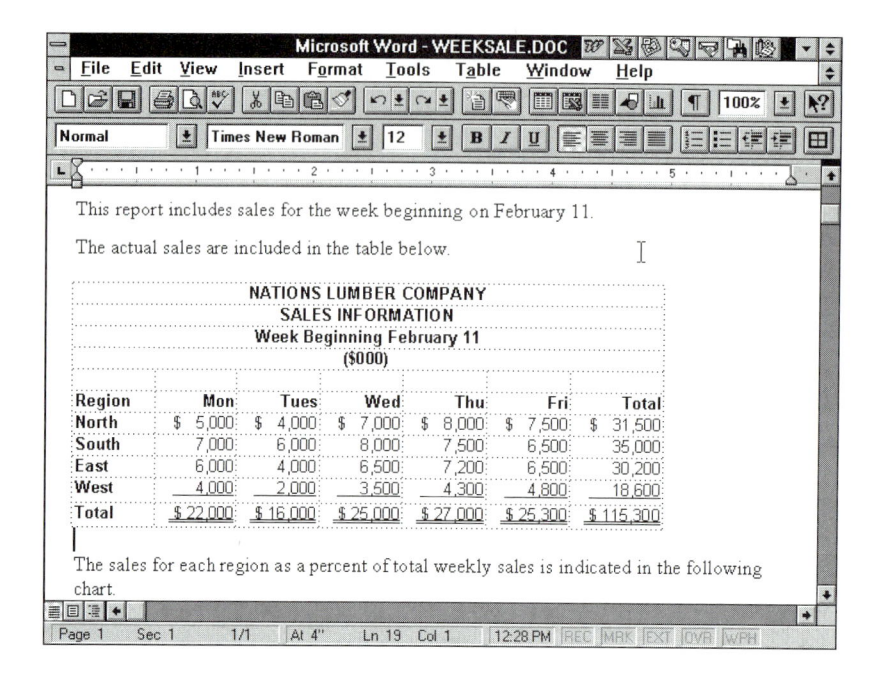

Figure 2-7

You can also use the Cut command on the Edit menu or the Cut button on the Standard toolbar to move data to the Clipboard. Unlike the Copy command, which duplicates the information, the Cut command removes the information from the current location.

To copy the chart from the NATSALES.XLS worksheet into the Clipboard:

Click　　　　　the Excel button on the MOM toolbar

Click　　　　　on the down arrow on the vertical scroll bar until a chart is visible

Move　　　　　the mouse pointer into the chart area

Click　　　　　the mouse button to select the chart

Small black squares, called *sizing handles*, appear around the chart to indicate it is selected. These sizing handles will be used later in this chapter to change the size of the chart.

To copy the chart to the Clipboard using the Copy button on the Standard toolbar:

Click　　　　　the Copy button on the Standard toolbar

To paste the chart into the sales report using the Paste button on the Standard toolbar:

Click　　　　　the Word button on the MOM toolbar

Move　　　　　the I-beam to the end of the third sentence

Click　　　　　the mouse button

Quick Start for Office

Press   ⏎ ENTER twice

Click   the Paste button on the Standard toolbar

The chart now appears in the document. Your screen should look like Figure 2-8.

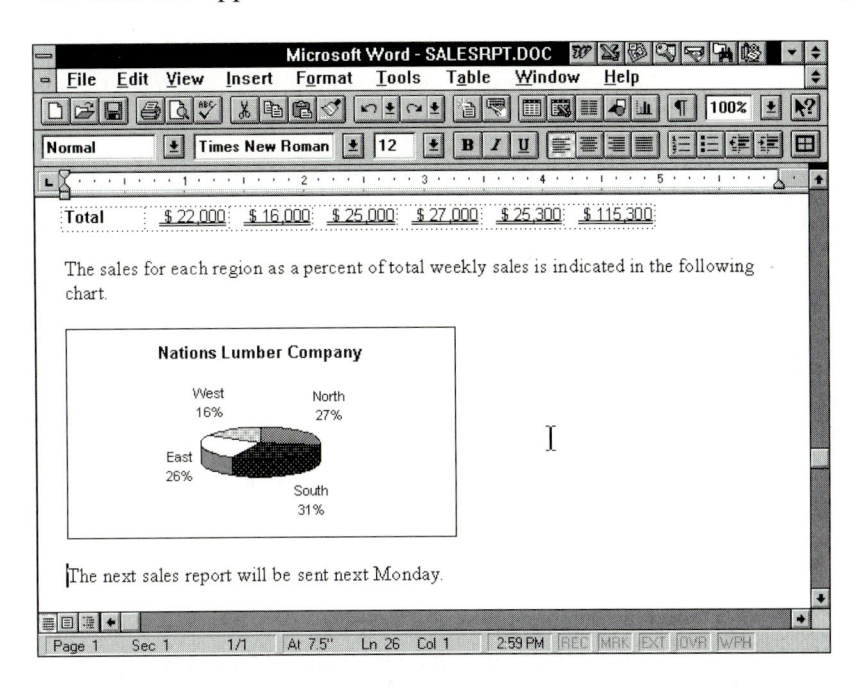

Figure 2-8

To indicate that you prepared the report:

Click   the mouse button at the end of the last sentence

Press   SPACEBAR

Type   `Your Name.`

Be sure and place a period after your name. The sales report is complete.

To save the sales report:

Choose   **File**

Choose   Save **As**

Type   `WEEKSALE` in the File **Name** text box

Click   the OK command button

When the Summary Info dialog box appears, you can enter documentation information if you so wish. To complete the saving process:

Click   the OK command button

The document is now saved on the diskette.

You can print the document.

- You can choose the **P**rint command button on the **F**ile menu.
- You can click the Print button on the Standard toolbar.

If you use the menu method, a dialog box appears allowing you to change the print settings. If you use the Print button on the Standard toolbar, the document is printed using the default settings and no dialog box appears.

To print the document with the current print settings using the menu method:

Choose   File

Choose   Print

Click   the OK command button

You will learn more about printing options in later chapters.

Copying Information from Excel to PowerPoint

Suppose that the sales manager needs to use the chart in the Excel worksheet for a presentation. PowerPoint is used to create such presentations. In this situation, assume that the presentation consists of only one slide. The presentation has been saved on your floppy diskette in a PowerPoint file named WEEKPRES.PPT.

To copy the chart on the Excel worksheet to the Clipboard:

Click   the Excel button on the MOM toolbar

Select   the chart (if necessary)

Click   the Copy button on the Standard toolbar

You must now place the chart into the sales manager's presentation.

To initiate the use of PowerPoint:

Click   the Microsoft PowerPoint button on the MOM toolbar

The PowerPoint Tip of the Day dialog box may appear. Close the Tip of the Day dialog box, if necessary, by clicking the OK command button. The PowerPoint dialog box appears. Your screen should look like Figure 2-9.

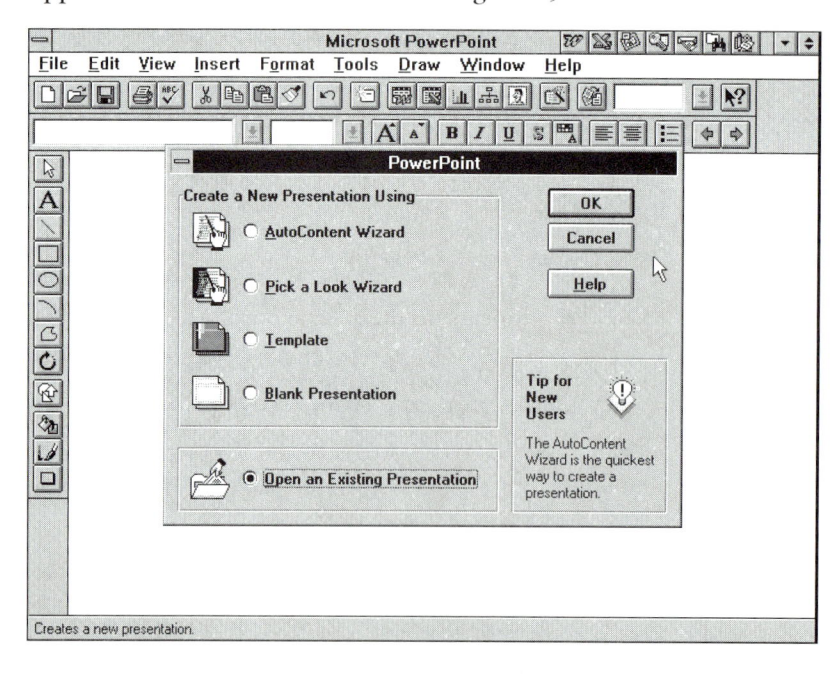

Figure 2-9

Quick Start for Office

To place the information in the presentation:

Click the **O**pen an Existing Presentation option button (if necessary)

Click the OK command button

The Open dialog box appears. To open the presentation file:

Click WEEKPRES.PPT in the File **N**ame text box

Click the OK command button

The presentation appears. Your screen should look like Figure 2-10.

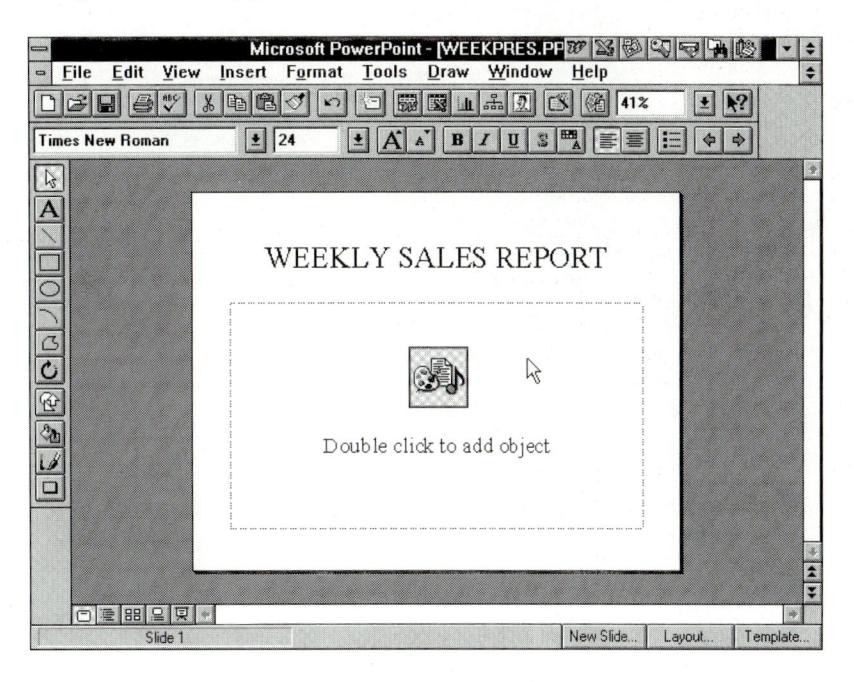

Figure 2-10

To place the chart on the presentation slide:

Move the mouse pointer inside the dotted line area

Click the mouse button to select the area

Click the Paste button on the Standard toolbar

The chart appears on the slide and has sizing handles surrounding it. The sizing handles are used to change the size of the chart on the slide. To resize the chart, move the mouse pointer to one of the sizing handles. The mouse pointer will be a double-headed arrow. Drag in the desired direction and release the mouse button. After you have used the mouse and sizing handles to modify the appearance of the chart, your screen should look similar to Figure 2-11.

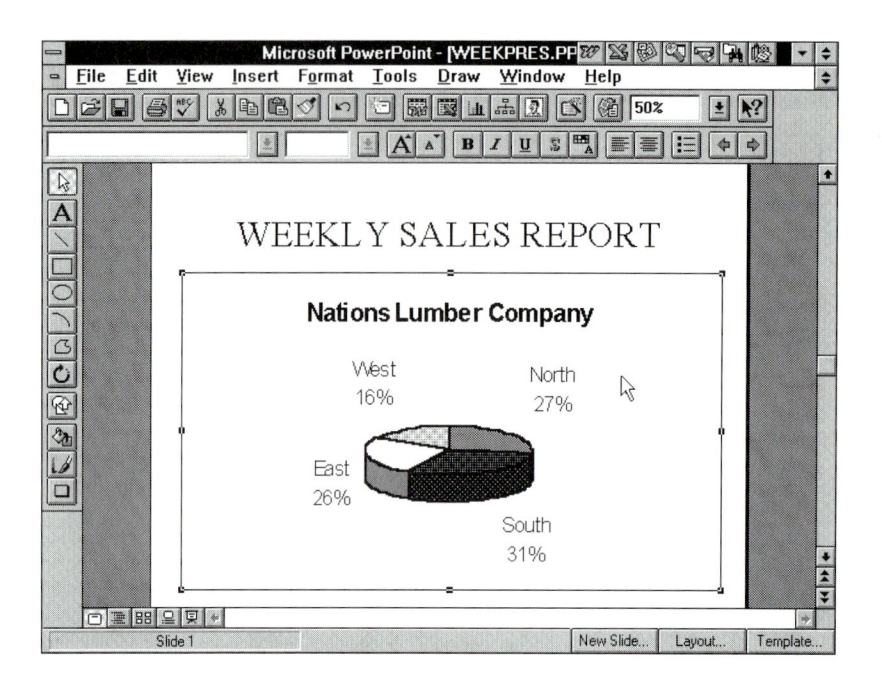

Figure 2-11

To save the new data in the PowerPoint presentation file:

Choose	File
Choose	Save **A**s
Type	FINPRES in the File **N**ame text box
Click	the OK command button

The Summary Info dialog box may appear, allowing you to place additional information about the file in text boxes. The Summary Information feature is available in many Microsoft Office applications. If the Summary Info dialog box appears, click the OK command button.

At this point, you have copied or integrated information among Word, Excel, and PowerPoint.

As a next step, you could prepare a cover letter and distribute the weekly sales report to appropriate personnel. You could save the mailing list in a database using Access. The actual document preparation can be accomplished using the Merge feature in Word and the database saved in Access.

Close all files, saving any changes to them. Close the three applications used in this chapter. Only the Program Manager window and the MOM toolbar should be visible on your screen.

Utilizing the Help Feature

The online Help feature allows you to learn more about Microsoft applications quickly. To display Help Contents, choose the **C**ontents command on the **H**elp menu or press the F1 key.

A **jump topic** is text that appears underlined and in a different color. Jump topics move you to another Help subtopic. You can select any jump topic by clicking on it or by pressing the TAB key to select it. If you cannot see all the jump topics on the screen, use the scroll bars or the pointer-movement keys to view the additional topics.

To display Help Contents:

Choose   Help

Choose   Contents

The Help Contents window is displayed.

To access instructions for a particular topic:

Move   the mouse pointer to any jump topic

Click   the mouse button to display the contents of the selected subtopic

Sometimes a Help topic will include words or phrases in a different color and with a dotted underline. When you click on such a word or phrase, a definition of the word or phrase appears on the screen. To remove the definition, click anywhere on the screen or press the ESC key.

In some applications, you can display step-by-step instructions while you perform the task. Some applications include a Glossary or Index feature. You can click on a desired topic and the screen will display Help about the specified topic.

To close the Help Window:

Double-click   the Control-menu box on the Help window title bar

Another way to receive help about specific commands is to use **context-sensitive Help**. Context-sensitive Help is available in two ways. You may use the Help button on the Standard toolbar to get help on any screen item, including menu commands and other toolbar buttons. When you click the Help button, a large question mark appears near the mouse pointer on the screen. You can then click on any menu item, button, or part of the window. A Help window will appear on your screen with information about the particular topic on which you clicked.

The Help button on the Standard toolbar looks like this:

Double-clicking the Help button on the Standard toolbar displays the Help Search dialog box, which is used to look up specific topics in online Help.

The other context-sensitive Help is within most dialog boxes. A **H**elp command button is usually available to offer assistance about the current feature you are using. When you click the **H**elp command button, the Help Window displays information about the current dialog box.

Summary

Microsoft applications can be used together to improve the work effectiveness of individuals. People can copy information between documents created in the various software packages such as Word, Excel, PowerPoint, Access, and Mail.

Exercise 1

INSTRUCTIONS: Define or explain the following:

1. Dialog box _____
   _____

2. Jump topic _____
   _____

3. Check boxes _____
   _____

4. Context-sensitive Help _____
   _____

5. Option buttons _____
   _____

6. List boxes _____
   _____

7. Spin boxes _____
   _____

8. Command buttons _____
   _____

9. Text boxes _____
   _____

Exercise 2

INSTRUCTIONS: Circle T if the statement is true and F if the statement is false.

T   F   1. The menu method and the toolbar method are two common ways to access commands.
T   F   2. A dialog box provides options within a command.
T   F   3. Text boxes provide a list of names from which you can make a choice.
T   F   4. In a dialog box, only two option buttons can be active.
T   F   5. If a check box contains an X, then that feature is off, or inactive.
T   F   6. List boxes allow you to type an option in them.
T   F   7. Only Excel and Word allow you to exchange data.
T   F   8. In a Help window, a jump topic is text that appears underlined and in a different color.

Exercise 3

INSTRUCTIONS:

1. Open the Word application.
2. Open the EXPRPT.DOC document. This file can be found on the floppy diskette at the back of this book.
3. Open the Excel application.
4. Open the MAYEXP.XLS worksheet. This file can be found on the floppy diskette at the back of this book.
5. Copy the district expense information in cells A1 through E12 to the Clipboard.

Quick Start for Office

6. Paste the district expense information into the EXPRPT.DOC Word document between the second and third sentences.
7. Save the Word document in a file using the name CH02EX03.
8. Print the document.
9. Close the Word and Excel applications.

Exercise 4

INSTRUCTIONS:

1. Open the Word application.
2. Open the CH02EX03.DOC document created in Exercise 3.
3. Open the Excel application.
4. Open the MAYEXP.XLS worksheet. You can find this file on the floppy diskette at the back of this book.
5. Copy the embedded chart to the Clipboard.
6. Paste it into the CH02EX03.DOC Word document at the end of the document.
7. Save the Word document in a file using the name CH02EX04.
8. Print the document.
9. Close the Word and Excel applications.

Exercise 5

INSTRUCTIONS:

1. Open the Excel application.
2. Open the MAYEXP.XLS worksheet. You can find this file on the floppy diskette at the back of this book.
3. Copy the embedded chart to the Clipboard.
4. Open the PowerPoint application.
5. Open the EXPTPRES.PPT presentation file. You can find this file on the floppy diskette at the back of this book.
6. Paste the chart on the presentation slide.
7. Resize the chart so that it is more legible.
8. Save the presentation in a file using the name CH02EX05.
9. Print the slide.
10. Close the PowerPoint and Excel applications.

Using the Microsoft Office Manager Toolbar

3

Objectives

In this chapter you will learn to:
- Identify the Microsoft Office Manager toolbar buttons
- Access the Microsoft Office Manager menu
- Customize the Microsoft Office Manager toolbar
- Modify the appearance and location of the Microsoft Office Manager toolbar
- Change the contents of the Microsoft Office Manager menu

Chapter Overview

The Microsoft Office Manager (MOM) toolbar allows you to efficiently switch among the various Microsoft applications. In this chapter, you will learn to describe the MOM toolbar, access the MOM menu, customize the MOM toolbar for your own requirements, modify the appearance of the MOM toolbar, alter the location of the MOM toolbar, and change the contents of the MOM menu.

Identifying the Microsoft Office Manager Toolbar Buttons

The MOM toolbar is used to switch among various applications represented by buttons on the toolbar. Initially, the MOM toolbar appears in the top-right corner of your screen. In this book, it is assumed that the MOM toolbar contains the following buttons:

Button	Application
	Microsoft Word
	Microsoft Excel
	Microsoft PowerPoint
	Microsoft Access
	Microsoft Mail
	Find File
	Microsoft Office

To complete the exercises in this chapter, first make sure that the MOM toolbar appears in the top-right corner of the screen. If you are unfamiliar with displaying the MOM toolbar, refer to Chapter 1. Assuming that you have the MOM toolbar on your screen, open the Word application. *Note*: To complete the exercises in this chapter, you do not need to have an application open.

Click the Microsoft Word button on the MOM toolbar so that a blank document appears on the screen. The MOM toolbar still appears in the top-right corner of your screen.

Accessing the Microsoft Office Manager Menu

To access the MOM menu:

Click the Microsoft Office button on the MOM toolbar

The MOM menu is displayed. Your screen should look like Figure 3-1. If your MOM toolbar looks different, you will learn how to customize it in a later section of this chapter.

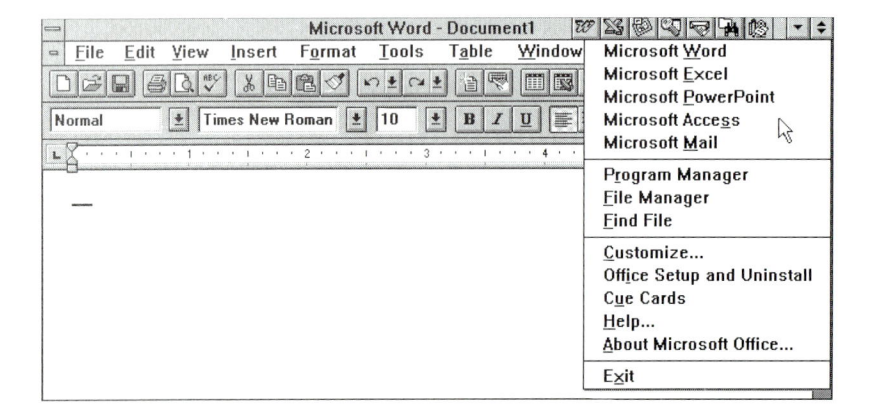

Figure 3-1

The first section of the menu includes the applications on the MOM menu. Notice that when the MOM menu appears on the screen, you can open one of the applications by clicking the mouse pointer on the application name appearing on the menu or by pressing the underlined letter for the application.

Using the Microsoft Office Manager Toolbar

The second part of the menu contains the Program Manager, File Manager, and Find File commands. By clicking the mouse pointer on one of the commands or by pressing the appropriate underlined letter, you can choose one of the commands.

The third segment of the menu contains the Customize, Office Setup and Uninstall, Cue Cards, Help, and About Microsoft Office commands. You can select each of these commands by clicking the mouse button with the mouse pointer on the command or by pressing the appropriate underlined letter for the command.

The last portion of the menu contains the Exit command. You can remove the MOM toolbar from the screen by choosing the Exit command. If you do not wish to make any selection, you can remove the menu from your screen by clicking elsewhere on the screen, clicking the Microsoft Office button, or by pressing the ESC key.

To remove the MOM menu:

Click elsewhere on the screen

Customizing the Microsoft Office Manager Toolbar

In some situations, you may want to add or delete or change the location of one of the application buttons on the MOM toolbar.

Adding an Application Button

Suppose you want to add the Program Manager application button to the MOM toolbar. To add the Program Manager button:

Click the Microsoft Office button on the MOM toolbar

Choose Customize

The Customize dialog box appears. Click the Toolbar tab, if necessary. Your screen should look similar to Figure 3-2.

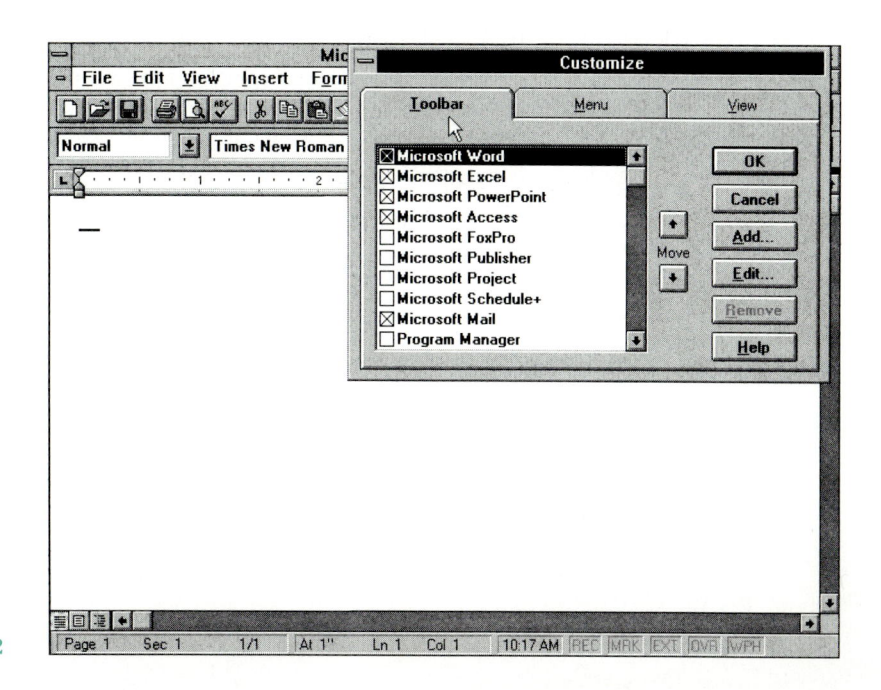

Figure 3-2

An "X" appears in the check box to the left of the Word, Excel, PowerPoint, Access, and Mail applications indicating that these applications appear on the MOM toolbar.

To include the Program Manager button on the MOM toolbar:

Click	the down scroll arrow in the list box until Program Manager appears (if necessary)
Click	the Program Manager check box to insert an X
Click	the OK command button

A button for the Program Manager appears on the MOM toolbar. The top part of your screen should look like Figure 3-3.

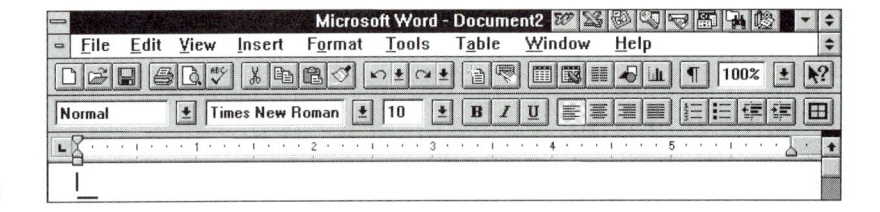

Figure 3-3

Notice that when a new button is added to the MOM toolbar, it appears near the end of the toolbar. The Microsoft Office button is always the last button appearing on the MOM toolbar. Later in this section, you will learn how to move buttons on the MOM toolbar.

> An alternative method for accessing the Customize dialog box is to move the mouse pointer to any position on the MOM toolbar and click the alternate mouse button. Then choose **Customize** from the menu.

Deleting an Application Button

You can also delete an application button from the MOM toolbar. Suppose you want to remove the Program Manager button from the MOM toolbar.

To remove the Program Manager button from the MOM toolbar:

Click	the Microsoft Office button on the MOM toolbar
Choose	Customize
Click	the **T**oolbar tab (if necessary)
Click	the down scroll arrow until Program Manager appears (if necessary)
Click	the Program Manager check box to remove the X
Click	the OK command button

The Program Manager button no longer appears on the MOM toolbar.

Moving an Application Button

In some situations, you may want to change the order of the buttons on the MOM toolbar. For example, you may want to have the Microsoft Excel button appear before the Microsoft Word button or the Microsoft PowerPoint button appear as the first button on the MOM toolbar.

Using the Microsoft Office Manager Toolbar

To move the Excel button before the Word button:

Click	the Microsoft Office button on the MOM toolbar
Choose	Customize
Click	the **T**oolbar tab (if necessary)
Click	Microsoft Excel in the list box
Click	the Up arrow button above the word Move
Click	the OK command button

The Excel button appears in front of the Word button on the MOM toolbar. The top part of your screen should look like Figure 3-4.

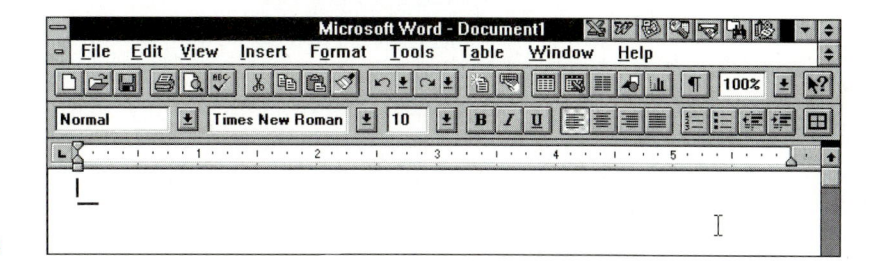

Figure 3-4

You can place a button to the right of another button.

To move the Excel button after the Word button:

Click	the Microsoft Office button on the MOM toolbar
Choose	Customize
Click	the **T**oolbar tab (if necessary)
Click	Microsoft Excel in the list box (if necessary)
Click	the Down arrow button below the word Move
Click	the OK command button

The Excel button again appears to the right of the Word button on the MOM toolbar.

Modifying the Appearance and Location of the Microsoft Office Manager Toolbar

When you initiate the use of Microsoft Office Manager, the default location of the MOM toolbar is in the top-right corner of your screen. The default appearance is small buttons. You can customize the size of the buttons. When you choose a larger button size, a Control-menu box, title bar, and Minimize button appear on the MOM toolbar. Once you select Regular or Large size buttons, you can move the MOM toolbar to other locations on the screen.

To change the size from the default small buttons to a larger size:

Click	the Microsoft Office button on the MOM toolbar
Choose	Customize
Click	the **V**iew tab

Click the Regular **B**uttons option button in the **T**oolbar Button Size group box

Click the OK command button

The appearance of the MOM toolbar changes. The toolbar is now in its own window with a Control-menu box, title bar, and Minimize button. The top part of your screen should look similar to Figure 3-5.

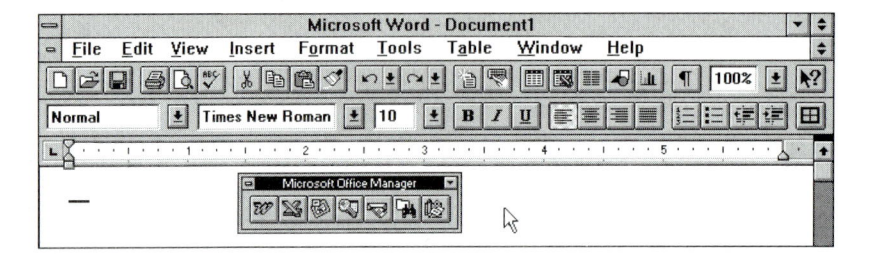

Figure 3-5

Since the toolbar can be moved to different places on the screen, the position of your MOM toolbar may vary, depending on where a previous user placed it.

You can select the various application software in the same manner as before (by clicking on the appropriate application button).

> An alternative method for changing the size of the buttons is to move the mouse pointer to any place on the MOM toolbar and click the alternate mouse button. Then choose the appropriate button size from the menu.

When the MOM toolbar is in its own window, you can place it in a different location on your screen. Whenever the small button size is used, the MOM toolbar always appears in the top-right corner of your screen.

To change the location of the MOM toolbar:

Move the mouse pointer to the title bar on the MOM toolbar

Drag the MOM toolbar to another location on the screen

If you move the MOM toolbar to the top-left corner of your screen, your screen should look similar to Figure 3-6.

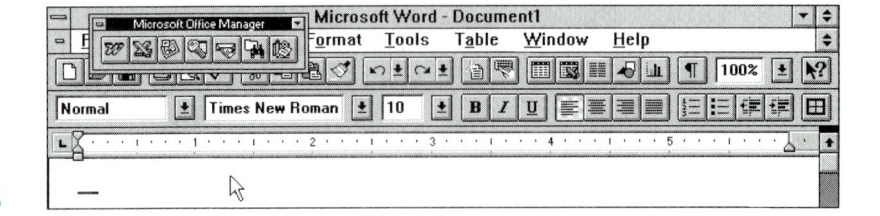

Figure 3-6

To return the MOM toolbar to its default appearance and location:

Click the Microsoft Office button on the MOM toolbar

Choose Customize

Click the **V**iew tab (if necessary)

Using the Microsoft Office Manager Toolbar

Click the **S**mall Buttons option button in the Toolbar Button Size group box

Click the OK command button

The MOM toolbar now appears in the upper-right portion of your screen and does not contain a Control-menu box, title bar, or Minimize button.

Changing the Contents of the Microsoft Office Manager Menu

You can modify the contents of the menu. For example, suppose you want to remove PowerPoint from the MOM menu.

To remove the PowerPoint option from the MOM menu:

Click the Microsoft Office button on the MOM toolbar

Choose **C**ustomize

Click the **M**enu tab

Click the Microsoft **P**owerPoint check box to remove the X

Click the OK command button

After you have clicked the Microsoft Office button to display the MOM menu, your screen should look like Figure 3-7.

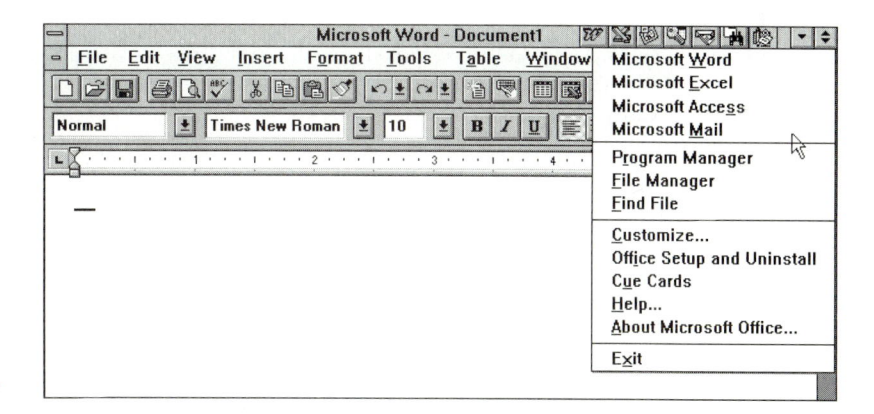

Figure 3-7

Notice that PowerPoint no longer appears on the menu. Click elsewhere on the screen to remove the MOM menu.

To place PowerPoint on the MOM menu:

Click the Microsoft Office button on the MOM toolbar

Choose **C**ustomize

Click the **M**enu tab (if necessary)

Click the Microsoft **P**owerPoint check box to insert an X

Click the OK command button

To view the MOM menu again:

Click the Microsoft Office button on the MOM toolbar

Notice that PowerPoint appears on the MOM menu again.

To remove the MOM menu:

Click elsewhere on the screen

Summary

The Microsoft Office Manager toolbar allows you to efficiently use the available applications. With Microsoft Office Manager, you can customize the contents, appearance, and location of the MOM toolbar.

Exercise 1

INSTRUCTIONS: Circle T if the statement is true and F if the statement is false.

T F 1. You cannot change the location of the MOM toolbar.
T F 2. Application buttons can be added or deleted on the MOM toolbar.
T F 3. You can move an application button on the MOM toolbar.
T F 4. When you initiate the use of Microsoft Office Manager, the default location of the MOM toolbar is in the top left corner of your screen.
T F 5. The default appearance of the buttons on the MOM toolbar is regular buttons.
T F 6. When you change the button size to a large button, a control-menu box, title bar, and minimize button appear on the MOM toolbar.
T F 7. When the MOM toolbar is in its own window, you can place it in a different location on your screen.
T F 8. The contents of the Microsoft Office Manager menu cannot be modified.

Exercise 2

INSTRUCTIONS:

1. Add the File Manager application button to the MOM toolbar.
2. Remove the File Manager application button from the MOM toolbar.

Exercise 3

INSTRUCTIONS:

1. Move the PowerPoint button before the Word button.
2. Move the PowerPoint button after the Excel button.

Exercise 4

INSTRUCTIONS:

1. Change the size of the buttons to large buttons.
2. Move the MOM toolbar to the bottom right corner of your screen.
3. Change the size of the buttons to small buttons.

Exercise 5

INSTRUCTIONS:

1. Remove the Excel option from the MOM menu.
2. Place Excel on the MOM menu.

Microsoft Excel 5.0

1. Quick Start for Excel
2. Organizing Workbooks and Designing Worksheets Properly
3. Creating and Enhancing Worksheets
4. Printing Features
5. Creating and Printing Charts
6. Creating and Using Multiple Worksheets and Workbooks
7. Introduction to Lists, Sorting, and Filtering
8. Introduction to Macros
9. Integrating Word and Excel

Quick Start for Excel

1

Objectives

In this chapter you will learn to:
- Identify the components of the Excel window
- Move around the workbook window
- Create a worksheet
- Edit a worksheet
- Save a workbook
- Print a worksheet
- Close a workbook
- Open a new workbook
- Open an existing workbook
- Exit Excel

Chapter Overview

This chapter explains elements of the Excel document window. Various methods of moving around the Excel document window are illustrated. When you create a worksheet in a workbook using Excel, you usually go through the following steps:

1. Access the Excel software
2. Create a worksheet by keying in the text and data
3. Make modifications or changes to the worksheet
4. Save the workbook in a file on a disk
5. Print the worksheet

Mastering and Using Microsoft Office Professional

In other situations, you may open an existing workbook file from a disk and make changes to a worksheet in the workbook. After you have completed the changes, save the workbook again. You may also print it.

When you are finished using a workbook, you will probably choose to close it before you start working on another workbook. You should exit the Excel application software when you are finished.

This chapter gives a quick overview of the processes of creating, editing, and printing a worksheet as well as saving a workbook. It also introduces the concept of closing the Excel workbook. You will open an existing workbook, make some changes to a worksheet, and save the workbook again. You will also learn to create a new workbook. Finally, the procedure for exiting Excel is presented.

To start Excel:

Click the Microsoft Excel button on the MOM toolbar

The program title appears on your screen. In a few seconds, the Excel window is displayed on your screen; it should look similar to Figure 1-1.

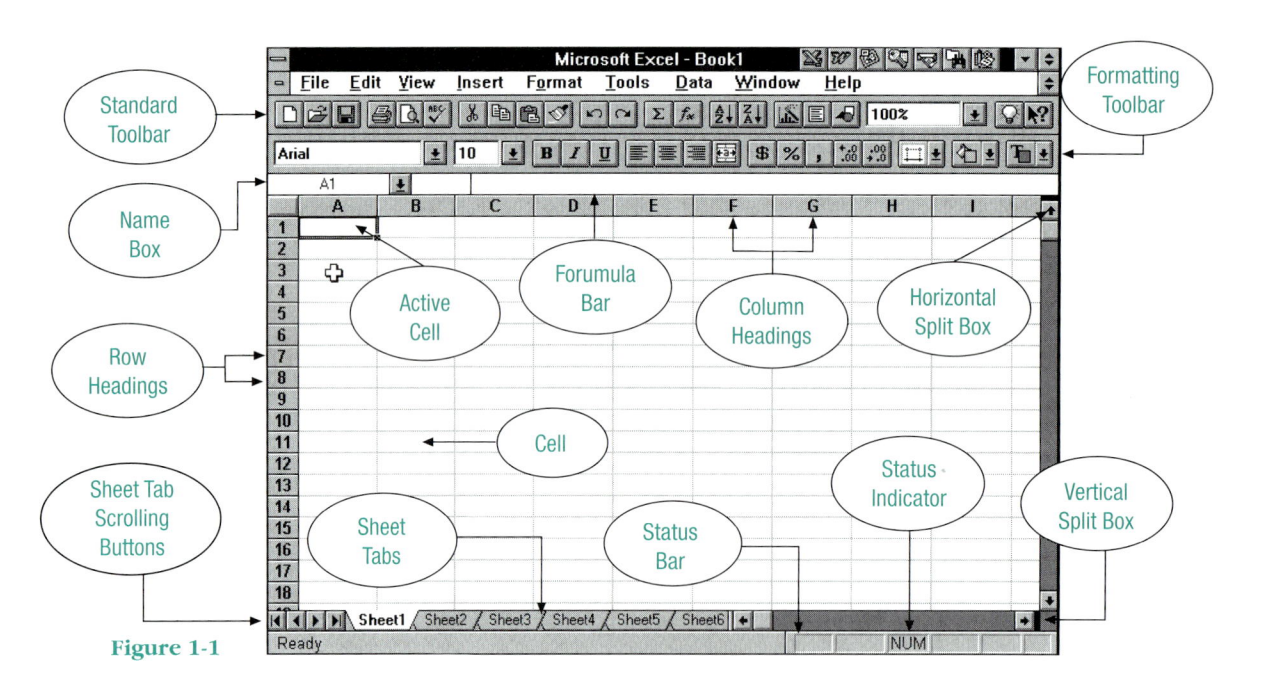

Figure 1-1

Identifying Components of the Excel Window

Each file you use is called a **workbook**. Notice the title bar contains the text "Book1." A workbook can include many sheets, including, for example, worksheets, charts, and macros. The sheet names appear on the tabs at the bottom of the screen.

Figure 1-1 is the standard form of the Excel window. Elements specific to the Excel application are noted in Figure 1-1 and are described below.

Standard and Formatting Toolbars

The **Standard** and **Formatting** toolbars appear below the menu bar. Use the toolbar buttons to quickly perform common commands. When the mouse pointer is positioned on a toolbar button, a ToolTip appears identifying the name of the button. You can change the buttons on a toolbar. For more information about changing toolbar buttons, consult your Excel *User's Guide*.

Name Box

The **Name box** is located below the Formatting toolbar on the left side of the window. This area displays the location of the active cell or name of a group of cells. If a range of cells is selected, the name box shows the initial cell in the range.

Formula Bar

The **formula bar** is located below the Formatting toolbar and to the right of the name box. This bar displays characters and formulas that you enter into a cell.

Column Headings

Across the top border of the worksheet on your screen is a set of letters called **column headings**. These headings identify columns with the letters A through Z, AA through AZ, BA through BZ, and so forth, until the letters IV are reached for a total of 256 column headings in a worksheet.

Row Headings

Along the left border of a worksheet is a set of numbers called **row headings**. There are a total of 16,384 rows available in a worksheet.

Cell

A **cell** is the area on a worksheet at the intersection of a column and a row. Data are stored in a cell. The cell reference, A1, refers to the cell at the intersection of column A and row 1.

Active Cell

The **active cell** is distinguished by a thick, heavy border. The next data entry or operation affects this cell. The contents of the active cell are displayed in the formula bar. The name box displays the address of the active cell. To make a cell active, move the mouse pointer to the cell and click the mouse button. You can also use the pointer-movement keys on the keyboard to make a cell active.

Sheet Tabs

The **sheet tabs** appear just below the last visible row in a workbook window. When you click on a particular sheet tab name, that sheet becomes the active worksheet.

Sheet Tab Scrolling Buttons

Scrolling buttons appear to the left of the sheet tab names. Use the tab scrolling buttons to display sheet tab names. The right-pointing triangle displays the next sheet name. The right-pointing triangle with the vertical line displays the last few sheet names. The left-pointing triangle displays the previous sheet name. The left-pointing triangle with the vertical line displays the first few sheet names.

Horizontal and Vertical Split Boxes

The vertical **split box** appears to the right of the horizontal scroll bar as a thick, black line. Use it to split the worksheet window into two vertical panes. The horizontal split box located above the vertical scroll bar is also a thick, black line. Use this split box to split the worksheet window into two horizontal panes.

Status Bar

The **status bar**, located at the bottom of the Excel window, includes the name of the currently selected command or current activity. **Status indicators** are activated only when certain conditions are present: For example, when you press the Caps Lock key, the CAPS indicator is activated.

Moving Around the Workbook Window

As mentioned earlier, the active cell is highlighted by a thick, heavy border. Using the mouse pointer and the pointer-movement keys to move around the worksheet window, you can make any cell the active cell.

Selecting the Active Cell Using the Mouse

You can use the mouse to make a cell the active cell. Move the mouse pointer to the desired cell. It should appear as a white cross. Click the mouse button. If the desired cell is not visible, use the scroll bars described below to display the cell location and then click on the desired cell.

Viewing Different Parts of a Worksheet Window Using the Scroll Bars

You can use the vertical and horizontal **scroll bars** to quickly view a different area of a worksheet in a workbook. The following table describes various locations on a worksheet and tells how to use the scroll bars to view the specified locations.

You may wish to open the NATSALES.XLS workbook you used in Chapter 2 of the Office unit before practicing the techniques below. Make cell A1 the active cell.

Movement	Mouse Technique
Down one row	Click the down scroll arrow on the vertical scroll bar
Up one row	Click the up scroll arrow on the vertical scroll bar
Down several rows	Click the gray shaded area below the vertical scroll box
Up several rows	Click the gray shaded area above the vertical scroll box
Beginning of a worksheet	Drag the vertical scroll box to the top of the vertical scroll bar
End of a worksheet	Drag the vertical scroll box to the bottom of the vertical scroll bar
One or more column(s) to the right	Click the right scroll arrow on the horizontal scroll bar or click the gray shaded area right of the horizontal scroll box

Movement	Mouse Technique
One or more column(s) to the left	Click the left scroll arrow on the horizontal scroll bar or click the gray shaded area left of the horizontal scroll box

Notice that the active cell, A1, referenced in the name box, does not change when you use the scroll bars. If you want one of the visible cells to become active, position the mouse pointer on the desired cell and click the mouse button. The cell address in the name box would change from A1 to the cell address of the cell on which you click.

Selecting the Active Cell Using the Keyboard

You can use the keyboard to quickly move the active cell to a different position on the worksheet. The following table describes various locations on a worksheet and tells how to use the keyboard to move to the specified locations.

Before practicing the following techniques, make cell A1 the active cell:

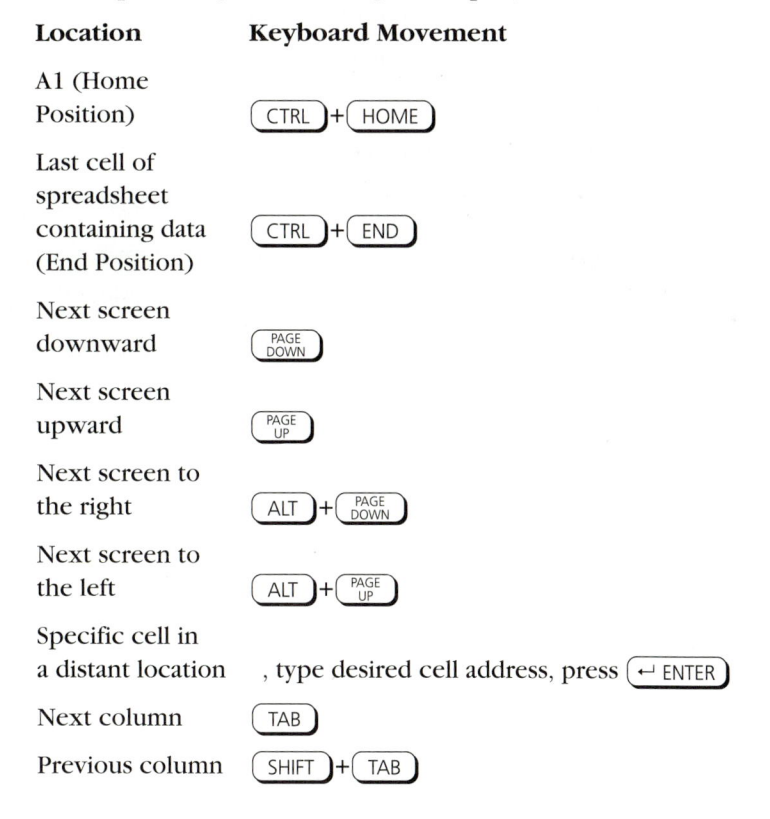

Location	Keyboard Movement
A1 (Home Position)	CTRL + HOME
Last cell of spreadsheet containing data (End Position)	CTRL + END
Next screen downward	PAGE DOWN
Next screen upward	PAGE UP
Next screen to the right	ALT + PAGE DOWN
Next screen to the left	ALT + PAGE UP
Specific cell in a distant location	, type desired cell address, press ENTER
Next column	TAB
Previous column	SHIFT + TAB

Creating a Worksheet

In this exercise, you will create the worksheet shown in Figure 1-2.

Figure 1-2

To specify the information to enter in cell A1:

Click   on cell A1 (if necessary)

Type   Sales

Your screen should look like Figure 1-3.

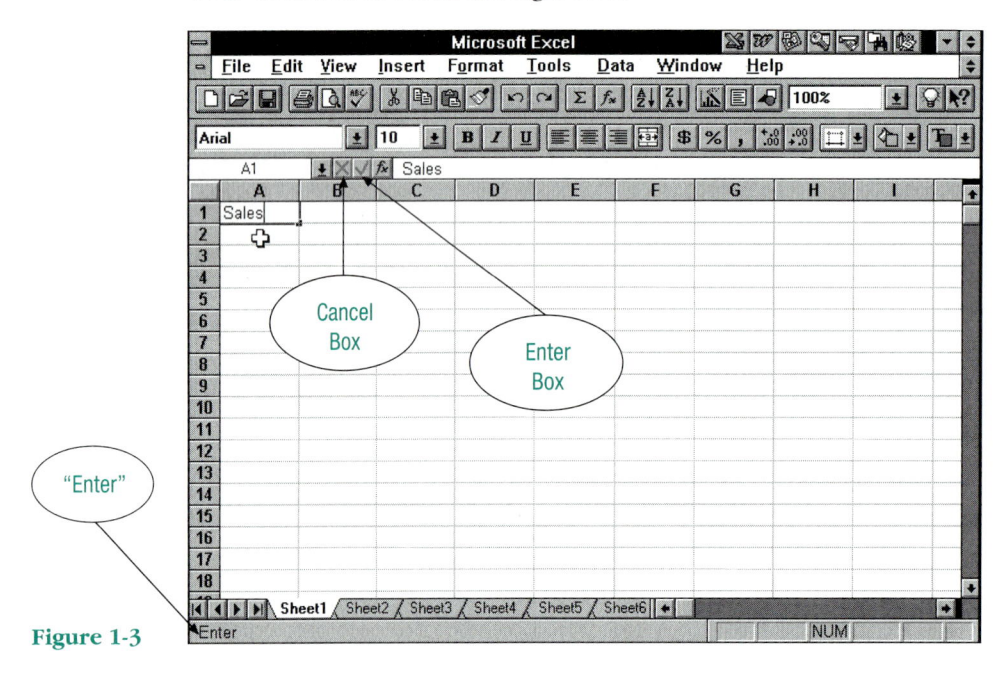

Figure 1-3

The word "Sales" appears in the formula bar and in the cell. Notice that when you enter the first character, the word "Enter" appears in the status bar indicating that you are entering something. The enter and cancel boxes also appear to the left of the formula bar.

To accept the information in cell A1:

Move   the mouse pointer to the enter box ✓

Click   the mouse button

The word "Sales" appears in cell A1 and will remain there until you delete it or enter other data. The word "Sales" also appears in the formula bar. The top part of your screen should look like Figure 1-4.

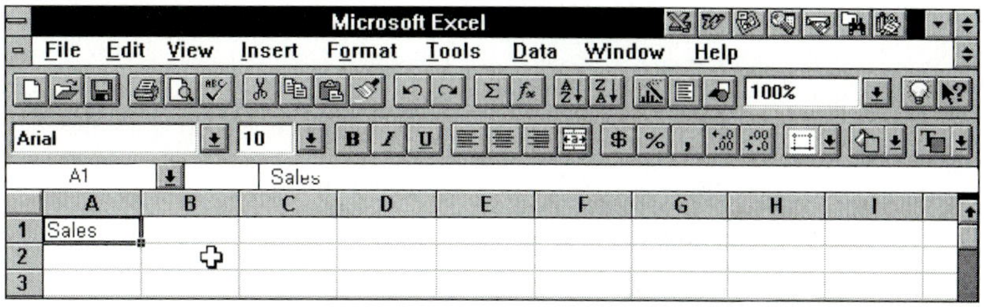

Quick Start for Excel

Figure 1-4

> You can also press the ENTER key to accept the cell contents instead of clicking the enter box. If you press the ENTER key to place text in a cell, the cell immediately below becomes the active cell.
>
> You may want the active cell to remain in the same position when you press the ENTER key. To change this default, choose the **O**ptions command on the **T**ools menu. Click the Edit tab and remove the X in the **M**ove Selection after Enter check box.

Notice that the text is left-aligned in cell A1. "Left-aligned" means that the characters begin at the leftmost position of the cell. When a number is entered, it is right-aligned. That is, the number appears in the rightmost part of the cell. Methods for changing alignment are discussed in Chapter 3.

To place the text "Nails" and "Bolts" in cells A3 and A4:

Move	the mouse pointer to cell A3
Click	the mouse button

To indent the product names two spaces and enter them:

Press	the space bar twice
Type	Nails
Move	the mouse pointer to the enter box ✓
Click	the mouse button
Move	the mouse pointer to cell A4
Click	the mouse button
Press	the space bar twice
Type	Bolts
Move	the mouse pointer to the enter box ✓
Click	the mouse button

> So far in this book, to make a cell active using the mouse, you have been instructed to move the mouse to a cell and then click the mouse button. For the remainder of the book, these two steps are combined by the instruction to click on the cell.
>
> When entering information using the mouse, so far you have been directed to move the mouse pointer to the enter box ✓ and click the mouse button. From this point forward, the steps to move the mouse pointer and click the enter box ✓ are eliminated. You will simply be told to enter the data in the cell. You can either click the enter box ✓ or press the ENTER key.

To enter the sales amount for Nails:

Click on cell B3

Enter 4000

To enter the sales amount for Bolts:

Click on cell B4

Enter 6000

The top part of your screen should look similar to Figure 1-5.

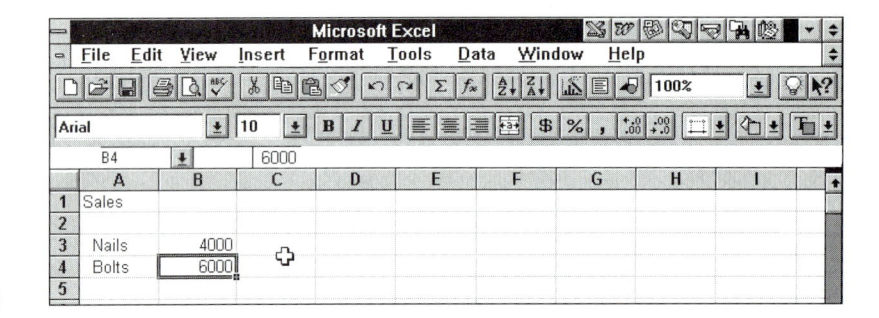

Figure 1-5

Editing a Worksheet

Suppose the sales value for Nails should have been 5000.

To change the number:

Click on cell B3

Enter 5000

The sales value for Nails is changed.

Using the Undo Feature

You will sometimes overwrite the contents of a cell accidentally. When this happens, you can use the **Undo** feature to return the original cell contents. The Undo feature creates a temporary copy of both the data and worksheet settings. Excel allows you to restore a cell entry to its previous form.

- You can choose the **Undo** command on the **Edit** menu to undo the previous action.
- You can also click the Undo button on the Standard toolbar to undo the previous action.

To illustrate the Undo feature:

Click on cell B3 (if necessary)

Enter 10000

The value "5000" has been replaced by "10000." Suppose you want to undo the action and have the value "5000" again appear in cell B3.

Click the Undo button on the Standard toolbar

The value "5000" again appears in cell B3.

The Undo Entry command does not work in all situations. For example, you cannot undo a print or file operation.

> Typing new contents in a cell automatically replaces the existing contents. You can edit the contents of a cell with three different methods.
>
> First, you can click the mouse button on the text in the formula bar area. An insertion point will appear. You can use the mouse pointer, the left and right arrow keys, as well as the HOME and END keys, to move the insertion point to various characters in an entry. To delete a character, move the insertion point to the left of the character you wish to delete and then press the DELETE key. You can also delete a character by placing the insertion point to the right of the character you wish to delete and then pressing the BACKSPACE key. To insert a character, move the insertion point to the place you want the new character(s) to appear and then type the text. After you edit the contents of a cell, click the enter box or press the ENTER key.
>
> The second method for editing the contents of a cell is to double-click on the cell itself. After an insertion point appears, you can use the methods mentioned above to edit the existing text.
>
> You can also use the F2 function key to edit information in a cell. When you press the F2 key, an insertion point appears at the end of the text in the cell. Move the insertion point using the mouse or keyboard and change the text as needed. You can then click the enter box or press the ENTER key.

Saving a Workbook

While you are creating or editing a worksheet, any changes you make are stored temporarily in your computer's memory. If the power to your computer fails, or if you turn off the computer, your work will be lost. You can prevent such a loss by placing a copy of the workbook in a file on a disk.

- You can choose the **S**ave or Save **A**s commands on the **F**ile menu to place a copy of the workbook in a file on a disk.
- You can also click the Save button on the Standard toolbar to place a copy of the workbook in a file on a disk.

The disk can be either a floppy diskette or a hard disk. When you are saving a file for the first time, it does not matter whether you choose the **S**ave command, the Save **A**s command, or click the Save button on the Standard toolbar. Regardless of which you do, the Save As dialog box will appear on your screen.

Once you have specified the directory for saving your workbooks, you will type the name of the workbook in the File **N**ame text box. A workbook name can have up to eight characters. Workbook names can contain letters, numbers, and some special characters in any combination. They cannot include spaces or the following special symbols: . ' / \ [ ] : ; | = , ? < > ~ ^

Excel automatically adds a period and a three-character extension (.XLS) to the end of the workbook name. By default, the File **N**ame text box contains the filename "book" based on the "Book1" name Excel assigned to the document window when you started the Excel program.

As you work, it is a good idea to save the workbook every 10 to 15 minutes. The **S**ave command on the **F**ile menu or the Save button on the Standard toolbar allows you to save a previously named document with the same name and location. Once you have named a file, the only time you will use the Save As command is when you wish to change the filename or its location. For simply saving your work periodically, it is faster to use the **S**ave button. No dialog box will appear, and your file is quickly saved with its original filename in its previous location.

Making cell A1 the active cell prior to saving a workbook is an optional step. If you make cell A1 the active cell before saving, the workbook is saved with A1 as the active cell. When the workbook file is opened, A1 is the active cell.

To make cell A1 the active cell:

Click on cell A1

To save the workbook to a file:

Click the Save button on the Standard toolbar

Because the file has not been previously saved, the Save As dialog box appears on your screen.

To save the worksheet with the filename EXAMPLE:

Type EXAMPLE in the File **N**ame text box

Click the OK command button

A Summary Info dialog box may appear on your screen. The Summary Info feature allows you to classify documents with a title, subject, author, keywords, and comments. You can use these categories to find files later. For more information about the Summary Info feature, see your Excel *User's Guide*.

If the Summary Info dialog box appears, enter a title for the workbook:

Type My first workbook in the **T**itle text box

Click the OK command button

Notice that the name of the workbook file (EXAMPLE) and its extension (XLS) now appear on the title bar.

Printing a Worksheet

Once you have created a worksheet, you may want to print it.

- You can choose the **P**rint command on the **F**ile menu to print a worksheet.
- You can also click the Print button on the Standard toolbar to print a worksheet.

To begin printing the worksheet:

Click the Print button on the Standard toolbar

The printer should print your worksheet. Printing options are discussed in Chapter 4.

Closing a Workbook

Before starting to work on a worksheet in another workbook, you usually close the current workbook and open a new workbook.

To close the current workbook using the menu:

Choose   File

Choose   Close

The Null screen is displayed on your screen. Your screen should look like Figure 1-6.

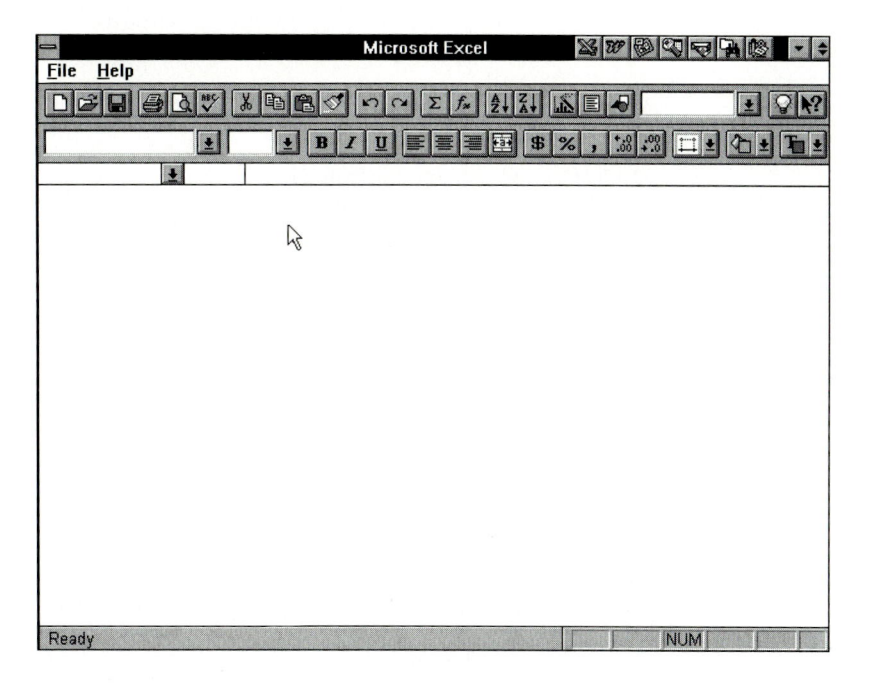

Figure 1-6

This screen appears when all workbooks are closed.

Opening a New Workbook

You can create a new workbook by using the menu or a button on the Standard toolbar.

- You can choose the **New** command on the **File** menu to create a new workbook.
- You can also click the New Workbook button on the Standard toolbar to create a new workbook.

To open a new workbook:

Click   the New Workbook button on the Standard toolbar

A new workbook similar to the one in Figure 1-1 appears on your screen. Before proceeding to the next chapter, you need to close the current workbook.

To close the workbook:

Choose   File

Choose   Close

The Null screen appears again.

Opening an Existing Workbook

You can open an existing workbook file by using the menu or a button on the Standard toolbar.

- You can choose the **O**pen command on the **F**ile menu to open an existing workbook file.
- You can also click the Open button on the Standard toolbar to open an existing workbook file.

You can open a document from any directory or any drive. If the document is stored in the current directory, just highlight the document name. If the document is stored in a different directory, you can change to the appropriate drive and directory before selecting the document name. The drive, directory, and filename can be typed instead of selected.

To open the EXAMPLE.XLS workbook file:

Click	the Open button on the Standard toolbar
Click	EXAMPLE in the File **N**ame list box
Click	the OK command button

The EXAMPLE.XLS workbook opens.

Enter the additional information that appears in Figure 1-7 to your worksheet.

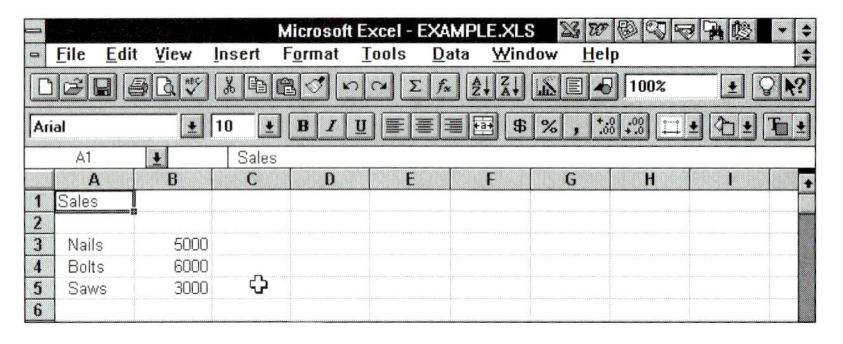

Figure 1-7

To continue:

Click	on cell A5
Press	the space bar twice
Enter	Saws
Click	on cell B5
Enter	3000

Instead of clicking on the desired cell, you can press pointer movement keys to accept the contents of a cell and move to a different cell.

After modifying a worksheet in a workbook, you usually save the workbook again using the same filename.

To save the workbook that contains your worksheet with the same filename:

Click	on cell A1
Click	the Save button on the Standard toolbar

Notice that because the file already has a name, the Save button uses the **S**ave command instead of the Save **A**s command.

Exiting Excel

When you finish using Excel, you need to exit from the software.

To exit Excel:

Choose	File
Choose	Exit

Summary

This chapter presents an overview of the processes for moving around a worksheet window, creating a worksheet, editing a worksheet, saving a workbook, printing a worksheet, closing a workbook, and opening an existing workbook. The process for exiting Excel is also illustrated.

Exercise 1

INSTRUCTIONS: Define or explain the following:

1. Sheet tabs _____

2. Formula bar _____

3. Cell _____

4. Split box _____

5. Scroll bars _____

6. Name box _____

Exercise 2

INSTRUCTIONS: Circle T if the statement is true and F if the statement is false.

T   F   1. You can replace the contents of a cell by typing over the current contents and pressing the ENTER key.
T   F   2. To use the keyboard to return to cell A1, press the CTRL key and the HOME key.
T   F   3. There is no limit to the number of characters that can appear in a workbook name.
T   F   4. When you use the keyboard to move through a worksheet, the active cell moves, too.
T   F   5. Excel will automatically save your work every 10 to 15 minutes.
T   F   6. A worksheet can have no more than 250 columns.

T F 7. The first time you save a file, it does not matter whether you choose the Save or the Save As command on the File menu.

T F 8. When you enter data into a cell, you cannot see the contents until you press the ENTER key.

Exercise 3

INSTRUCTIONS:

1. Create the worksheet shown in Figure 1-8.
2. Save the workbook in a file using the name E01EX03.
3. Print the worksheet.
4. Close the workbook.

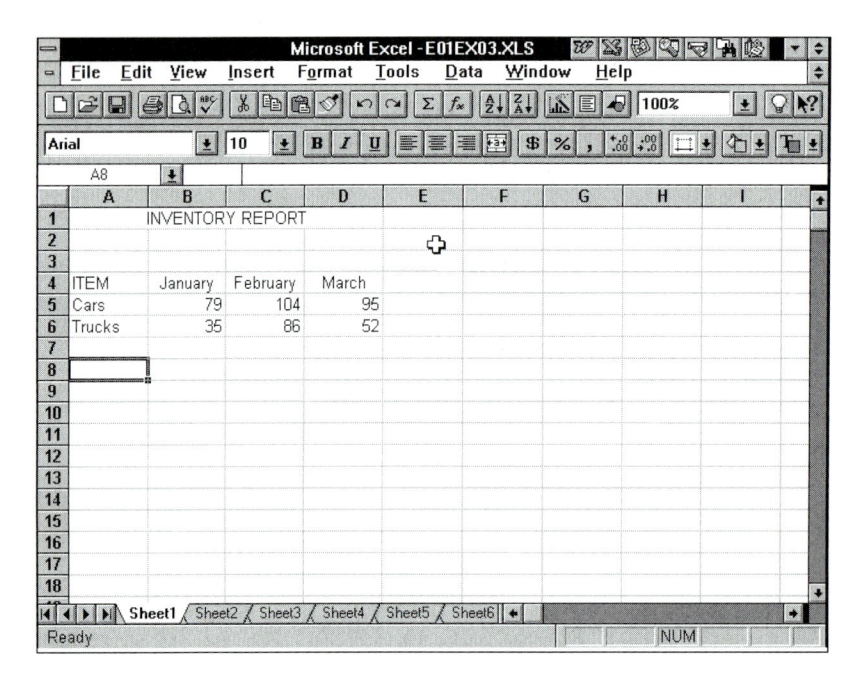

Figure 1-8

Exercise 4

INSTRUCTIONS:

1. Open the E01EX03.XLS workbook created in Exercise 3.
2. Change the value for inventory of Cars in February to 95.
3. Change the value for inventory of Trucks in March to 61.
4. Add a new item to the Inventory Report. The new item is called Trailers. The inventory amounts are:

	January	February	March
Trailers	10	15	12

5. Save the workbook in a file using the name E01EX04.
6. Print the worksheet.
7. Close the workbook.

Organizing Workbooks and Designing Worksheets Properly

2

Objectives

In this chapter you will learn to:
- Design workbook and worksheet layout
- Design worksheets within a workbook
- Document a workbook
- Name a sheet tab

Chapter Overview

When you create workbooks consisting of multiple worksheets, remember to use good design principles. Properly laid-out workbooks and properly designed worksheets are easier for individuals to modify at a later date. Furthermore, if a workbook is organized effectively and worksheets are designed appropriately, it takes less effort for someone to understand how a worksheet prepared by someone else actually operates.

Designing Workbook and Worksheet Layout

Thommes (1992) and Ronen, Palley, and Lucas (1989) discuss some formats to use in designing the worksheet layout. The layout suggested by Ronen, Palley, and Lucas, and discussed in the work by Thommes, has been adapted for use in this book. Figure 2-1 shows the suggested layout. The suggested layout would appear on three or more worksheets in the workbook.

Identification Owner Developer User Date Prepared and Revised Workbook Filename	Worksheet Model	Macros
Map of Workbook		
Description, Assumptions, and Parameters		

Figure 2-1 **Documentation** **Worksheet Model** **Macro Module**

With this layout, the user can develop worksheets in a workbook to satisfy the five criteria for proper worksheet design discussed in the next section.

- The **identification area** usually appears on Sheet 1 of the workbook and includes information on the workbook owner, developer, and user. The dates the workbook was created and last revised are also specified in the identification area. The identification area also provides the filename for the workbook.
- The **map of the workbook** appears below the identification area. It resembles a table of contents, showing the order of the various areas in the workbook.
- The next area includes additional documentation about the workbook. This area includes a general **description** of the workbook and provides the **parameters** and **assumptions** used in the workbook. For example, it might show growth rates and interest rates.
- The next worksheet contains the **model**. In this section of the workbook, the rows and columns contain formulas that calculate values based on the parameters and assumptions specified for the workbook. Additional worksheets may be used for charts or other related data.
- Macros, which are used to improve the efficiency of processing a worksheet, appear on a separate **macro worksheet**. Macros can also be placed in the Personal Macro Workbook or in a separate workbook. Macros are discussed more thoroughly in Chapter 8.

Designing Worksheets within a Workbook

Excel is a tool that enhances productivity. Worksheets within a workbook should be designed so they are useful for the individuals who create them as well as for other people who may use them. A worksheet should be designed so that it is easy for the developer or any other user to modify in the future.

Organizing Workbooks and Designing Worksheets Properly

In designing a worksheet, Thommes (1992) has suggested several criteria to consider, including (1) accuracy, (2) clarity, (3) flexibility, (4) efficiency, and (5) auditability.

1. The first criterion is **accuracy**. That is, if a worksheet does not give correct results, it is worthless. As you will see later in this book, there are many situations in which you can enter the wrong formula or value that lead to incorrect answers. The formulas and functions used in Excel are not immediately visible to a worksheet user. Proper design and documentation can improve the worksheet so that people are less likely to use it improperly.

2. **Clarity** is the second design criterion. The creator and designer of a worksheet must understand how the worksheet works. Proper layout and documentation improve the clarity for everyone who uses a workbook and its worksheets.

3. The next criterion is **flexibility**. When designing and developing a worksheet, you should consider possible future modifications.

4. **Efficiency**, the fourth criterion, has three aspects. First, you should consider the amount of computer memory required to process the worksheet. Second, think of the time the computer requires to process the worksheet. Third, the user should be able to easily find the important sections of the worksheet.

5. The final criterion is **auditability**. In many situations, worksheets may require auditing for accuracy. An individual should be able to determine what items are used to calculate the value in a cell. Proper layout and documentation can ease the task of checking worksheets.

Documenting a Workbook

After you have completed a workbook, you should document it. Documentation should include at least: (1) a printout of the workbook, (2) a printout of worksheet cell formulas, (3) a copy of the workbook on a diskette, (4) information on the purpose of the workbook, (5) source of the input data, and (6) destination and users of the output information. Documentation is particularly useful when a worksheet must be changed or a workbook file is destroyed.

It is a good idea to keep the documentation in a fireproof file cabinet or in a separate location. You can usually obtain additional assistance on documentation and backup precautions from the information systems department in an organization.

Example Problem

Suppose you are asked to create a worksheet for Acme Wholesalers Company that computes the profit forecast for the next five years and displays the profit before and after taxes.

You will create and print the worksheet model in Chapter 3. In this chapter, you will create (1) the identification section, (2) a map of the workbook, and (3) the description, assumptions, and parameters section. You will place this information on the first worksheet of a new workbook.

Prior to entering the data for the identification area, it is a good idea to place the name of the company at the beginning of the worksheet. Make sure you have a blank workbook on your screen. If not, close the current workbook and open a new workbook.

Click	on cell A1 (if necessary)
Enter	`ACME WHOLESALERS COMPANY`

In the identification section, include the following items:

1. The name of the workbook owner.
2. The name of the person who developed the workbook.
3. The workbook user(s).
4. The date the workbook was completed.
5. The date the workbook was last revised.

To enter the data for the identification section:

Click	on cell A3
Enter	`Identification:`
Click	on cell A4
Press	`SPACEBAR` twice
Enter	`Owner: Financial Planning Department`
Click	on cell A5
Press	`SPACEBAR` twice
Enter	`Developer: H. Albert Napier`
Click	on cell A6
Press	`SPACEBAR` twice
Enter	`User: Mary Jackson`
Click	on cell A7
Press	`SPACEBAR` twice
Enter	`Date Created: 9/19/95`
Click	on cell A8
Press	`SPACEBAR` twice
Enter	`Date Revised: 4/15/96`

To enter the filename where the workbook will be stored:

Click	on cell A10
Enter	`Workbook File: PROFFCST`

The top part of your screen should look like Figure 2-2.

Organizing Workbooks and Designing Worksheets Properly

Figure 2-2

[Screenshot of Microsoft Excel showing:
A1: ACME WHOLESALERS COMPANY
A3: Identification:
A4: Owner: Financial Planning Department
A5: Developer: H. Albert Napier
A6: User: Mary Jackson
A7: Date Created: 9/19/95
A8: Date Revised: 4/15/96
A10: Workbook File: PROFFCST]

Now enter the information for the map of the workbook. This area shows the order of the various parts of the worksheets in the workbook.

Use the information shown in Figure 2-3 to enter the data for the map of the workbook section. You will use cells A12 through B16.

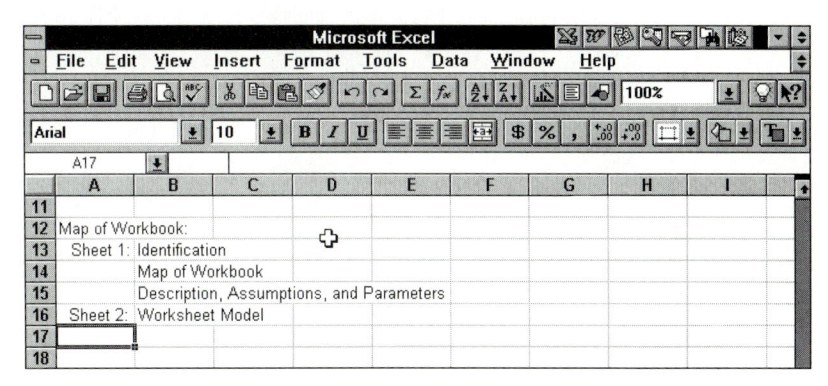

Figure 2-3

[Screenshot of Microsoft Excel showing:
A12: Map of Workbook:
B13: Sheet 1: Identification
C14: Map of Workbook
C15: Description, Assumptions, and Parameters
B16: Sheet 2: Worksheet Model]

The next segment of the worksheet is the description, assumptions, and parameters section. The inclusion of a brief description of the workbook and the assumptions and parameters used in the workbook simplifies both the developer's and user's understanding of the workbook.

Figure 2-4 includes the information to place on your worksheet for the description, assumptions, and parameters section. Enter the information shown in Figure 2-4.

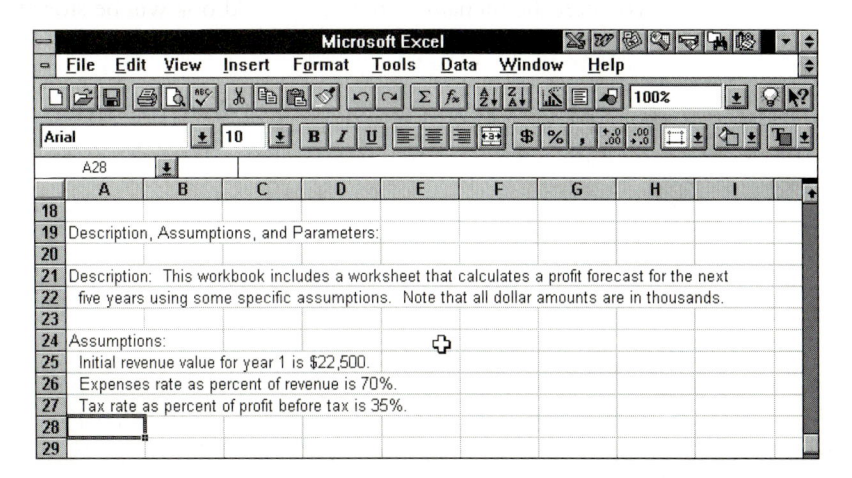

Figure 2-4

[Screenshot of Microsoft Excel showing:
A19: Description, Assumptions, and Parameters:
A21: Description: This workbook includes a worksheet that calculates a profit forecast for the next
A22: five years using some specific assumptions. Note that all dollar amounts are in thousands.
A24: Assumptions:
A25: Initial revenue value for year 1 is $22,500.
A26: Expenses rate as percent of revenue is 70%.
A27: Tax rate as percent of profit before tax is 35%.]

Naming a Sheet Tab

Since various information is placed on different worksheets, it is a good idea to name the various sheets using the sheet tabs.

- You can choose the **R**ename command under the **Sh**eet command on the **F**ormat menu to rename a sheet tab.
- You can also position the mouse pointer on the sheet tab and double-click the mouse button to rename a sheet tab.

To name the first sheet tab:

Double-click   the Sheet1 tab

The Rename Sheet dialog box appears. The top part of your screen should look like Figure 2-5.

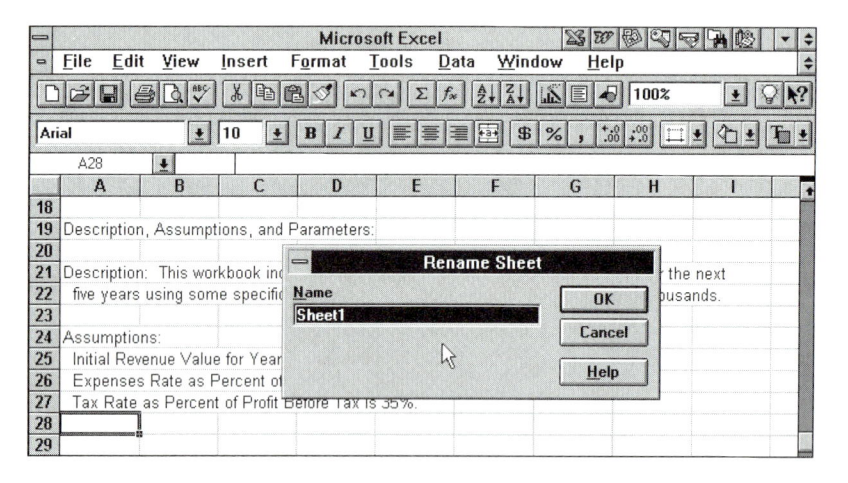

Figure 2-5

To name the Sheet1 tab:

Type   Documentation

Click   the OK command button

The next sheet is the worksheet model. This is where you enter the actual data and create calculations. The worksheet model will be placed on the second worksheet in the workbook. You will create the worksheet model in the next chapter.
To save the workbook:

Click   on cell A1 (to be in Home position before saving)

Click   the Save button on the Standard toolbar

The Save As dialog box appears:

Type   PROFFCST in the File **N**ame text box

Click   the OK command button

If the Summary Info dialog box appears:

Type   Profit Forecast Workbook in the **T**itle text box

Click   the OK command button

Organizing Workbooks and Designing Worksheets Properly

Summary

This chapter describes the basics of organizing workbooks and designing worksheets in a workbook. The layout described in this chapter is a popular workbook design. The areas include identification; map of the worksheet; description, assumptions, and parameters; the worksheet model; and the macros. The five criteria for good worksheet design are accuracy, clarity, flexibility, efficiency, and auditability. For more detailed information on designing workbooks, see the references at the end of this chapter.

Exercise 1

INSTRUCTIONS: Answer the questions in the space provided.

1. Briefly describe the following criteria for good worksheet design:
    a. Accuracy _____
    b. Clarity _____
    c. Flexibility _____
    d. Efficiency _____
    e. Auditability _____
2. Briefly describe the following sections:
    a. Identification area _____
    b. Macro worksheet _____
    c. Map of the workbook _____
    d. Description, assumptions, and parameters _____
    e. Worksheet model _____

Exercise 2

INSTRUCTIONS: Circle T if the statement is true and F if the statement is false.

T F 1. Identifying the Developer, User, Date, and so forth is a sound practice when creating a workbook.

T F 2. Documenting the parameters and assumptions in a worksheet is required for a worksheet to compute properly.

T F 3. You should not specify the name of the workbook developer.

T F 4. You should note the last date a workbook was changed on the second worksheet in a workbook.

T F 5. You cannot change sheet tab names.

References

Ronen, B., Palley, M. A., Lucas, Jr., H. C., "Spreadsheet Analysis and Design," Communications of the ACM, Volume 32, No. 1 (January 1989), pp. 84-93.

Thommes, M.C., Proper Spreadsheet Design, boyd & fraser publishing company, Danvers, MA, 1992.

Creating Worksheets 3

Objectives

In this chapter you will learn to:
- → Enter worksheet titles, column titles, and row titles
- → Expand the width of a column
- → Enter data and formulas and copy information in a worksheet
- → Select a format for the data
- → Correct rounding errors
- → Enhance the appearance of a worksheet
- → Use absolute cell references
- → Split a window into panes
- → Change the assumptions to complete a "what-if" analysis
- → Use the Spelling feature

Chapter Overview

One of the first difficulties facing you as a beginning Excel user in learning to create a worksheet within a workbook is how to begin! The next several sections provide step-by-step instructions for solving a business problem with a properly designed Excel worksheet. While guiding you through the worksheet-building process, the instructions detail Excel's capabilities as you need them. The instructions address typical beginners' problems, such as how to solve rounding problems and how to change the numeric format of a worksheet.

Entering Worksheet Titles, Column Titles, and Row Titles

In Chapter 2, you entered some information about the worksheet model you will create in this chapter. You may wish to refer to that information as you complete the activities in this chapter. Figure 3-1 displays the completed worksheet model.

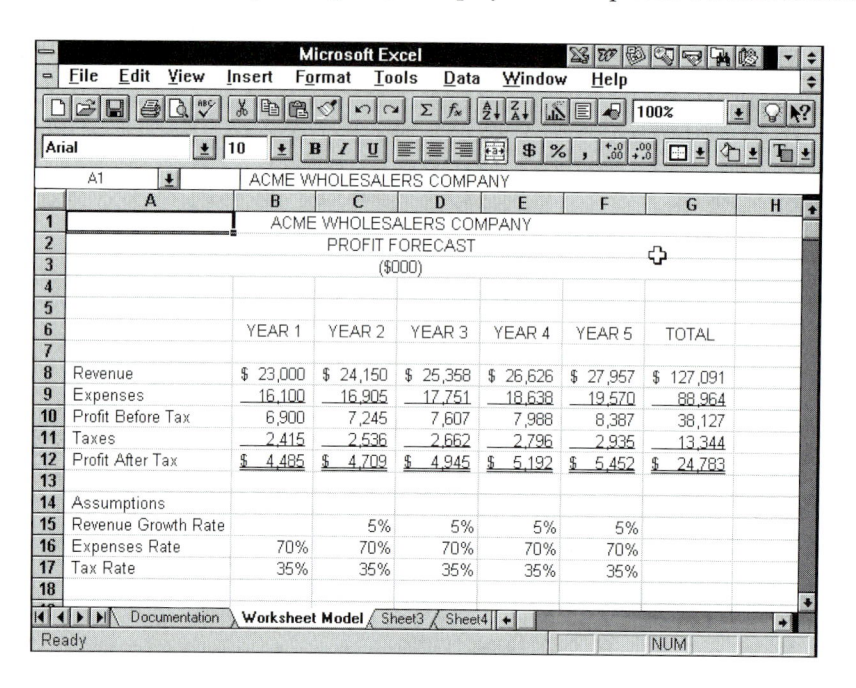

Figure 3-1

Open the PROFFCST.XLS workbook you created in Chapter 2.

To place the worksheet model on the second worksheet of the workbook:

    Click   the Sheet2 tab

Notice that the second worksheet is now the current worksheet. The Sheet2 tab name is in front of the other sheet tabs and is **boldfaced**.

To name the Sheet2 tab:

    Double-click   the Sheet2 tab

    Type   `Worksheet Model`

    Click   the OK command button

The bottom part of your screen should look like Figure 3-2.

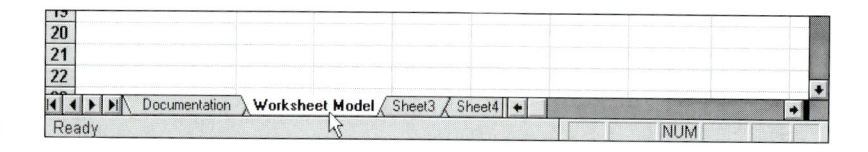

Figure 3-2

Creating Worksheets

Entering Worksheet Titles

Beginning in cell A1, you will enter the title of the worksheet.

> **FYI** In the previous two chapters, you were told to move to a new cell to make it the active cell. Then, you were instructed what to enter in the cell. From this point forward, you will be instructed to enter data in a cell. It is assumed that you will either click on the cell to make it the active cell or use pointer-movement keys to move to the desired cell.

To enter the title:

Enter   ACME WHOLESALERS COMPANY in cell A1

Enter   PROFIT FORECAST in cell A2

You wish to enter the text ($000) in cell A3 to indicate that all numeric values are in thousands of dollars. When you simply enter the text ($000) in cell A3, Excel changes the appearance of the text to a value. To force Excel to display the text ($000), type an apostrophe or single quote before the first parenthesis. When you print the worksheet, the apostrophe will not print.

Enter   '($000) in cell A3

The worksheet title information appears in cells A1 through A3. The top part of your screen should look like Figure 3-3.

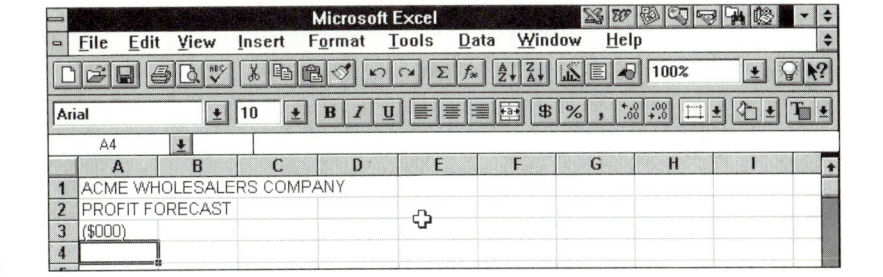

Figure 3-3

Centering Worksheet Titles

Now that you have entered the worksheet titles, you can center them across the columns in the worksheet. Before you can center text across several selected columns, select the cells containing the text and the range over which the text is to be centered.

- You can choose the **C**ells command on the **F**ormat menu to display the Format Cells dialog box. Click the Alignment tab and click the Center **a**cross selection option button to center text across columns.

- You can also click the Center Across Columns button on the Standard toolbar to center text across columns.

Refer to Figure 3-1 and observe that columns A through G will be used to complete this worksheet.

To select the columns over which the text is to be centered:

Click   on cell A1 (if necessary)

Verify   the mouse is positioned in cell A1 and appears as a white cross

Drag   to cell G3

The first selected cell remains white to indicate that it is the anchor cell. The other cells are blackened to indicate the area is selected. The selected cells, A1:G3, are called a **range**. Ranges are discussed in greater detail later in this chapter.

To center the worksheet title information:

Click the Center Across Columns button on the Formatting toolbar

The worksheet title information is now centered across the selected columns.

Entering Column Titles Using the AutoFill Feature

Excel has a feature called **AutoFill** that allows you to extend a sequential series of data from a cell(s) to other cells. To use the AutoFill feature, first enter the data to be extended to the other cells. Then position the mouse pointer on the Fill handle (the small, black square in the lower-right corner of the active cell containing the data). The mouse pointer appears as a small, black cross. Drag the mouse in the desired direction. When you release the mouse button, the selected cells contain a sequential series of text.

To enter the column titles using the AutoFill feature:

Enter	YEAR 1 in cell B6
Verify	B6 is the active cell
Move	the mouse pointer to the Fill handle in the lower-right corner of cell B6 (the mouse appears as a small, black cross)
Press and hold	the mouse button
Drag	to cells C6 through F6
Release	the mouse button

Years 2 through 5 are now automatically entered in cells C6:F6. The top part of your screen should look like Figure 3-4.

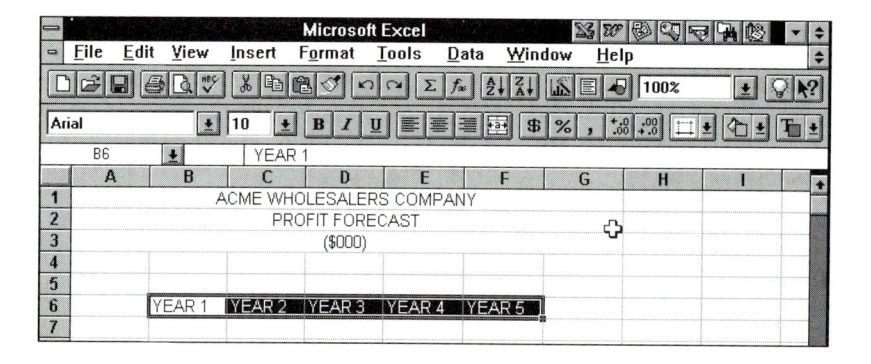

Figure 3-4

Creating Worksheets

> The AutoFill feature extends other series, such as "QTR 1, QTR 2...," "3/25/96, 3/26/96...," "Monday, Tuesday...," and "Jan, Feb...." AutoFill matches case and abbreviation when it increments numbers. To make the AutoFill feature display sequential numbers, such as "1,2,3...," type 1 in the anchor cell and press the CTRL key as you drag the Fill handle to create the sequential numbers in the desired range. If you need a series, such as "2,4,6...," type the text in the first two cells, select the two cells, and drag the Fill handle as needed.
>
> The AutoFill feature is also used later in this chapter to copy formulas from one cell to other cells. If you wish to use the menu, use the Fill command on the Edit menu. For more information about the Fill command, see your Excel *User's Guide*.

Centering Column Titles

By default, the column titles are left-aligned. Suppose you want to center-align the column titles.

- You can choose the Cells command on the Format menu to display the Format Cells dialog box. Click the Alignment tab and then click the Center option button in the Horizontal group to center text within a cell.

- You can also click the Center alignment button on the Formatting toolbar to center text within a cell.

To center the text in cells B6:F6:

Select   cells B6:F6 (if necessary)

Click   the Center ▤ button on the Formatting toolbar

The top part of your screen should look like Figure 3-5.

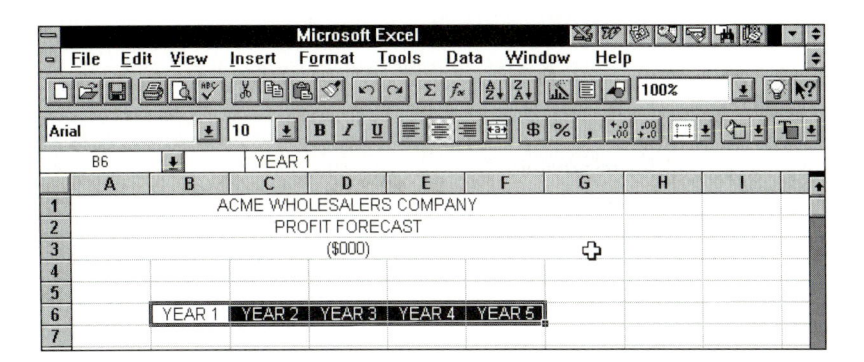

Figure 3-5

Selecting a Range

The highlighted cells, B6:F6, are called a range. A range of cells is usually a rectangular block of adjoining cells. A range can consist of cells within several columns or rows, single columns or rows, or even a single cell. The first selected cell remains white to indicate that it is the anchor cell. A range address consists of the cell addresses of two opposite corners of the range separated by a colon (:). Normally, the upper-left and lower-right cell addresses are used. For example, the address B2:C10 indicates a range of cells extending from row 2 through row 10 in columns B and C. If you think of the colon for the word "through," you would call the range of cells "B2 through C10." The address B1:B1 denotes a range consisting of the single cell B1.

Before entering information in Excel, you can select a range of cells and enter the data quickly in the selected area. In a selected range, the TAB key naturally moves the active cell to the right. However, if you select a horizontal range, you can press the ENTER key to move the active cell to the right. The ENTER key naturally moves the active cell down. However, when you select a vertical range, you can press the TAB key to move the active cell down. If your selected area contains multiple rows and columns, you can use a combination of ENTER, SHIFT+ENTER, TAB, and SHIFT+TAB to move the active cell.

Rather than use the specific cell addresses each time you refer to a range, you can create a range name. For example, you could create the range name TEXT for the range B2:C10. Then you can use the range name when referring to the range of cells B2:C10. Creating and using range names is discussed in Chapter 4.

You can select a range in one of three ways: (1) use the mouse to drag across the desired cells, (2) hold down the SHIFT key and select the cells with the arrow keys on the keyboard, or (3) make the first cell of the desired range the active cell, press the SHIFT key, and click on the last cell of the desired range.

> **FYI**
>
> In the remainder of the book, you are asked to select a range of cells. You can use any one of the three ways mentioned here to specify the range of cells.

If you need to reduce or enlarge a selected range, you can use the SHIFT key and either the mouse or pointer movement keys to alter the size of the range. To deselect a highlighted range of cells at any time, you can click on a specific cell or press any arrow key.

If you need to select the entire worksheet, move the mouse pointer to the **Select All button** (the button at the left of column A and above row 1), and click. Alternatively, you can select the entire worksheet by pressing CTRL+SHIFT+SPACEBAR or CTRL+A. You also can select nonadjacent cells. To select nonadjacent cells, first select the desired cell or range of cells. Then press the CTRL key and select the second cell or range of cells.

Entering Row Titles in a Selected Range

When you type the text or data for a cell and click the enter box, press the ENTER key, or press the TAB key, Excel enters the text or data and moves the active cell to the next cell in the selected range. In the following steps, use whichever method you prefer to advance to the next cell.

In cells A7 through A11, enter the row titles that describe the contents of the rows.

To select the cells and enter the row titles:

Select	cells A7:A11
Enter	Revenue in cell A7
Enter	Expenses in cell A8
Enter	Profit Before Tax in cell A9
Enter	Taxes in cell A10
Enter	Profit After Tax in cell A11

After you have made cell A6 the active cell, the top part of your worksheet should look like Figure 3-6.

Creating Worksheets

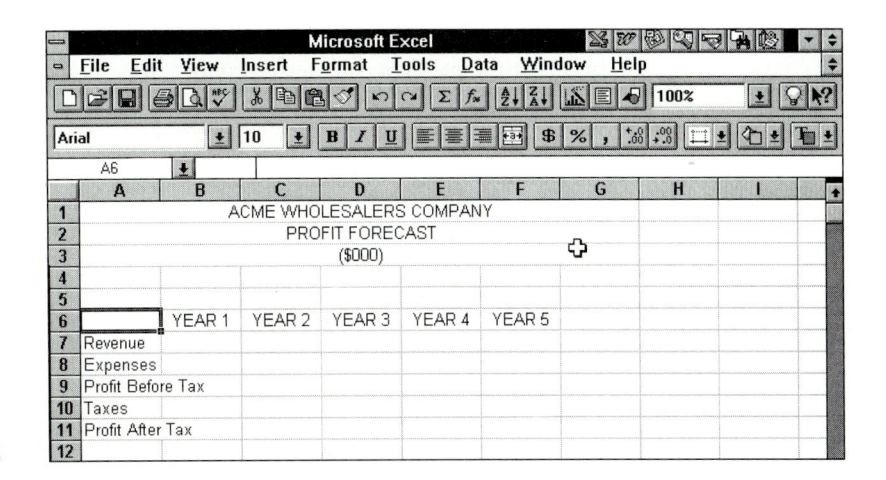

Figure 3-6

> When you create a worksheet, you can use some **Assumptions** to compute your data. Assumptions allow you to do "what-if" analysis on the worksheet. "What-if" means that you can change various Assumptions to see the impact on the calculations. It is a good idea to note the Assumptions in a separate part of the worksheet. If someone else looks at the worksheet, it is much easier for that person to determine how the values appearing in the worksheet are computed. In this example, you place the Assumptions below the worksheet. "What-if" analysis is demonstrated later in this chapter.

To enter the row titles for the Assumptions:

Select	cells A13:A16
Enter	`Assumptions` in cell A13
Enter	`Revenue Growth Rate` in cell A14
Enter	`Expenses Rate` in cell A15
Enter	`Tax Rate` in cell A16

After you have made cell A12 the active cell, the bottom part of your screen should look like Figure 3-7.

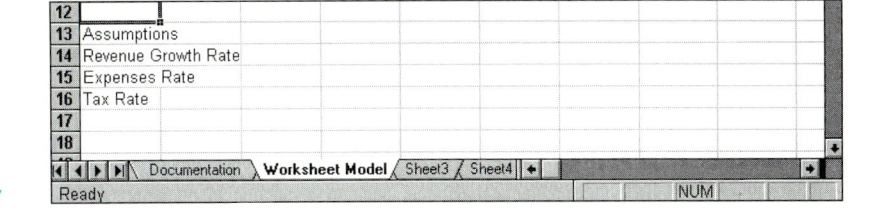

Figure 3-7

Expanding the Width of a Column

Notice that several row titles extend into column B. When you enter data in column B, the text in column A is truncated. You can widen column A so that you can see all the row and column titles.

- You can choose the **W**idth command under the **C**olumn command on the **F**ormat menu. Type the desired width and click the OK command button to widen selected columns.

- You can also widen columns with the mouse pointer. To do this, first position the mouse pointer on the right boundary of the column header. The mouse pointer will become a two-headed horizontal arrow. Press and hold the mouse button down. Drag the double-headed arrow to the right of the longest data entry in the narrow column. As you drag the mouse, the column width is indicated in the reference area. When you release the mouse button, the column width will be changed.

To widen column A:

Move	the mouse pointer to the column heading area of the screen
Position	the mouse pointer on the boundary between column A and B (the mouse appears as a double-headed arrow with a vertical line)
Press and hold	the mouse button
Drag	the mouse pointer to the right of the text in cell A14
Release	the mouse button

Because column A now occupies more space, column B has shifted to the right and part of column I no longer appears on the screen. Your screen should look like Figure 3-8.

> When the mouse is positioned on the right boundary of a column header, you can also double-click. When you double-click, the column is automatically widened to the width of the longest entry.

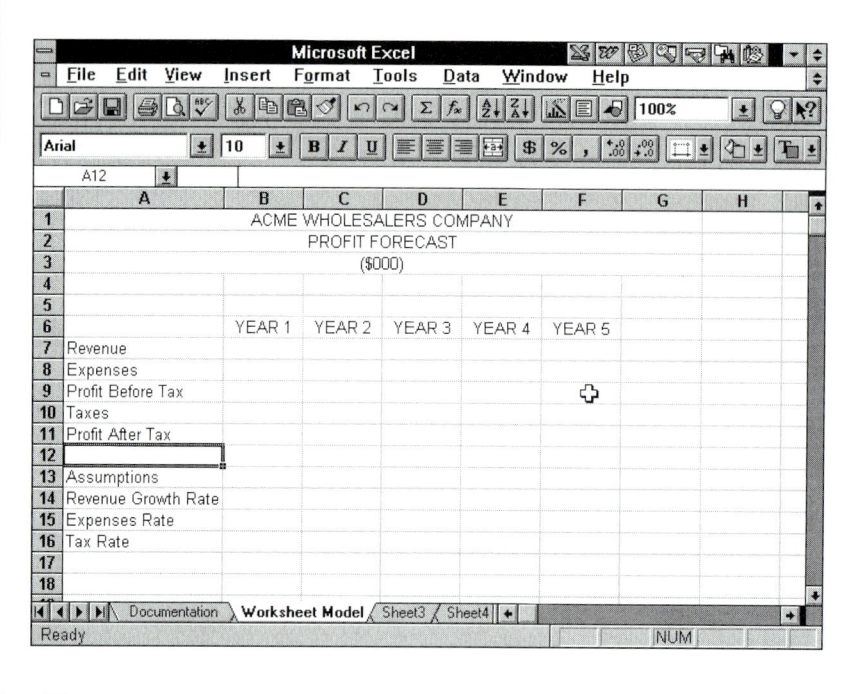

Figure 3-8

> You can increase row size in much the same way that you increase column width. Choose the Height command under the **R**ow command on the **F**ormat menu. Using the mouse, you can position the mouse pointer on the line separating row header numbers and drag in the desired direction.

Creating Worksheets

Entering Data and Formulas and Copying Information in a Worksheet

Entering Assumptions

> Excel allows you to format numbers with the keyboard. To display ".05" as a percent, you could have typed "5%" in cell C14. Excel would display "5%" in the cell and ".05" would display in the formula bar. This feature is called "automatic" formatting.
>
> You will learn another method for changing the decimal number to a percent later in this chapter.

To input the assumed Revenue Growth Rate for Year 2:

| **Enter** | .05 in cell C14 |

The Revenue Growth Rate is not placed in column B because the rate is not needed for Year 1.

To use the AutoFill feature to copy the Revenue Growth Rate to cells D14 through F14:

Click	on cell C14 (if necessary)
Move	the mouse pointer to the Fill handle in the lower-right corner of cell C14
Press and hold	the mouse button
Drag	to cells D14:F14
Release	the mouse button

The contents of cell C14 are copied to cells D14 through F14.

To indicate the Expenses Rate and the Tax Rate for Year 1:

| **Enter** | .7 in cell B15 |
| **Enter** | .35 in cell B16 |

To use the AutoFill feature to copy the rates to Years 2 through 5:

Select	cells B15:B16
Move	the mouse pointer to the Fill handle
Press and hold	the mouse button
Drag	to cells C15:F16
Release	the mouse button

The contents of cells B15:B16 are copied to cells C15 through F16. After you have made cell G13 active, the bottom of your screen should look like Figure 3-9.

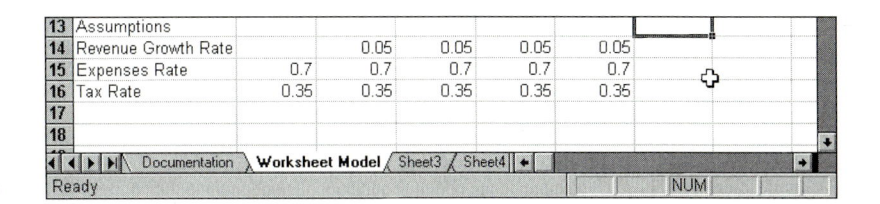

Figure 3-9

Creating Formulas

In this section, you will learn to create **formulas**. A formula is an equation that can include cell addresses, range names, numbers, arithmetic operators, and parentheses. A formula is an effective way to compute values in Excel.

> The three types of formulas that you can enter into a cell in Excel are arithmetic, text, and comparison. Arithmetic formulas are used to calculate numeric values using arithmetic operators such as + and –. Text formulas are used to calculate labels using the text operator (&). Comparison formulas are used to compare values in two or more cells using comparison operators such as < and >. For more information about the different formula types, see your Excel *User's Guide*.

To enter the Revenue amount for Year 1:

Click on cell B7

Enter 23000

To enter the Revenue amount for Year 2, you need to show a 5% increase over the Revenue in Year 1. The formula for Revenue in Year 2 multiplies the Revenue amount in Year 1 by 1.05 to show the 5% projected increase.

To make sure the active cell is the cell where the formula will be entered:

Click on cell C7

All formulas begin with an equal sign (=). The equal sign indicates that some calculation will take place.

To begin entering the formula:

Type =

Click on cell B7 (Revenue for Year 1)

Notice that a moving border, called a "marquee," appears around the referenced cell B7, and the formula in cell C7 now contains a reference to cell B7.

To continue creating the formula:

Type *

The asterisk (*) is the symbol for multiplication.

To continue creating the formula:

Type (1+

Click on cell C14 (Revenue Growth Rate for Year 2)

Type)

Click the enter box ✓

or

Press ⏎ ENTER

The number 24150 should now appear in cell C7. Click on cell C7 and look at the formula bar. The formula =B7*(1+C14) is displayed as the formula used to calculate the number 24150. The top part of your screen should look like Figure 3-10.

Creating Worksheets

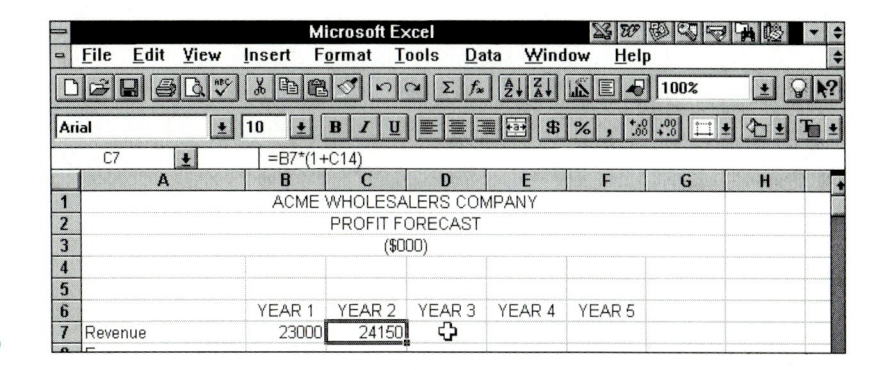

Figure 3-10

Rather than clicking on the cells to be used in a formula, you can type a formula directly into a cell. For example, by typing =B7*(1+C14) in cell C7 and clicking the enter box or pressing the ENTER key, you will obtain the same result. However, it is best to point to the cells when creating a formula because you tend to make fewer errors in creating the formula.

Order of Precedence

Parentheses were needed around the addition portion of the formula because of a rule in mathematics called "order of precedence" or "order of operations." When a formula contains a combination of operations (for example, multiplication and addition as shown in cell C7), you may need to use parentheses to change the natural calculation order.

The operators are listed below in the order that operations are completed:

( )   Parentheses

+ –   Positive and Negative values

^   Exponentiation

*/   Multiplication, Division

+ –   Addition, Subtraction

The operations higher on the list are performed before the operations lower on the list. For example, if the arithmetic formula =10+5^2 is used, the result is 35 (10 + 25 (5 squared)), not 225 (15 raised to the power of two).

Multiplication and division operations are performed before addition and subtraction. For example, if a cell contains the formula =7–3/2, the value is 5.5 (7–(3/2)), not 2 ((7–3)/2).

Excel can tell the difference between a + or – sign that means a positive or negative number as opposed to the + or – sign meaning addition or subtraction. For example, in the formula =10/–5+10, the result is 8, (–2+10), not 2 (10/5).

You can change the order in which operations are completed by using sets of parentheses. If more than one set of parentheses is included in a formula, Excel begins with the innermost set of parentheses and proceeds to the outermost set. For example, the formula =(10/(2+3))*4 produces a value of 8.

Relative Cell Location

The formulas in Excel are based on **relative cell location**. For example, the formula in cell C7, =B7*(1+C14), tells Excel to "multiply the contents of the cell immediately to the left of the formula location times the quantity 1 plus the number appearing 7 cells below the formula location." The Revenue for Years 3, 4, and 5 are also projected to increase from the previous year (the previous cell) by 5 percent. Therefore, the formula =B7*(1+C14) can be copied to cells D7, E7, and F7, and Excel adjusts the formulas to =C7*(1+D14), =D7*(1+E14), and =E7*(1+F14), respectively.

An absolute cell reference is one that does not change when the formula is copied to other locations. An example of using absolute cell references appears at the end of this chapter.

Copying Formulas

You can use the menu commands or the mouse to copy formulas.

- You can use the **C**opy and **P**aste commands on the **E**dit menu or the Copy and Paste buttons on the Standard toolbar to duplicate the formula for Years 3, 4, and 5.
- You can use the AutoFill feature to copy formulas.

Verify that cell C7 is the active cell.

To copy the contents of cell C7 to the Clipboard:

Click   the Copy button on the Standard toolbar

Notice that cell C7 has the marquee around it.

To paste the formula from the Clipboard to cells D7 through F7:

Select   cells D7:F7

Click   the Paste button on the Standard toolbar

The formula in cell C7 has been copied to cells D7 through F7 (Years 3, 4, and 5). After you have made cell G7 the active cell, the top part of your screen should look like Figure 3-11.

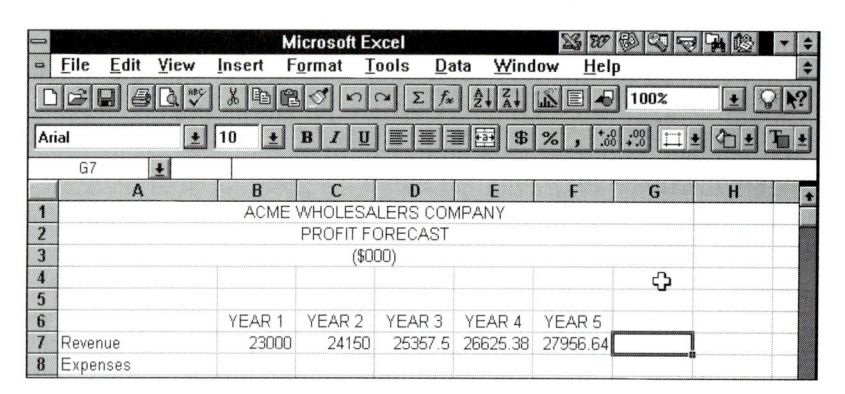

Figure 3-11

Notice that the marquee around cell C7 did not disappear. The marquee indicates the contents are still on the Clipboard. To remove the marquee, press the ESC key. This action removes the data from the Clipboard.

An alternative method for pasting the contents is to press the ENTER key. When you press the ENTER key, the marquee disappears and the data is removed from the Clipboard.

Expenses are 70% of Revenues.

To create a formula to calculate the Expenses for Year 1:

Click   on cell B8

Type   =

Click   on cell B7 (Revenue for Year 1)

Creating Worksheets

Type	*
Click	on cell B15 (Expense Rate for Year 1)
Click	the enter box ✓
	or
Press	⏎ ENTER

The number 16100 appears in cell B8, and if B8 is still the active cell, the formula =B7*B15 appears in the formula bar. The Expenses formulas for Years 2 through 5 are completed later in this chapter.

The Profit Before Tax is the difference between Revenue and Expenses.

To calculate the Profit Before Tax:

Click	on cell B9 (if necessary)
Type	=
Click	on cell B7 (Revenue for Year 1)
Type	-
Click	on cell B8 (Expenses for Year 1)
Click	the enter box ✓
	or
Press	⏎ ENTER

The number 6900 appears in cell B9, and if B9 is still the active cell, the formula =B7-B8 is displayed in the formula bar. The Profit Before Tax formulas for Years 2 through 5 are completed later in this chapter.

Taxes for Year 1 are computed by multiplying the Profit Before Tax by the Tax Rate.

To compute the Taxes for the first year:

Click	on cell B10 (if necessary)
Type	=
Click	on cell B9 (Profit Before Tax for Year 1)
Type	*
Click	on cell B16 (Tax Rate for Year 1)
Click	the enter box ✓
	or
Press	⏎ ENTER

The number 2415 appears in cell B10, and if B10 is still the active cell, the formula =B9*B16 is displayed in the formula bar. The formulas for Taxes for Years 2 through 5 are completed later in this chapter.

The Profit After Tax is computed by subtracting Taxes from the Profit Before Tax.

To calculate the Profit After Tax for the first year:

Click	on cell B11 (if necessary)
Type	=

Click	on cell B9 (Profit Before Tax for Year 1)
Type	-
Click	on cell B10 (Profit After Tax for Year 1)
Click	the enter box ✓
	or
Press	⏎ ENTER

The number 4485 appears in cell B11, and if B11 is still the active cell, the formula =B9-B10 is displayed in the formula bar. The top part of your screen should look like Figure 3-12.

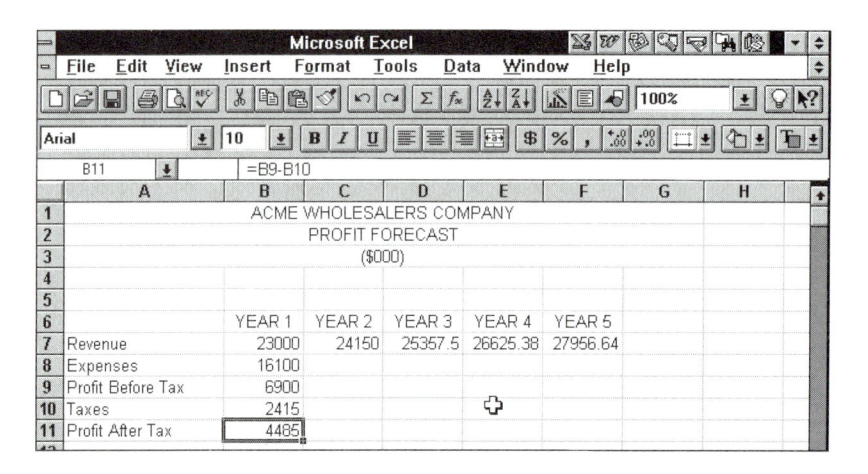

Figure 3-12

The formulas for the Profit After Tax for Years 2 through 5 are completed below.

To copy the formulas for Expenses, Profit Before Tax, Taxes, and Profit After Tax using the AutoFill feature:

Select	cells B8:B11
Move	the mouse pointer to the Fill handle in the bottom-right corner of cell B11
Press and hold	the mouse button
Drag	the mouse pointer to cells C8:F11
Release	the mouse button

The formulas in cells B8 through B11 that project Expenses, Profit Before Tax, Taxes, and Profit After Tax have been copied to cells C8 through F11 for Years 2 through 5. After you have made cell F12 the active cell, your screen should look like Figure 3-13.

Creating Worksheets

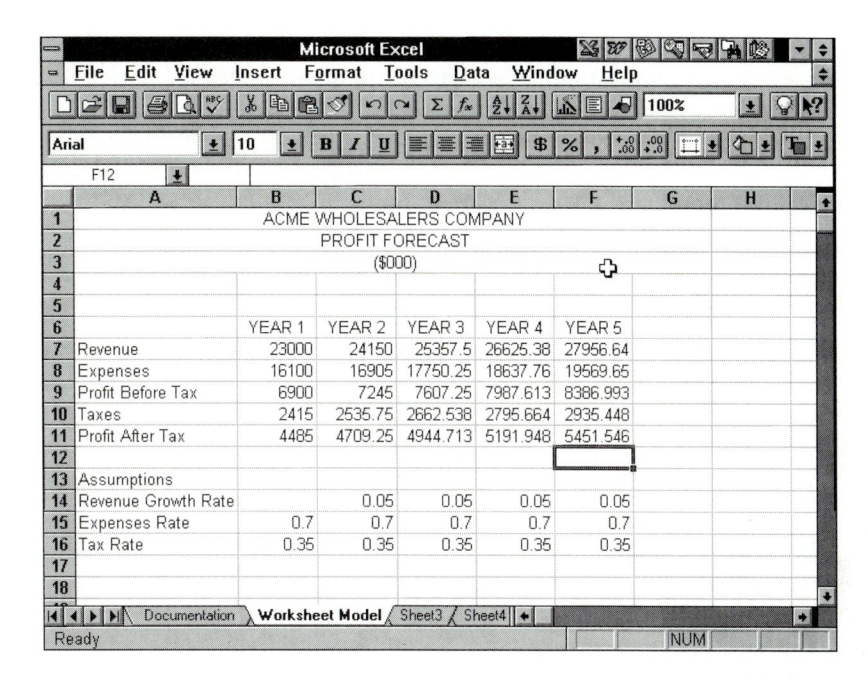

Figure 3-13

Later in this chapter, you will learn how to properly format the numbers.

Using the SUM Function

You now need to **sum** the values for the various items to obtain totals for the five years. Excel has a **function** that makes it easy to sum the values. Functions are built-in formulas in Excel that perform special calculations. Excel has hundreds of functions categorized in different ways. See the online Help feature for a complete listing of the functions.

The general format for the SUM function is:

    =SUM(first cell:last cell)

Notice that a range of cells is specified within the set of parentheses. By placing the = character prior to the word SUM, you have indicated that you will perform a calculation using the SUM function. Typing the function name in all caps is not required. This text uses all caps to emphasize function names.

To use the SUM function for calculating Total Revenue for the five years:

Enter	TOTAL in cell G6
Center	the text in cell G6
Click	on cell G7
Type	=SUM(
Select	the range B7:F7
Click	the enter box ✓
	or
Press	⏎ ENTER

The number 127089.5 appears in cell G7, and if G7 is still the active cell, the formula =SUM(B7:F7) is displayed in the formula bar. Notice that even though you did not type the closing parenthesis, Excel inserted it for you.

Using the AutoSum Feature

An alternative method for summing the contents of adjoining cells is to use the **AutoSum** button on the Standard toolbar.

To compute the Total Expenses for the five years:

Click   on cell G8 (if necessary)

Click   the AutoSum ∑ button on the Standard toolbar

The SUM function and a suggested range appear in cell G8 and are displayed in the formula bar. The marquee appears around the suggested range. If the range is incorrect, drag the mouse pointer across the correct cells.

> A feature in Excel 5.0 called the Function Wizard guides you in the selection and completion of functions. You can display the Function Wizard dialog box by clicking the Function Wizard f_* button on the Standard toolbar. For more information about using the Function Wizard, see your Excel *User's Guide*.

If the suggested range is correct:

Click   the enter box ✓

or

Click   the AutoSum ∑ button again

or

Press   (← ENTER)

The number 88962.66 appears in cell G8, and if G8 is still the active cell, the formula =SUM(B8:F8) appears in the formula bar.

Using the Shortcut Menu to Copy Cell Contents

The Copy and Paste commands were demonstrated earlier in this chapter in the discussion on copying formulas. Another method is to select the cell or range of cells to be copied and click the alternate mouse button. A shortcut menu appears on the screen. Choose **C**opy. Then select the cell or cells to which the information is to be copied. Click the alternate mouse button and choose **P**aste.

To copy the contents of cell G8 to cells G9 through G11 using the alternate menu:

Click   on cell G8 with the alternate mouse button

The shortcut menu appears. The bottom part of your screen should look like Figure 3-14.

Figure 3-14

Creating Worksheets

Choose	Copy
Select	cells G9:G11
Move	the mouse pointer onto the selected range
Click	the alternate mouse button
Choose	Paste

The formula =SUM(B8:F8) has been copied from cells G8 to cells G9 through G11.

> You can use the AutoSum feature to place formulas in a range of cells. In this example, you could have selected cells G7:G11 and clicked the AutoSum button. All the formulas would have been calculated.
>
> *Note:* AutoSum prefers to add vertically. Thus, if you have numeric data displayed vertically and horizontally, the AutoSum feature highlights the vertical range of cells. If you clicked on the AutoSum button and the selected range is incorrect, simply drag across the desired range of numbers and then click the enter box or the AutoSum button, or press the ENTER key.

Selecting a Format for the Data

Excel provides several different formats for numeric data. You can choose a format that will insert commas.

- You can choose the **C**ells command on the **F**ormat menu to display the Format Cells dialog box. Click the **N**umber tab. Click Number in the **C**ategory list box. Several different comma appearance options appear in the **F**ormat Codes list box. Click the desired option.

- You can click the Comma Style button on the Formatting toolbar to format a cell or range of cells with the Comma Style.

To format a range of numbers:

Select	the range B7:G11
Click	the Comma Style button on the Formatting toolbar

The numbers in the selected range now display two decimal places and a comma if they are thousands or greater. After you have made cell A6 the active cell, your screen should look like Figure 3-15.

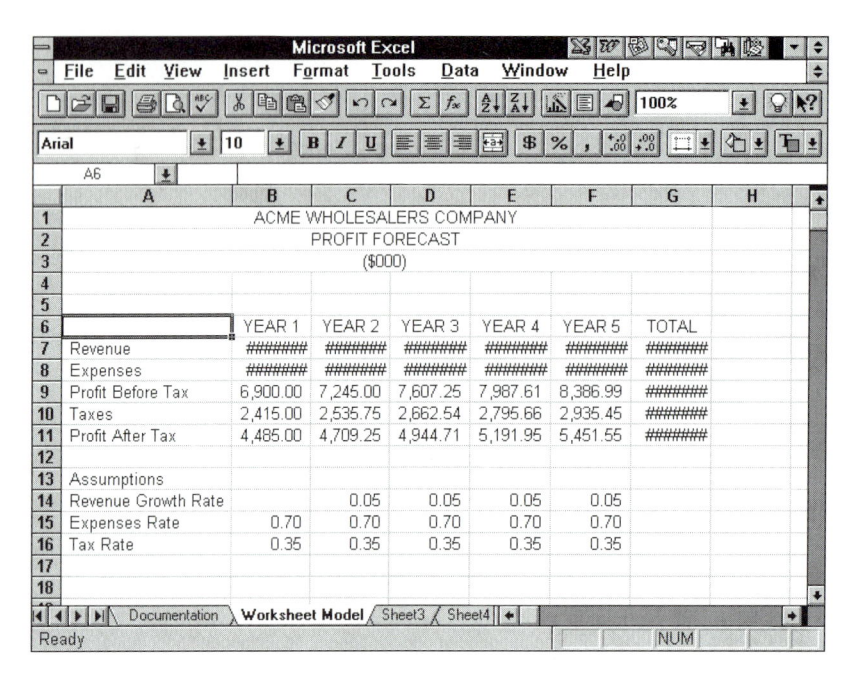

Figure 3-15

The number signs (#) that appear in some cells represent numbers that are too long to fit in the current cell width. You can increase the column width as demonstrated earlier in this chapter.

Instead of widening the columns, you can remove the display of one or more of the decimal places.

To remove the display of any decimal places:

Select   cells B7:G11

Click   the Decrease Decimal button on the Formatting toolbar twice

After you have made cell A6 the active cell, your screen should look like Figure 3-16.

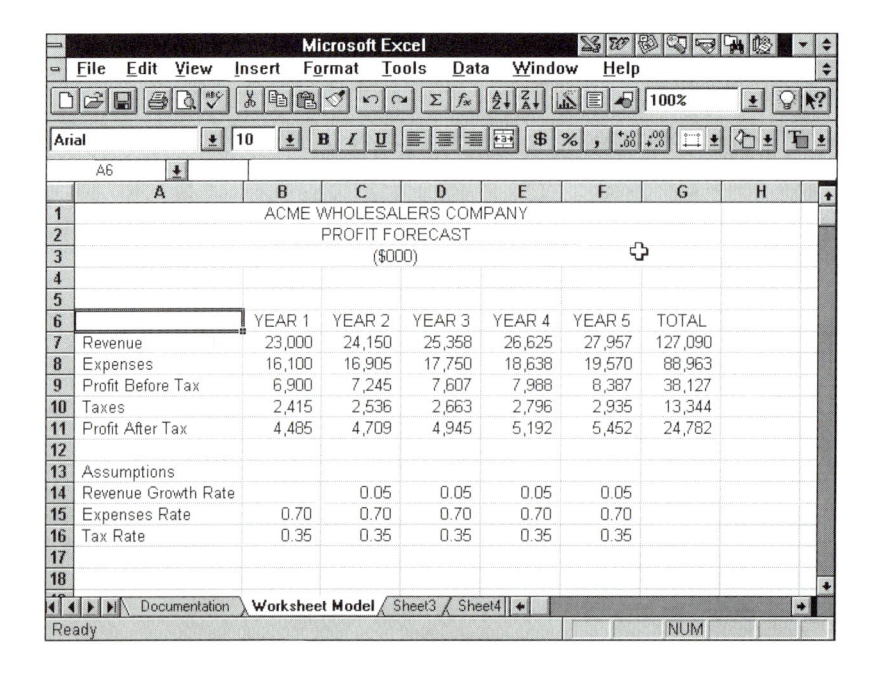

Figure 3-16

Creating Worksheets

Using the Percent Format

To display the proper format for the Assumptions, select the range of cells from B14 through F16 and include percent signs.

> You can choose the Cells command on the Format menu to display the Format Cells dialog box. Click the Number tab. Click Percentage in the Category list box. Click the desired option in the Format Codes list box.

> You can click the Percent Style button on the Formatting toolbar to format a cell or range of cells with the Percent Style.

To change to the Percent format using the menu method:

Select	cells B14:F16
Choose	Format
Choose	Cells
Click	the **N**umber tab (if necessary)
Click	Percentage in the **C**ategory list box
Click	0% in the **F**ormat Codes list box (if necessary)
Click	the OK command button

After you have made cell G14 the active cell, the bottom part of your screen should look like Figure 3-17.

Figure 3-17

13	Assumptions					
14	Revenue Growth Rate		5%	5%	5%	5%
15	Expenses Rate	70%	70%	70%	70%	70%
16	Tax Rate	35%	35%	35%	35%	35%

Documentation \ **Worksheet Model** / Sheet3 / Sheet4
Ready — NUM

Using the Currency Format and Selecting Noncontiguous Ranges

In this exercise, you will alter the Revenue and Profit After Tax rows to display dollar signs.

> You can choose the Cells command on the Format menu to display the Format Cells dialog box. Click the Number tab. Click Currency in the Category list box. Click the desired option in the Format Codes list box.

> You can change to the Currency format by clicking the Currency Style button on the Formatting toolbar. When you use the Currency Style button to display dollar signs, the accounting format with two decimal places is used. The accounting format aligns the dollar signs near the left side of the cells. If you want the dollar sign to appear immediately next to the number, you must use the menu method to select the appropriate format code from the Currency category of the Number tab in the Format Cells dialog box.

Before formatting the Revenue and Profit After Tax rows, you must select the appropriate cells. The CTRL key allows you to select ranges of cells that are separate from one another.

To select noncontiguous ranges:

Select	cells B7:G7
Move	the mouse pointer to cell B11
Press and hold	CTRL

Select	cells B11:G11
Release	the mouse button
Release	CTRL

Notice that two noncontiguous ranges have been selected.

To format the selected cells with the Currency format:

Click	the Currency Style $ button on the Formatting toolbar

To remove the display of any decimal places:

Click	the Decrease Decimal button on the Formatting toolbar twice

Widen column G to display all the numbers for the column.

After you have made cell A1 the active cell, the top part of your screen should look like Figure 3-18.

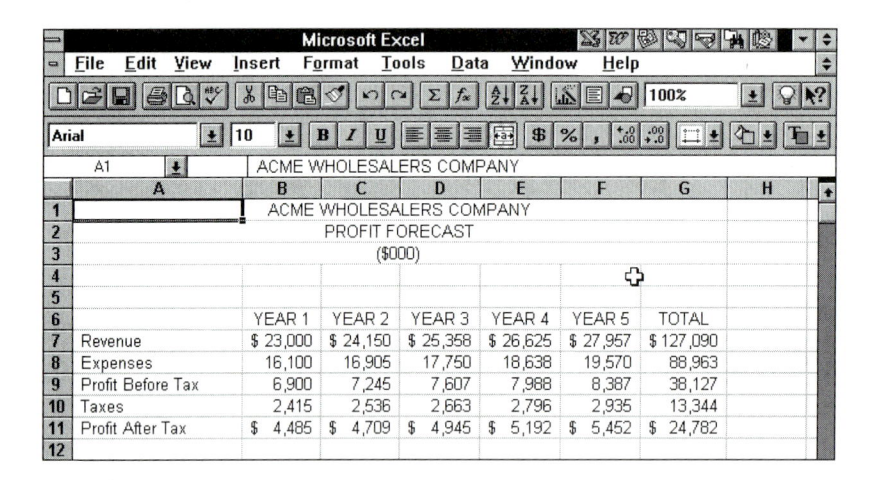

Figure 3-18

Correcting Rounding Errors

Notice that rounding errors occur when the total for Profit After Tax is computed for the five years (e.g., Profit Before Tax is 38,127 minus Taxes of 13,344 should equal 24,783 rather than 24,782). The rounding error occurred because the numbers are formatted to show 0 decimal places on the worksheet, but the values in the cells are not rounded to 0 decimal places. Excel uses the hidden decimal places in computation, which sometimes results in rounding errors.

When you use multiplication, division, or exponents in a formula, you can use the ROUND function to round a number to a specific number of decimal places before the calculation is performed. The following steps can be used to round the appropriate formulas where necessary.

You should immediately use the ROUND function when creating formulas rather than editing them later. This example was completed differently to show the results of not using the ROUND function.

The formulas for Revenue, Expenses, and Taxes use multiplication, so you need to edit them to use the ROUND function. Formulas that use only addition or subtraction, such as Profit Before Tax and Profit After Tax, do not cause rounding problems. For more information about the ROUND function, see online Help.

Creating Worksheets

The format of the ROUND function is:

=ROUND(number or formula, number of digits to round to)

The formula for projecting Revenue for Year 3 is =C7*(1+D14). The value of the computation is 25,357.50.

See the summary below of the difference when rounding is used:

Formula	Value	Number Used in Computation
=C7*(1+D14)	25,357.50	25,357.50
=ROUND(C7*(1+D14),0)	25,358	25,358

Revenue is the first formula edited.

To round the Revenue projections to 0 decimal places:

Click	on cell C7
Click	after the = sign near the beginning of the formula in the formula bar
Type	ROUND(
Click	at the end of the formula

To indicate zero decimal places:

Type	,0)
Click	the enter box ✓
	or
Press	⏎ ENTER

The formula =ROUND(B7*(1+C14),0) appears in the formula bar for cell C7. The formula =B7*(1+C14) is rounded to 0 decimal places. The top part of your screen should look like Figure 3-19.

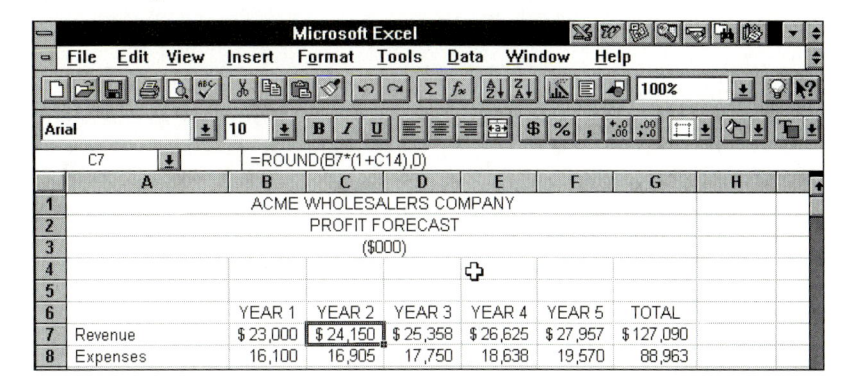

Figure 3-19

To copy the formula to the other cells containing Revenue data:

Move	the mouse pointer to the Fill handle in cell C7
Press and hold	the mouse button
Drag	the Fill handle to cell F7 (be careful not to drag across to cell G7, which contains a different formula)
Release	the mouse button

The projections for Revenue for Years 2 through 5 are now rounded to 0 decimal places.

The second set of formulas you need to round is for Expenses. Use the steps above to round the formulas for Expenses for Years 1 through 5.

After you have rounded Revenue and Expenses, the rounding error is corrected in cell G11. However, in the event that any values change later, it is a good idea to round the Taxes in row 10. Use the steps to round the formulas for Taxes as well.

After you have made cell A1 the active cell, the top part of your screen should look like Figure 3-20.

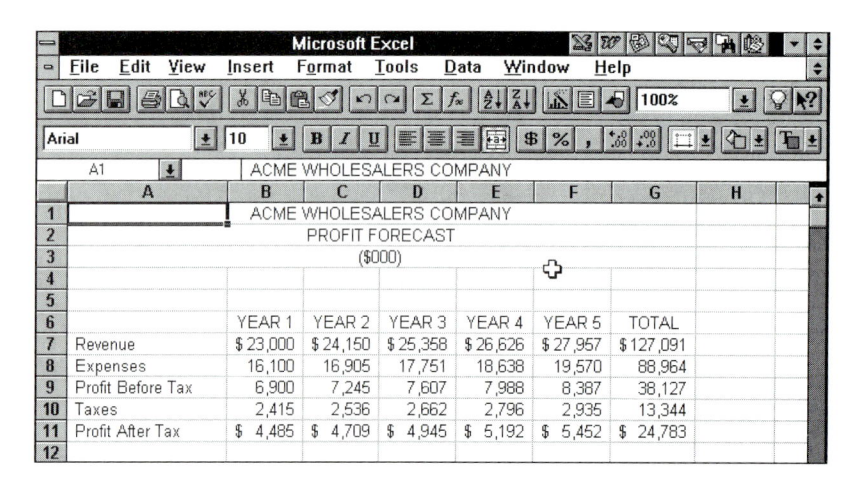

Figure 3-20

Enhancing the Appearance of a Worksheet

Once you have created the worksheet, you can use various features available in Excel to enhance the appearance of the worksheet.

Suggested enhancements follow:

- Enter underlines and double underlines
- Insert blank rows
- Change the font appearance and font size of selected text
- Boldface text
- Move cell contents
- Add degrees of shading to selected areas on a worksheet
- Add a box border to a cell or a range of cells
- Change colors of selected text or background when a color printer is available

All of these enhancements are discussed below.

Entering Underlines

You can underline the contents in a cell, or you can place a bottom border beneath an entire cell. Borders are discussed in a later section of this chapter.

Creating Worksheets

- You can choose the **C**ells command on the F**o**rmat menu to display the Format Cells dialog box. Click the Font tab in the Format Cells dialog box. Click the drop-down arrow in the **U**nderline text box. Click the desired line appearance.

- You can also click the Underline button on the Formatting toolbar to underline the contents of a cell or range of cells.

To underline the Expense entries in row 9 and the Taxes in row 11:

Select	cells B8:G8
Press and hold	CTRL
Select	cells B10:G10
Release	the CTRL key
Click	the Underline U button on the Formatting toolbar

When you make cell A13 the active cell, the top part of your screen should look similar to Figure 3-21.

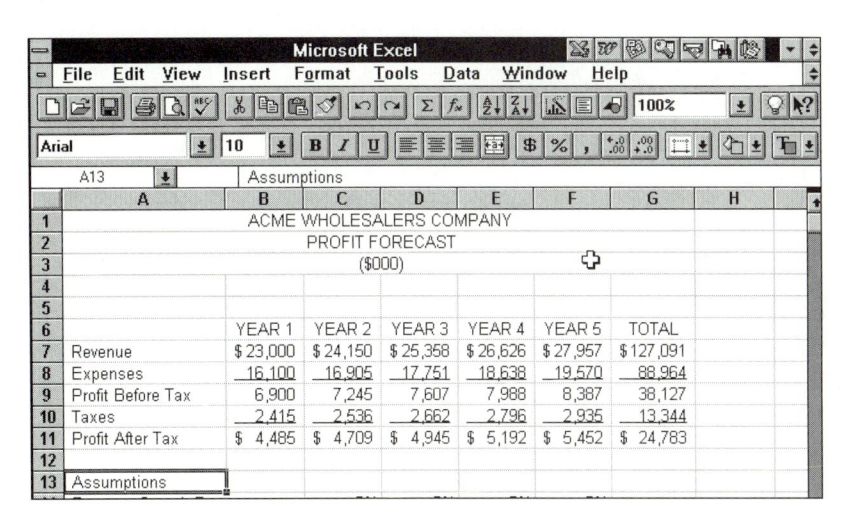

Figure 3-21

Now place double underlines below the Profit After Tax data in cells B11:G11.

To apply double underlining to cells B11:G11:

Select	cells B11:G11
Choose	Format
Choose	Cells
Click	the Font tab (if necessary)
Click	the down arrow on the Underline list box
Choose	Double Accounting
Click	the OK command button

After you have made cell A1 the active cell, the top part of your screen should look like Figure 3-22.

Figure 3-22

> Now that you have entered underlines, you may wish to print the worksheet without gridlines. To print the worksheet without gridlines, open the Print dialog box by choosing the **Print** command on the **File** menu. Click the Page Set**u**p command button in the Print dialog box. Click the Sheet tab in the Page Setup dialog box. Remove the X from the **Gridlines** check box in the Print group box. Additional printing options are discussed in the next chapter.

Inserting Blank Rows in a Worksheet

You may need to insert rows or columns in a worksheet.

To insert a blank row between the row titles and the Revenue data:

Click on any cell in row 7

Notice that the entire row does not have to be highlighted. Also notice that the active cell does not have to be in column A to insert rows; it can be in any column.

Choose Insert

Choose R**o**ws

Notice that the new row is inserted above the current position. After you have made cell A1 the active cell, the top part of your screen should look like Figure 3-23.

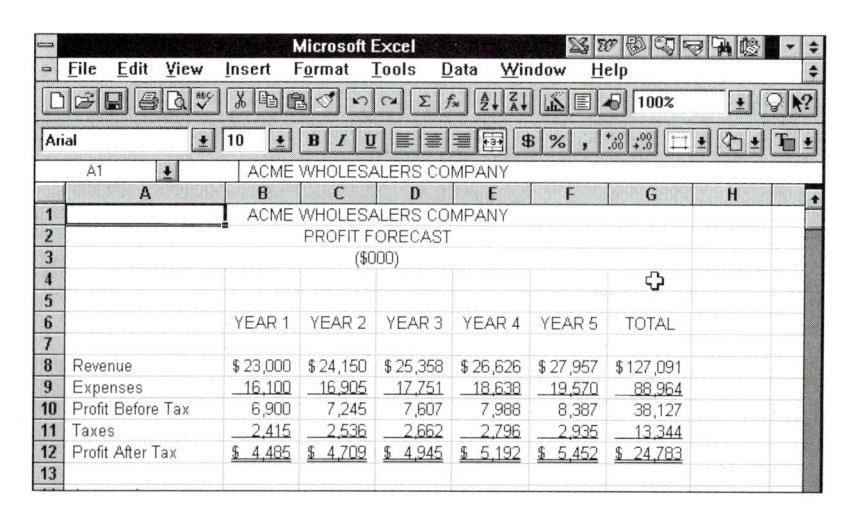

Figure 3-23

Because of relative cell referencing, the worksheet formulas and values remain correct and are adjusted to the new location. For example, the formula for Revenue for Year 2 has changed from =ROUND(B7*(1+C14),0) to =ROUND(B8*(1+C15),0).

If you insert too many rows, you can delete a row, column, or range of rows or columns. First, select the row or column to be deleted. Then use the **Delete** command on the **Edit** menu to delete rows or columns.

Save the workbook.

> In this example, instead of inserting a row, you could have increased the size of the row. Unless you print gridlines, you will not be able to tell the difference between an inserted row or increased row height. Printing with and without gridlines is discussed in the next chapter.
>
> You can also insert only a portion of a row or column rather than an entire row or column. This is especially helpful when a worksheet contains multiple ranges of information, and you only need to alter one range. To insert a portion of a row or column, select a range in the area in which you wish to create new space. Choose Cells on the Insert menu and then choose the appropriate option to shift cells down or to the right.
>
> To insert an entire column, you would choose the **Column** command on the **Insert** menu. A new column would be inserted to the left of the current position. You can insert more than one row or column by selecting multiple row numbers or column letters before choosing the **Row** or **Column** command on the **Insert** menu.
>
> You can also use the Insert command on the shortcut menu to insert a row or column.

Changing the Font Appearance

Fonts are sets of printed characters with the same size and appearance. You can describe a font in four ways: typeface, weight, style, and point size. Some typefaces include:

Courier	Times New Roman
Book Antiqua	Arial

Typeface refers to the design and appearance of the characters on a printed document. **Weight** refers to bold, medium, or light print density. Normal print is in medium weight. **Font style** refers to upright or *italic* print. **Point size** refers to the height of the printed characters.

- You can choose the Cells command on the Format menu to change the font for a cell or range of cells. First, select the Font tab in the Cells dialog box. Click the desired font in the Font list box. You may have to scroll to observe all the choices. The Font tab also allows you to apply boldfacing and other appearance changes. The Preview box in the lower-right corner displays the selected choices.

- You can also change the appearance of text using buttons on the Formatting toolbar. Click the down arrow on the Font text box and the Font Size text box. Select the desired typeface and size from the drop-down lists.

To change the font of the worksheet titles to Times New Roman, 14 point, bold:

| **Select** | cells A1:A3 |
| **Click** | the down arrow on the Font `Arial` drop-down list box on the Formatting toolbar |

Click	Times New Roman (scroll to view the font name)
Click	the down arrow on the Font Size [10] drop-down list box on the Formatting toolbar
Click	14
Click	the Bold [B] button on the Formatting toolbar

Notice that the row height for rows 1 through 3 automatically increased when the point size changed. After you have made cell A4 the active cell, the top part of your screen should look like Figure 3-24.

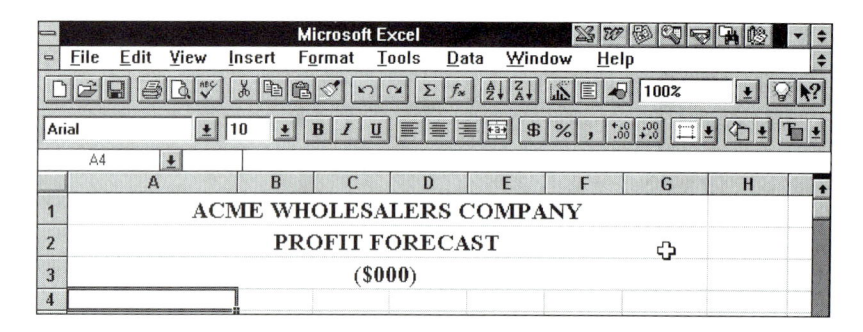

Figure 3-24

To boldface the column titles and the row headings:

Select	cells B6:G6
Press and hold	CTRL
Select	A8:A17
Click	the Bold [B] button on the Formatting toolbar

The column titles are now boldfaced. Notice that part of the contents of cell A15 appear in cell B15. Widen column A so that no text appears in column B.

Using Drag-and-Drop to Move or Copy Cell Contents

The Drag-and-Drop feature allows you to quickly copy or move the contents of one or more cells. Select the cell or range of cells to be moved or copied. Move the mouse pointer to a boundary of the range. The mouse appears as a left-pointing arrow. To move the contents, drag to a new location and release the mouse button.

Suppose you want to move the Assumption section down one row.

To move the Assumption data using drag-and-drop:

Select	cells A14:F17
Move	the mouse pointer to the bottom boundary of cell F17 (the mouse appears as a selection arrow)
Press and hold	the mouse button
Drag	down one row
Release	the mouse button

To copy the contents of a cell or range of cells, press the CTRL key as you drag the contents to a new location. Release the mouse button before you release the CTRL key and the contents are duplicated.

The Assumption information appears in rows 15 through 18, and the formulas have adjusted to the new location of the assumption data.

Creating Worksheets

Applying Shading to Selected Cells

You can shade the background of selected cells.

- You can choose the Cells command on the Format menu to display the Format Cells dialog box. Click the Patterns tab. Click the desired Color in the Cell Shading group box.
- You also can use the Color button on the Formatting toolbar to add shading to a cell or range of cells.

To place a light shading in the cells containing the column titles:

Select	cells B6:G6
Click	the down arrow on the Color button on the Formatting toolbar
Click	the desired shade

After you have made cell A4 the active cell, your screen should look similar to Figure 3-25.

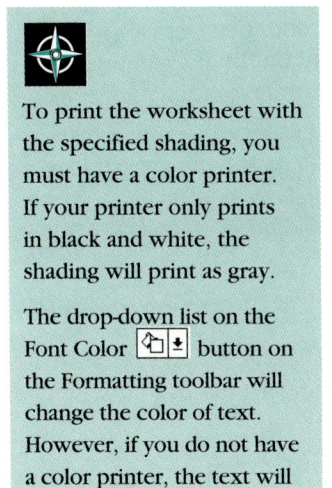

> To print the worksheet with the specified shading, you must have a color printer. If your printer only prints in black and white, the shading will print as gray.
>
> The drop-down list on the Font Color button on the Formatting toolbar will change the color of text. However, if you do not have a color printer, the text will print in black and white.

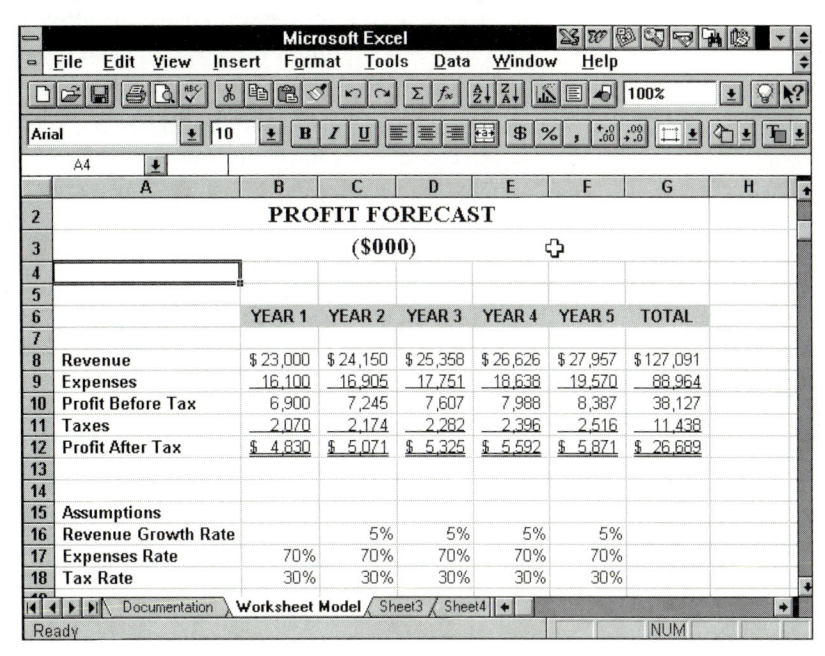

Figure 3-25

Placing a Box Border Around Selected Cells

You can place a border below, above, to the left, to the right, or completely around selected cells.

- You can choose the Cells command on the Format menu to display the Format Cells dialog box. Click the Border tab. Click the desired line style in the Style group box. Click the desired position for the line in the Border group box. If you use the menu method, you can change the color of the lines and alter the line appearance.
- You can click the Borders button on the Formatting toolbar to apply borders to a cell or range of cells. If you use the Borders button, you cannot change the color of the lines or alter the line appearance.

To place an outline around the cells containing the values for the Growth Rate Assumptions:

Select	cells A15:F18
Click	the down arrow on the Borders button on the Formatting toolbar
Click	the last square in the last row

After you have made cell A13 the active cell, the bottom part of your screen should look like Figure 3-26.

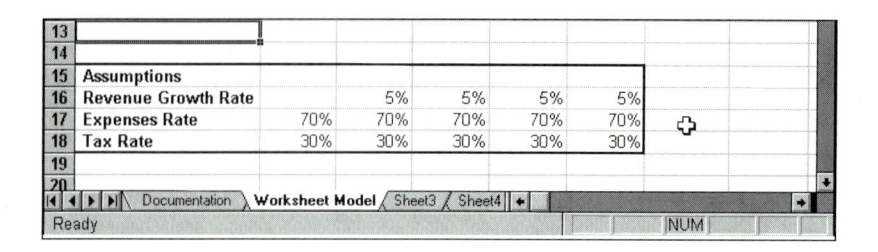

Figure 3-26

Copying Formats

You may wish to copy the shading and alignment of cells B6:G6 to the row labels in cells A8:A12.

- First, make one of the formatted cells the active cell, and then copy the data. Use the For**mat**s option in the Paste **S**pecial command on the **E**dit menu to paste only the formatting.

- You can use the Format Painter button on the Standard toolbar to copy formats. First, make one of the formatted cells the active cell. Then click the Format Painter button on the Standard toolbar. Then drag across the cells to be formatted. When you release the mouse button, the cells are formatted and the Format Painter automatically turns off.

To copy the shading and alignment of cell B6 to the row labels section of the worksheet:

Select	cell B6
Click	the Format Painter button on the Standard toolbar
Move	the mouse pointer to cell A8
Press and hold	the mouse button
Drag	across cells A8:A12
Release	the mouse button

The row labels are now shaded and centered. After you have made cell A1 the active cell, the top part of your screen should look like Figure 3-27.

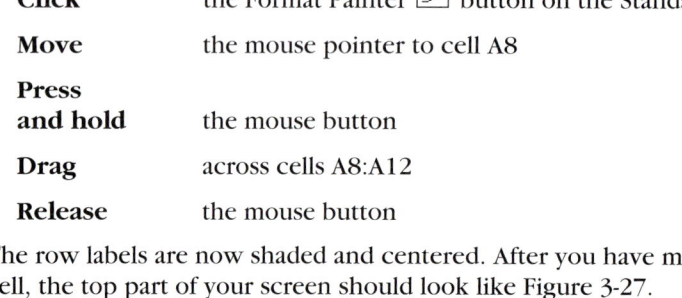

If you want to use the Format Painter multiple times before turning it off, double-click the Format Painter button on the Standard toolbar. It will remain on until you click the Format Painter button again.

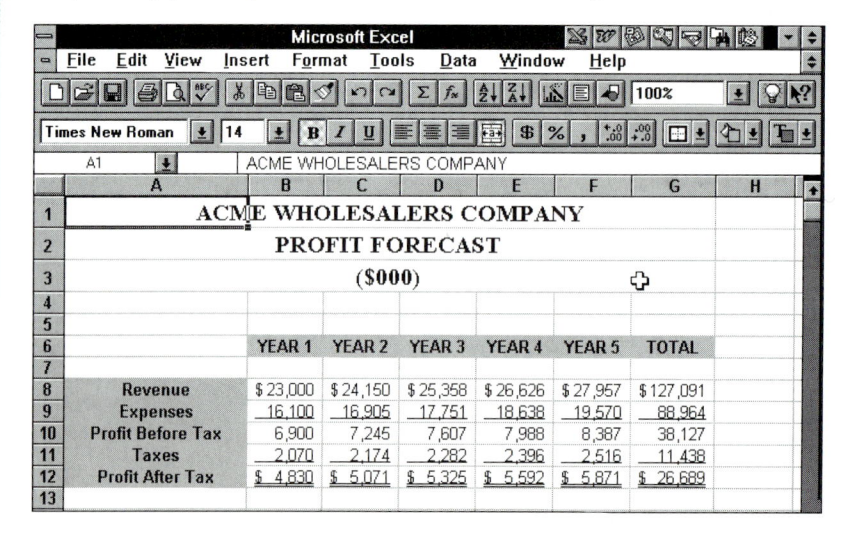

Figure 3-27

Creating Worksheets

Save the workbook in a file using the name PROF-ENH.

Close the workbook.

> Once you have formatted a worksheet in a particular way, you may wish to use the Style feature to name your formatting. A **style** is a set of formats that can be applied to one cell or a range of cells. There are three ways to create a style: (1) by example, (2) by definition, or (3) by copying styles from another worksheet. You can use the Style command on the Format menu to create a style name. For more information about creating styles to repeat formatting, see your Excel *User's Guide*.
>
> Excel provides some formats for tables of information. You can access these formats by choosing the **AutoFormat** command on the **Format** menu. The range of cells in the table must be selected prior to using the available formats.

Using Absolute Cell References

Open the NATSALES.XLS workbook. This file may be found on the diskette in the back of this book.

To enter a formula that computes the commission for each division:

Enter	`Com Rate:` in cell I1
Enter	`5%` in cell J1
Enter	`Commissions` in cell H6
Type	`=` in cell H7
Click	on cell G7
Type	`*`
Click	on J1
Click	the enter box ☑
	or
Press	⏎ ENTER

Cell H7 displays the number 1575.

To copy the formula to the remaining cells:

Verify	cell H7 is the active cell
Move	the mouse pointer to the Fill handle in cell H7
Press and hold	the mouse button
Drag	the Fill handle to cell H10
Release	the mouse button

Zeros appear in cells H8 through H10. After you have made cell H8 the active cell, the top part of your screen should look like Figure 3-28.

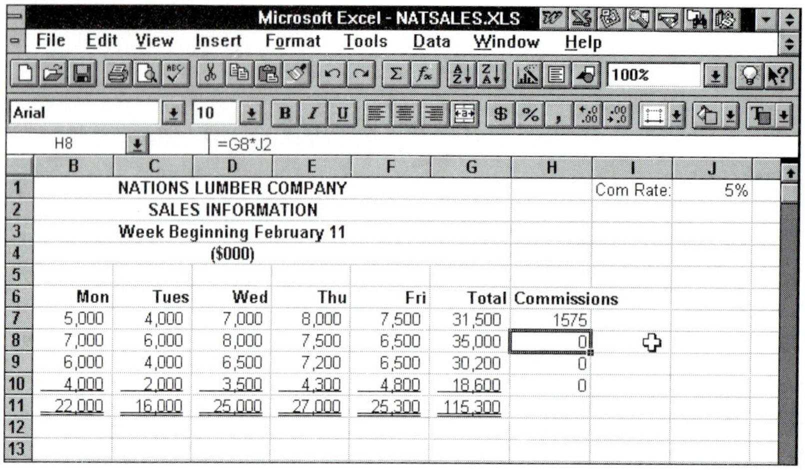

Figure 3-28

Look at the formula in the formula bar. The formula that was intended to be copied was =G8*J1. However, when the formula =G7*J1 was copied, it became =G8*J2.

Similar results occurred for the formula in cells H9 and H10. Formulas are based on relative location. Excel interprets the formula that was copied not as =G7*J1 but, rather, as "multiply the number one cell to the left by the number two columns to the right and six rows up."

Since cells J2, J3, and so forth are blank and are interpreted as the number 0 in formula calculations, the multiplied value using these blank cells is zero.

The F4 key, called the "reference key," has four options or ways of changing a cell. The following options provide ways to change rows and columns using the reference key:

Option	Example	Column	Row
1	J1	Absolute	Absolute
2	J$1	Relative	Absolute
3	$J1	Absolute	Relative
4	J1	Relative	Relative

To cycle through the four options, press the F4 key after you enter the cell address until the proper option is selected.

To enter a formula that computes the commission for each region and holds the commission rate constant when the formula is copied to other cells:

Click   on cell H7

Type   =G7*J1

Press   F4

A dollar sign appears in front of the J and in front of the 1. These dollar signs indicate that the column (J) and the row (1) will remain constant, or absolute, when copied.

Click   the enter box ✓

or

Press   ← ENTER

The formula in cell H7 is now =G7*J1. Cell H7 should still display the number 1575.

Creating Worksheets

To copy the formula in cell H7 to cells H8 through H10:

Click on cell H7

Move the mouse pointer to the Fill handle in cell H7

Drag the Fill handle to cell H10

The correct computation for cells H8 through H10 occurs. After you have made cell A1 the active cell, the top part of your screen should look like Figure 3-29.

> Instead of retyping the formula, you could double-click on J1 in the formula bar. This would select J1. You then could press F4 until the desired absolute reference positions appear. Then click the enter box or press the ENTER key.

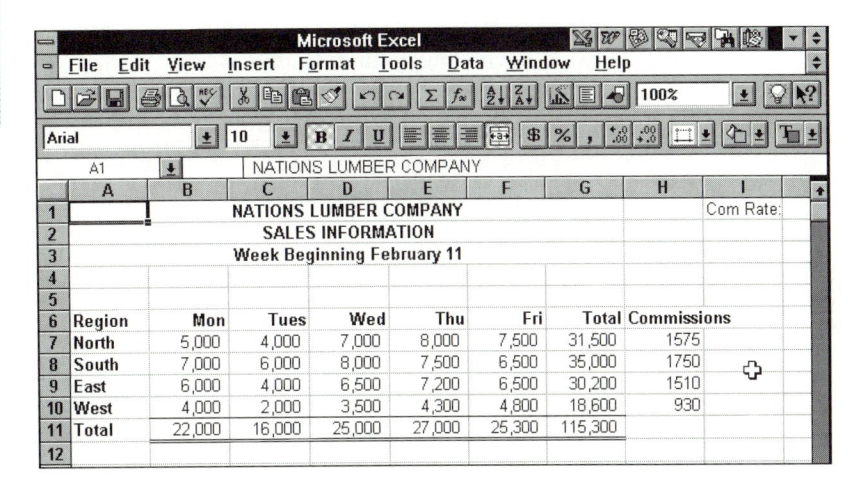

Figure 3-29

To see how the formula =G7*J1 was copied correctly:

Click on cell H8

The formula =G8*J1 appears in the formula bar. If you wish, also click on cells H9 and H10 to see that J1 is held constant in the formulas for these cells.

Save the workbook in a file using the name ABSOLUTE. Leave the workbook on the screen for the next exercise.

Splitting a Window into Panes

Excel allows you to view different areas of the worksheet at the same time by splitting the worksheet window into panes.

- You can split the worksheet window by choosing the **S**plit command on the **W**indow menu. By default, Excel splits the window above and to the left of the active cell.

- You can split the worksheet window into panes by using the horizontal or vertical split bar and the mouse. The vertical split bar appears at the right edge of the horizontal scroll bar. The horizontal split bar appears at the top of the vertical scroll bar.

To split the screen vertically to aid in viewing row titles:

Press CTRL + HOME

Move the mouse pointer to the vertical split box (the mouse appears as a double-headed arrow with a vertical line in the middle)

**Press
and hold**   the mouse button

Drag   the split bar to the boundary line between columns A and B

Release   the mouse button

Two vertical panes are visible on the screen. With the screen split vertically, you can display column A at all times and still be able to view data that may be hidden from view in columns I through IV. Notice that two horizontal scroll bars are displayed. Using the horizontal split box, you can use the same steps to split the screen horizontally to aid in viewing column titles.

To move to the right pane:

Click   on any cell in the right pane

Any cell in either pane can be accessed.

To move to the left pane:

Click   on any cell in the left pane

To display columns C through J in the right pane:

Click   the right arrow on the horizontal scroll bar

By splitting the window into panes, you can see the effect of changing a number in one area of the worksheet on another area of the worksheet. The top part of your screen should look like Figure 3-30.

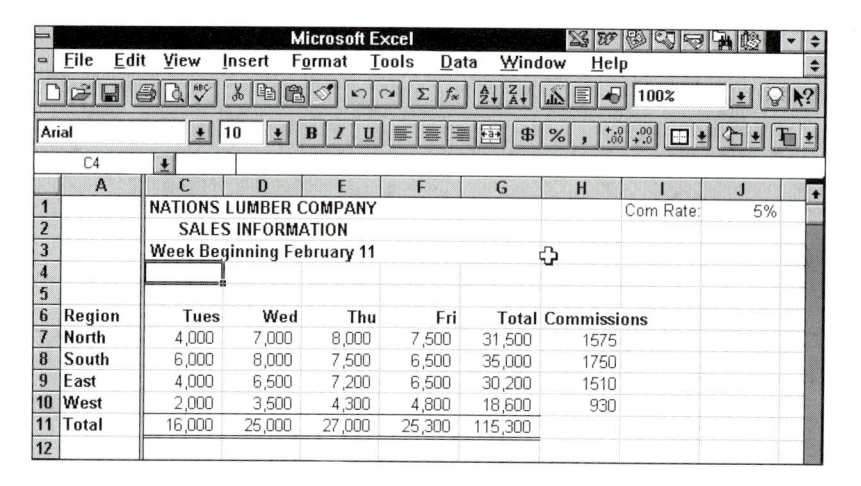

Figure 3-30

Once the window is split into panes, you can use the menu or the mouse to remove the split view.

- You can remove the panes from the screen by choosing the Remove **S**plit command on the **W**indow menu.

- You can double-click the gray line separating the panes to remove the split appearance.

To clear the window panes:

Move   the mouse pointer onto the gray line separating the two windows

Double-click   the mouse button

The split view of the worksheet is removed from your screen. Close the workbook without saving changes.

Creating Worksheets

Changing the Assumptions to Complete a "What-If" Analysis

One advantage of using Excel is the ability to change the Assumptions and see the impact of the changes on other values in the worksheet. For example, suppose you show your supervisor the PROFFCST worksheet results. Your supervisor may then ask some "what-if" questions and request that you complete some further analysis. Open the PROFFCST.XLS workbook. Suppose you are asked to determine the impact on Profit After Tax if the Tax Rate is 30%.

To place the new Tax Rate on your worksheet:

Select cell B17

Enter .3

Your worksheet is recalculated to reflect the new Tax Rate for Year 1. Use the Fill handle to change the Tax Rate for Years 2 through 5. You can now see the new values for Profit After Tax that were calculated using these new assumptions. If desired, you can change some of the other assumptions. After you have made cell A18 the active cell, the bottom of your screen should look like Figure 3-31.

Figure 3-31

Close the workbook. Do not save any changes.

Using the Spelling Feature

When you complete a worksheet, it is a good idea to spell check the text used in headings and column and row labels. The Spelling feature in Excel is similar to the Spelling feature in other Windows applications. Open the ABSOLUTE.XLS workbook.

- You can check the spelling in a worksheet by choosing the **S**pelling command on the **T**ools menu.
- You can also click the Spelling button on the Standard toolbar to check the spelling in a worksheet.

To spell check the ABSOLUTE.XLS workbook:

Press CTRL + HOME

Click the Spelling button on the Standard toolbar

The Spelling dialog box appears. The top part of your screen should look like Figure 3-32.

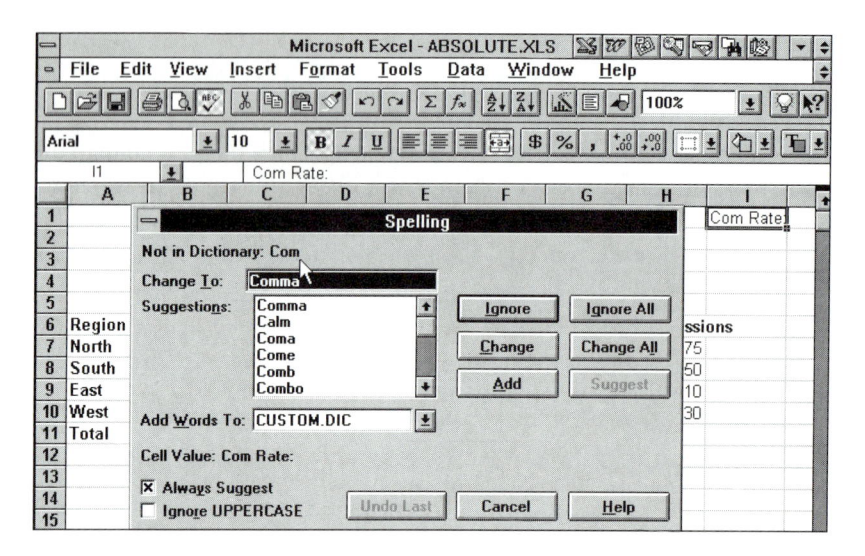

Figure 3-32

> Only the current worksheet is spell checked. If you wish to check the spelling on other sheets of the workbook, you must make each sheet active before opening the Spelling dialog box.

The abbreviation "Com" in cell I1 appears next to the phrase "Not in Dictionary:". A word is suggested in the Change To text box. Additional words are suggested in the Suggestions list box.

To select one of the suggested words, click the desired word; it will then appear in the Change To text box. Once the correct word appears in the Change To text box, click the Change or Change All command button to place the correct word in the cell. The Spelling feature automatically advances to the next word. In this instance, you do not wish to change the word. You could either choose to skip the word by clicking the Ignore or Ignore All command button, or you could choose to add the word to the dictionary by clicking the Add command button.

Continue spell checking the worksheet and click the Ignore command button when the Spell Checker stops on the abbreviated days of the week. When all the cells have been examined, Excel displays a confirmation box to indicate that the Spell Checking procedure is complete. Click the OK command button.

Close the workbook. Do not save any changes.

Summary

Creating worksheets is faster and more effective when you use a software package like Excel than when you prepare a worksheet by hand. You can create formulas and include values that can be copied. Inserting and deleting rows and columns with Excel commands is easy. A saved worksheet is simple to edit later. Excel provides commands that permit you to enhance the appearance of a worksheet. You can include various fonts, boldface the contents of a cell, shade a cell, and include boxes around a cell or range of cells. Excel also includes features for automatically formatting a table of data and removing the gridlines from a worksheet. Different parts of a worksheet can be easily viewed using the Split feature. Errors can be prevented using the ROUND function, the absolute reference on cell addresses, and the Spelling feature. These are just a few of the advantages of the Excel software package.

Creating Worksheets

Exercise 1

INSTRUCTIONS: Define or explain the following:

1. Assumptions _____
   _____

2. AutoFill _____
   _____

3. AutoSum button _____
   _____

4. Range _____
   _____

5. Relative cell location _____
   _____

6. Select All button _____
   _____

7. Replacing a workbook file _____
   _____

8. Formula _____
   _____

9. SUM function _____
   _____

Exercise 2

INSTRUCTIONS: Circle T if the statement is true and F if the statement is false.

T   F   1. One method to correct data in a cell is to type the entry again and click the enter box.
T   F   2. The formula =SUM(B3:B10) will add the values in cells B3 through B10.
T   F   3. You can change the tab name for a sheet only once.
T   F   4. The = sign must appear as the first character in any formula.
T   F   5. The File Save As command must be used the first time you save a workbook to a file.
T   F   6. The character "\" is used in Excel to indicate division.
T   F   7. You can print a worksheet without specifying the range of cells to print.

Exercise 3

INSTRUCTIONS:

1. Create the worksheet displayed in Figure 3-33.
2. Place appropriate information on the Documentation worksheet, and put the worksheet itself on the Worksheet Model worksheet.
3. The width of column A is 11.
4. The font size for the company name and report title is 12. Center the title text in rows 1 and 2 across columns A through G.
5. Create a formula using the SUM function to calculate each region's weekly sales and total daily sales.
6. Format the numbers in the Comma format with no decimal places. Format the North region and Daily Total rows in the Currency format with no decimal places.

7. Apply the boldface format to the column headings and row headings.
8. Add the appropriate underlines.
9. Save the workbook in a file using the name E03EX03.
10. Print the worksheet.
11. Close the workbook.

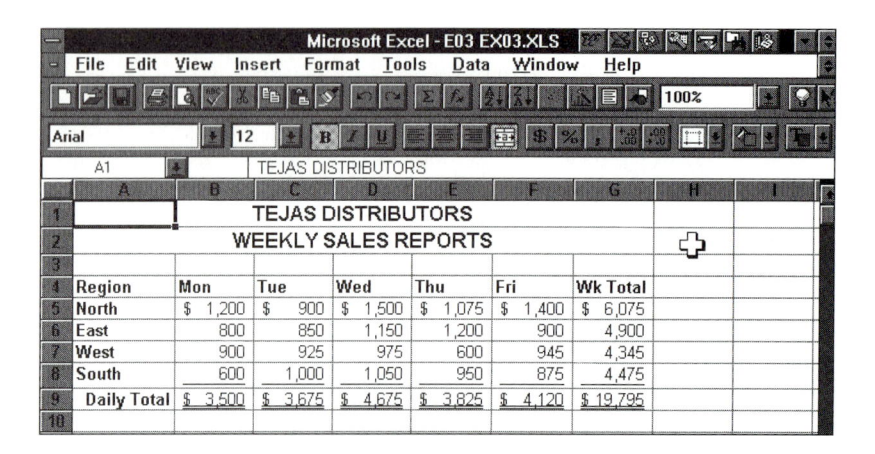

Figure 3-33

Exercise 4

INSTRUCTIONS:

1. Create the worksheet displayed in Figure 3-34.
2. Place appropriate information on the Documentation worksheet, and put the worksheet itself on the Worksheet Model worksheet.
3. The worksheet calculates a projection of expenses.
4. The initial values for the expense categories appear as assumptions.
5. Create a formula in the appropriate cells so the initial values are utilized. Use the Round function in your formulas to correct any rounding errors.
6. Save the workbook in a file using the name E03EX04.
7. Print the worksheet.
8. Change the initial value for Salaries to $29,500 and the growth for materials in the fourth quarter to 4.7%.
9. Print the worksheet.
10. Close the workbook. Do not save any changes.

Creating Worksheets

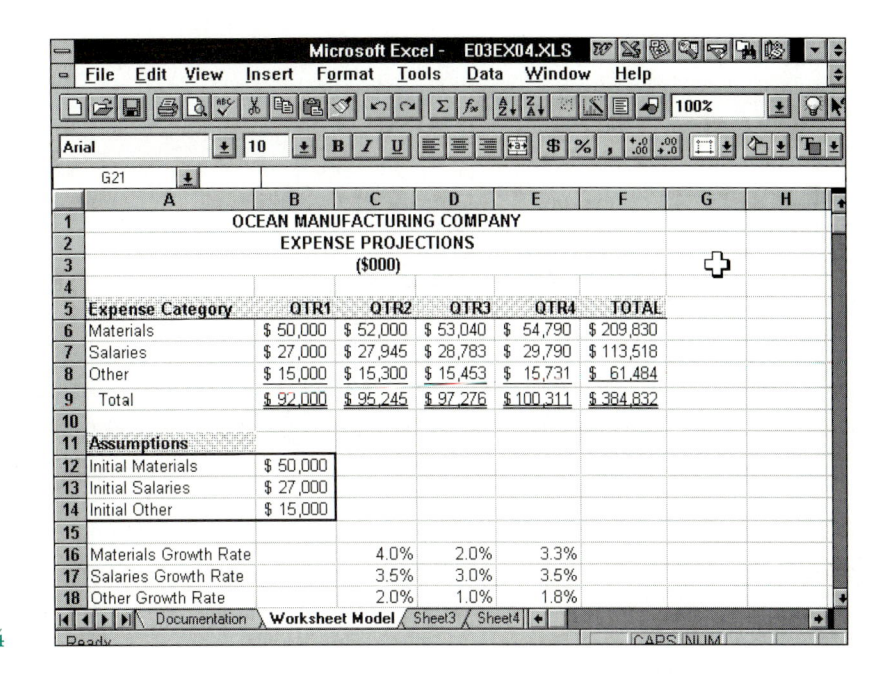

Figure 3-34

	A	B	C	D	E	F	G	H
1		OCEAN MANUFACTURING COMPANY						
2		EXPENSE PROJECTIONS						
3		($000)						
4								
5	Expense Category	QTR1	QTR2	QTR3	QTR4	TOTAL		
6	Materials	$ 50,000	$ 52,000	$ 53,040	$ 54,790	$ 209,830		
7	Salaries	$ 27,000	$ 27,945	$ 28,783	$ 29,790	$ 113,518		
8	Other	$ 15,000	$ 15,300	$ 15,453	$ 15,731	$ 61,484		
9	Total	$ 92,000	$ 95,245	$ 97,276	$ 100,311	$ 384,832		
10								
11	Assumptions							
12	Initial Materials	$ 50,000						
13	Initial Salaries	$ 27,000						
14	Initial Other	$ 15,000						
15								
16	Materials Growth Rate		4.0%	2.0%	3.3%			
17	Salaries Growth Rate		3.5%	3.0%	3.5%			
18	Other Growth Rate		2.0%	1.0%	1.8%			

Printing Features

4

Objectives

In this chapter you will learn to:
- Use Print Preview and the Print feature
- Insert a page break
- Create and use a range name

Chapter Overview

This chapter discusses printing features. The Preview Window and its various command options are covered. Options in the Page Setup dialog box are discussed. Creating page breaks and range names is illustrated.

Using Print Preview and the Print Feature

Open the PROFFCST.XLS workbook you modified in Chapter 3.

Before you print a worksheet, it is a good idea to preview it. You can adjust margins and column widths in Print Preview. If you do not select a particular range of cells, the entire worksheet is previewed.

- You can choose the Preview command on the File menu to preview a worksheet.
- You can also click the Print Preview button on the Standard toolbar to preview a worksheet.

To preview the Worksheet Model sheet workbook before printing it:

Click the Preview button on the Standard toolbar

The top part of your screen should look like Figure 4-1.

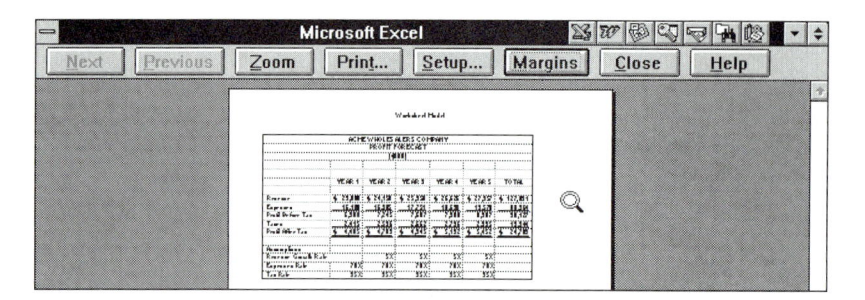

Figure 4-1

The lower-left corner indicates how many pages the print job contains and which page you are currently viewing. If the worksheet is more than one page in length, you can view the next page by clicking the **N**ext command button. You can view previous pages by clicking the **P**revious command button.

Using the Zoom Command in Print Preview

The **Z**oom command button enlarges the document view. Once the document is enlarged, you can use the scroll bars or pointer-movement keys to view other parts of the previewed page. Clicking the **Z**oom command button again returns the view to a miniature size. You also can zoom the viewing size by clicking the mouse pointer anywhere on the previewed worksheet. The mouse pointer appears as a magnifying glass. The area on which you click is enlarged. You can click again to return to a miniature view.

Using the Margins Command in Print Preview

When you click the **M**argins command button in the Preview window, vertical and horizontal lines appear on the previewed document. When you move the mouse pointer onto one of these lines, the mouse appears as a double-headed arrow. You can drag in the desired direction to change the position of the margin, headers or footers, or change the size of column widths. As you drag the mouse, the current measurement appears in the lower-left corner of the screen.

Printing Features

Figure 4-2 illustrates the vertical and horizontal lines and the double-headed arrow used to change margins, headers, footers, and column widths.

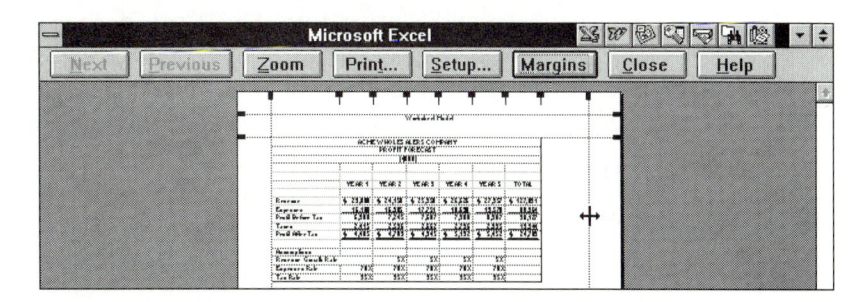

Figure 4-2

Using the Print Command in Print Preview

The **Print** command button in the Preview window displays the Print dialog box, allowing you to select a different printer or change other elements, such as number of copies and number of pages.

To display the Print dialog box:

Click   the Print button on the Print Preview toolbar

The Print dialog box appears. Your screen should look similar to Figure 4-3.

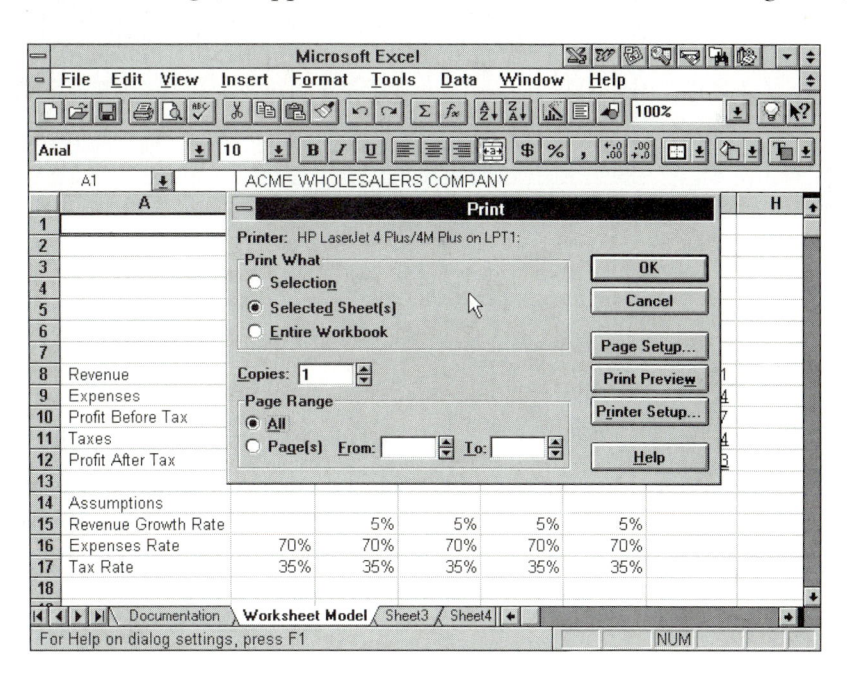

Figure 4-3

Notice that the default option in the Print What group box is to print the Selecte**d** Sheet(s). However, you could select a range before displaying the Print dialog box and then click the Selectio**n** option button in the Print What group box. Range names, which are described in a later section of this chapter, provide an efficient way for you to print particular sections of a worksheet. You can also print the entire workbook by clicking the **E**ntire Workbook option button in the Print What group box. Notice that when you print the entire workbook, each worksheet is printed on a separate page.

Using the Setup Command in Print Preview

The **S**etup command button in the Print Preview window is the same as the Page Set**u**p command button in the Print dialog box. Either command button displays the Page Setup dialog box. The Page Setup dialog box has many elements to consider before you print: margins, vertical and horizontal alignment, page orientation, scaling, paper size, page number order, headers, and footers. Many of these options are discussed below.

You should still be viewing the Print dialog box from the previous topic.

To display the Page Setup dialog box:

Click the Page Set**u**p command button

The top part of your screen should look like Figure 4-4.

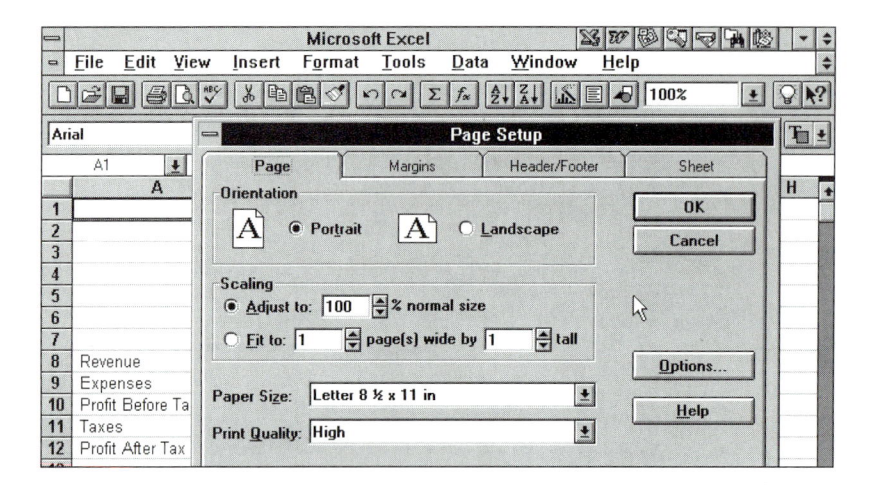

Figure 4-4

Orientation

In printing operations, the standard **orientation** for printing a worksheet is Portrait.

To change the orientation to Landscape:

Click the **P**age tab (if necessary)

Click the **L**andscape option button in the Orientation group box

Other options in the Page Tab include scaling, paper size, print quality, and starting page number. For more information about these features, click the **H**elp command button in the Page Setup dialog box or see your Excel *User's Guide*.

To change the orientation back to Portrait:

Click the **Po**rtrait option button in the Orientation group box

Using the Margins Tab

The Margins tab in the Page Setup dialog box is displayed in Figure 4-5. The Margins tab provides an alternate way to change margins and the vertical position of headers and footers. You can type the desired increment in each text box. Changes to these settings affect all the printed pages of the worksheet. To center the worksheet horizontally or

Printing Features

vertically on the page, click in the desired check box to insert an X. For more information about these features, click the **H**elp command button in the Page Setup dialog box or see your Excel *User's Guide*.

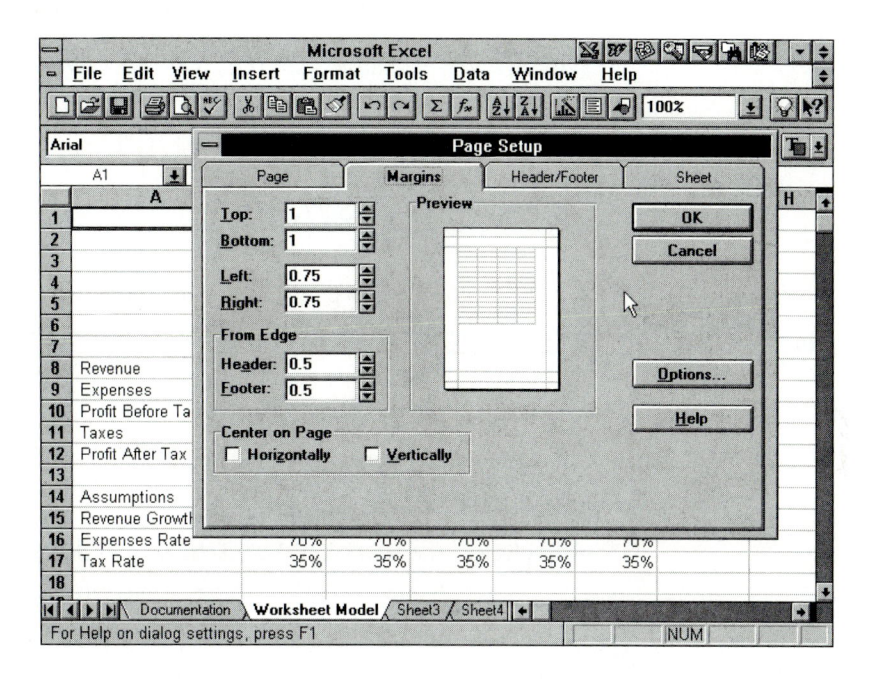

Figure 4-5

Customizing Headers and Footers

A **header** is a line of text that appears above the top margin of every page. A **footer** is a line of text that appears below the bottom margin of every page. By default, Excel includes the worksheet tab name as the header and the page number as the footer on each printed page. By default, headers are printed 0.5" from the top and 0.75" from each side of the page. The vertical position of headers can be changed and header text can be placed at the left margin, right margin, or centered.

Your screen should still display the Page Setup dialog box from the previous activity.

To change the default header at the top of each page, use the following procedure:

Click the Header/Footer tab

Click the **C**ustom Header command button

The Header dialog box appears.

The top part of your screen should look like Figure 4-6.

You can type your own text in the header or footer text boxes, or you can use the buttons in the Header and Footer dialog boxes.

The buttons are explained below in the order they appear above the **C**enter Section edit box:

To format the header or footer text

To insert a page number

To insert the total number of pages

To insert the current date

To insert the current time

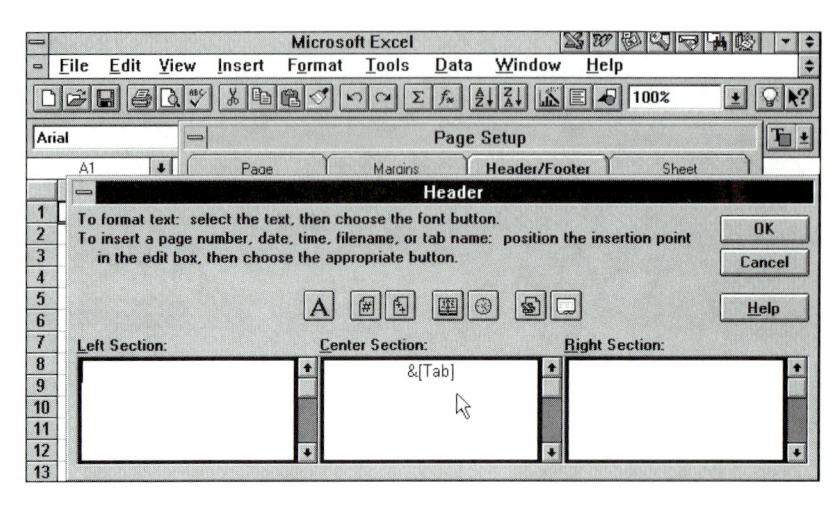

Figure 4-6

To insert the workbook filename

To insert the worksheet tab name

To create a custom header:

Double-click the text "&[Tab]" in the **Center** Section edit box

Type ACME WHOLESALERS COMPANY in the **Center** Section edit box

Click the OK command button

You enter headers only once, but they are reproduced on each printed page. You can change header text by repeating the procedure. You can delete a header by repeating the procedure, then selecting the text in each of the Section edit boxes, and pressing the DELETE key.

By default, footers are printed 0.5" from the bottom of the page and 0.75" from the side of the page.

To create a footer that will result in a right-aligned page number:

Click the Custom Footer command button

The Footer dialog box appears.

To delete the footer text:

Select the default text in the **Center** Section edit box

Press DELETE

To enter the footer:

Click the **Right** Section edit box

Type Page

Press SPACEBAR

Click the Page Number button

Click the OK command button

Your screen should look like Figure 4-7.

Printing Features

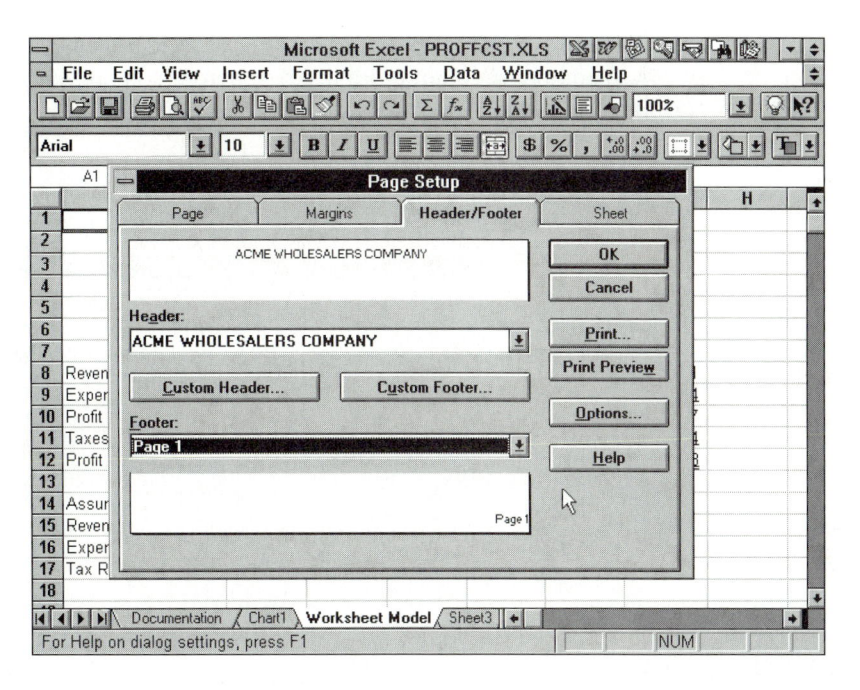

Figure 4-7

Notice that the example header and footer appear in the Header and Footer edit boxes.

To close the Page Setup dialog box and close the Print dialog box without printing:

Click	the OK command button in the Page Setup dialog box
Click	the Cancel command button in the Print dialog box

Setting Row and Column Print Titles

Sometimes, you may work with large worksheets that contain more than one page. It is useful to include **row print titles** on each page when there are several pages to a report. These titles provide descriptive information at the top of each page. You can print a **column print title** on the left side of each page for ease in reading the worksheet rows. By setting column A as a print title, you ensure that the data in column A are printed at the left edge of additional pages if the worksheet data spread across more than one page horizontally.

Print titles are created in the Sheet tab of the Page Setup dialog box.

To display the Page Setup dialog box:

Choose	File
Choose	Page Setup
Click	the Sheet tab (if necessary)

To specify column A as the column to repeat at the left of the worksheet:

Click	the Columns to Repeat at Left text box in the Print Titles group box
Type	$A:$A
	or
Click	on any cell in column A on the worksheet

The dollar signs in front of the column letters indicate an absolute reference to column A. If additional columns are inserted before column A, the data in this column will still be used for the print titles. The top part of your screen should look like Figure 4-8.

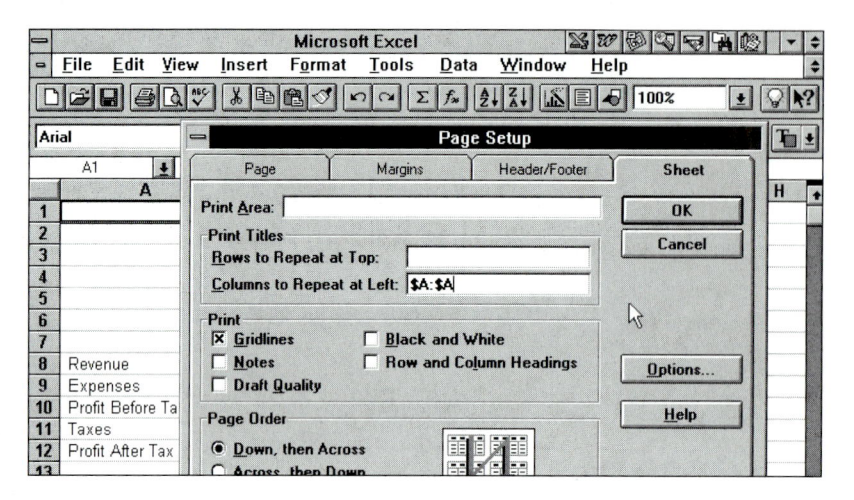

Figure 4-8

Gridlines and Row and Column Headings

You can use the check box in the Sheet tab in the Page Setup dialog box to include or exclude cell **gridlines** and the row and column headings on your printouts. The default condition is to include gridlines but to exclude row and column headings. When you have placed single underlines and double underlines on a worksheet, the gridlines may prevent you from distinguishing between the single and double underlines.

To exclude the gridlines:

Click   the **Gridlines** check box in the Print group box to remove the X

To close the Page Setup dialog box:

Click   the OK command button

> Excel automatically includes gridlines in a worksheet. In some situations, you may not want gridlines on your worksheet. You can use the Options command on the Tools menu to remove the gridlines.
>
> To remove the gridlines, choose the **V**iew tab in the Options dialog box. To display the Options dialog box, choose the **O**ptions command on the **T**ools menu. Click the **G**ridlines check box in the Window Options group box to remove the X. Click the OK command button. The gridlines are removed from the worksheet. When you print the document, no gridlines appear on the printout.

Inserting Page Breaks

Excel has a number of default settings when you print a worksheet. You can change these settings using various print commands. When you are printing a worksheet in Excel using the default settings, the software prints as much as it can on a single page based on the default page length. The remaining rows are printed on the next page or set of pages. Sometimes, you may wish to specify where you want **page breaks** to occur. You can use the Page **B**reak command on the **I**nsert menu in such situations.

Printing Features

To insert a page break above the Assumptions in the PROFFCST.XLS worksheet:

Click   on cell A14

Choose   Insert

Choose   Page **B**reak

Dashes appear on the horizontal boundary separating rows 13 and 14 to indicate a page break has been set. You may wish to preview the worksheet to see the two pages.

> When creating a vertical page break, it is important that the active cell be in row 1. The break will occur in the column boundary to the left of the active cell location. When you create a horizontal page break, the break occurs above the current row location. The active cell should be in column A.

After you have made cell A14 the active cell, your screen should look like Figure 4-9.

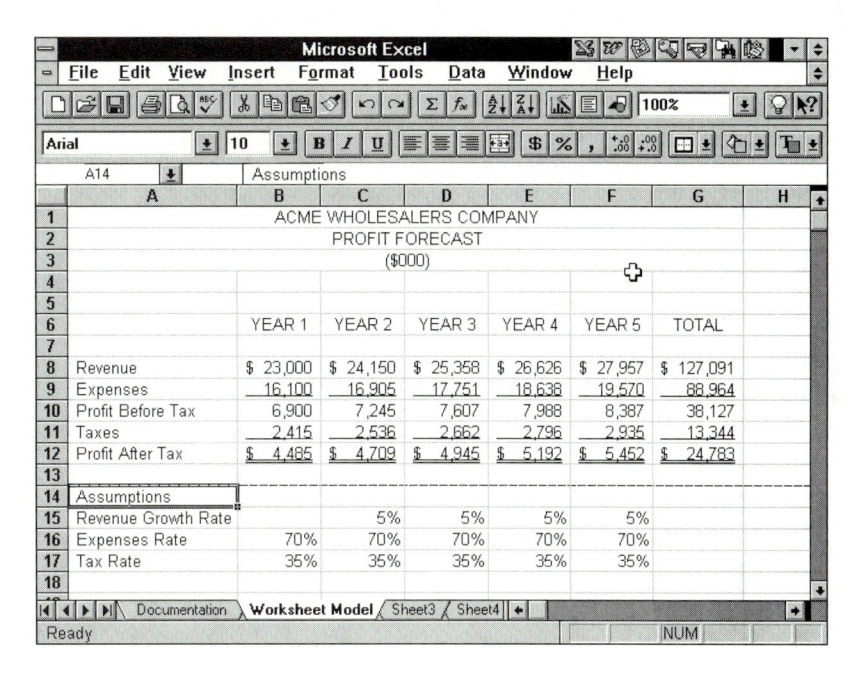

Figure 4-9

To remove the page break:

Click   on cell A14 (if necessary)

Choose   Insert

Choose   Remove Page **B**reak

The dashes no longer appear on the horizontal boundary between rows 13 and 14.

Creating and Using Range Names

A **range name** is a name given to a selected range of cells. You can use range names rather than cell addresses to make it easier to remember the location of cells or to quickly select a range of cells. Range names can also be used to print special sections of a worksheet.

- You first select the desired range of cells. Then choose the **D**efine command under the **N**ame command on the **I**nsert menu. Type the desired name in the Define Name dialog box.

- You first select the desired range of cells. Click the Name box and type the name to be used for the range. Then press the ENTER key.

To assign a range name to the cells containing the total values for the five years:

Select	cells G8:G12
Click	in the Name box
Type	TOTAL
Press	(← ENTER)
Deselect	the range

Using a Range Name to Select a Range of Cells

You can use a range name to select a range of cells.

To select the range of cells used in the name "TOTAL":

Click	the down arrow next to the Name box
Click	TOTAL

The range G8:G12 is selected. You can also use range names in formulas in place of cell addresses. You can use range names to quickly move to a particular area of a worksheet or to select a range of cells for printing.

Deleting a Range Name

When you delete a range name, the contents of the cell or range of cells do not change.

To delete the range name you created:

Choose	**I**nsert
Choose	**N**ame
Choose	**D**efine
Click	TOTAL in the Names in **W**orkbook list box
Click	the **D**elete command button
Click	the OK command button

Printing Features

> At times, you may want to see the cell formulas that comprise a worksheet. Having a printout of cell formulas is especially helpful for documentation purposes. To change the format of the worksheet to see the cell formulas, choose the **O**ptions command on the **T**ools menu. Click the View tab and click the Fo**r**mulas check box in the Window Options group box to insert an X. Then click the OK command button. The formulas are now displayed on the worksheet itself. However, some cell formulas are not fully displayed because the column width cannot accommodate them. To view the full formulas, widen the columns and then print the worksheet that includes the formulas.

Close the workbook. Do not save any changes.

Summary

This chapter discussed printing features. The Preview Window and its various command options were illustrated. Options in the Page Setup dialog box were described. Creating page breaks and range names was demonstrated.

Exercise 1

INSTRUCTIONS: Define or explain the following:

1. Column print title _____
   _____

2. Row print titles _____
   _____

3. Footer _____
   _____

4. Header _____
   _____

5. Page breaks _____
   _____

6. Gridlines _____
   _____

7. Orientation _____
   _____

Exercise 2

INSTRUCTIONS: Circle T if the statement is true and F if the statement is false.

T   F   1. The margins cannot be changed in Print Preview.
T   F   2. Landscape orientation is the default orientation when a worksheet is printed.
T   F   3. Print titles allow row and column text to be printed on all pages of a multipage worksheet.
T   F   4. A name can be assigned to a set of cells in a worksheet.
T   F   5. Range names cannot be deleted.

Exercise 3

INSTRUCTIONS:

1. Open the E03EX03.XLS workbook created in Chapter 3, Exercise 3.
2. Create the following header and footer in the Center sections:

    Header: Weekly Sales Report

    Footer: Prepared by Your Name
3. Include the current date in the right section of the header.
4. Remove the gridlines from being displayed on the printed document.
5. Change the orientation to Landscape.
6. Save the workbook in a file using the name E04EX03.
7. Print the worksheet.
8. Close the workbook.

Exercise 4

INSTRUCTIONS:

1. Open the E03EX04.XLS workbook created in Chapter 3, Exercise 4.
2. Place a page break immediately above the cell containing the word "Assumptions."
3. Save the workbook in a file using the name E04EX04.
4. Print the worksheet.
5. Close the workbook.

Creating and Printing Charts

5

Objectives

In this chapter you will learn to:
- Identify parts of a chart
- Create a column chart on a new sheet
- Create an embedded chart
- Print an embedded chart
- Print an embedded chart and worksheet
- Delete an embedded chart from a worksheet
- Size and move an embedded chart
- Change the location of a legend
- Remove and change axes scales
- Change the fonts of chart text
- Change colors and hatch patterns
- Insert and remove gridlines
- Add unattached text and graphic objects to a chart

Chapter Overview

If a worksheet contains a large amount of data, it can be very difficult to detect trends and see relationships among various values. A **chart** depicting key elements of a worksheet can facilitate a more accurate analysis. You can use Excel to create charts using the worksheet data. The chart image can be viewed on your screen and can also be printed. The data points, selected from values on a worksheet, are grouped into a data series. Each data series has a distinguishing pattern or color.

Excel has 9 two-dimensional chart types and 6 three-dimensional chart types. Excel also provides a number of chart formats for the various chart types.

The 9 two-dimensional chart types available are: area, bar, column, line, pie, doughnut, radar, XY (scatter), and combination. The 6 three-dimensional chart types include: 3-D Area, 3-D Bar, 3-D Column, 3-D Line, 3-D Pie, and 3-D Surface.

Excel provides a tool named **ChartWizard** to assist you in creating a chart. ChartWizard is a series of five dialog boxes that guide you through the process of preparing a chart. You will use the ChartWizard in this chapter to create two charts.

This chapter demonstrates creating two of the most common two-dimensional chart types. One of the charts is created on its own sheet, and the other is embedded in the worksheet. This chapter also demonstrates how to change or enhance the appearance of a chart.

With the options available in Excel, you can change the location of a legend on a chart, remove and modify the axes scales, and change the fonts of text appearing on the chart. You can modify the chart colors, hatch patterns, gridlines, and borders. Text and graphic objects can be added to a chart. Finally, you can move and size embedded charts.

Identifying Parts of a Chart

Figure 5-1 includes a column chart on a separate chart sheet and identifies the various parts of the chart.

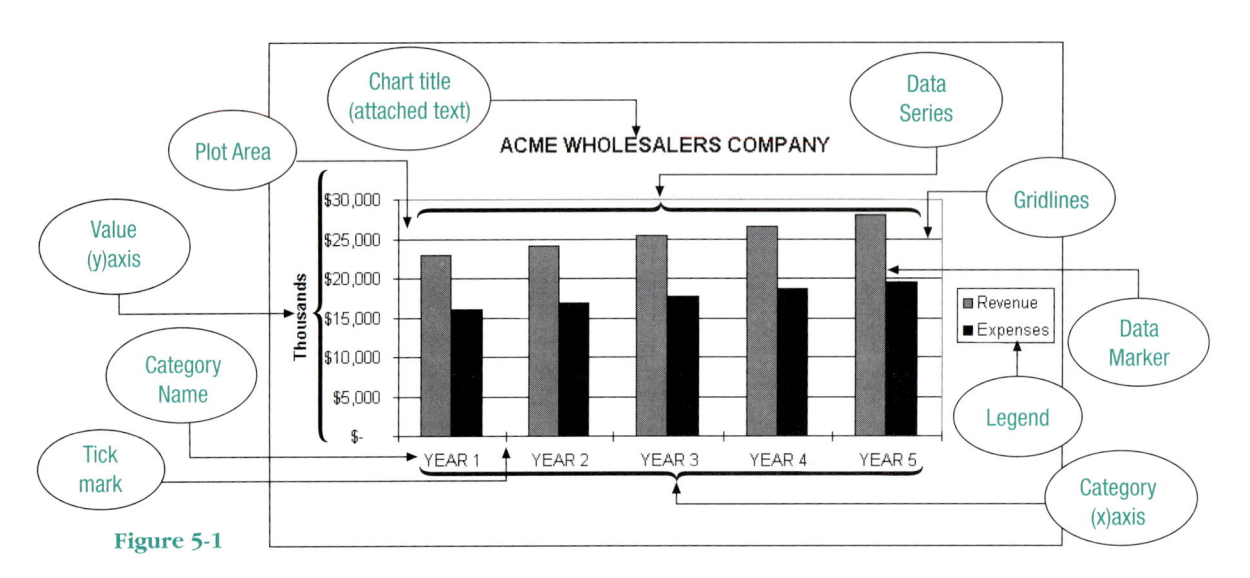

Figure 5-1

You will create this chart later in this chapter.

> The patterns and background of charts on your screen may not look exactly like those shown in the text. The patterns of charts in the text were chosen because they present a clear illustration.

Chart Area

The **chart area** includes all of the area in the chart sheet and all the elements in the chart.

Chart Toolbar

The **Chart toolbar** displays some tools for working with charts. With these tools, you can change the chart type, use the default chart type, use the ChartWizard, add or delete horizontal gridlines, and add or delete a legend.

Chart Title

The **chart title** describes the content of the chart.

Data Marker

The **data marker** is an item such as a bar, dot, area, or other symbol that marks an individual data point.

X-axis (Category Axis)

The x-axis, or **category axis**, is the horizontal axis along which you normally plot categories of data.

Y-axis (Value Axis)

The Y-axis, or **value axis**, is the vertical axis you usually use to plot the values associated with various categories.

Category Name

The **category name** is the label associated with a specific category on the x-axis.

Data Series

A chart **data series** is a group of related data, such as the values in a single row or column of a worksheet. In this case, Revenue for the various years is an example of a chart data series.

Gridlines

These lines are optional and are included to make a chart easier to read and understand. Horizontal and/or vertical gridlines can appear on a chart.

Tick Mark

Tick marks are small lines that appear on an axis. Use them to delineate a category, scale, or chart data series.

Data Label

A **data label** value or label is used to identify a data point on a chart.

Plot Area

The **plot area** includes the plotted data. The x-axis, y-axis, and data markers are located in the plot area.

Attached Text

Attached text is text associated with a specific object on the chart. For example, the chart title is considered attached text.

Unattached Text

You can include text on the chart inside or outside the plot area. Also, you can place graphics such as arrows on a chart.

Legend

A **legend** is a key that you use to identify the patterns, colors, or symbols associated with the markers for a chart data series. The chart data series name appears in the legend.

Creating a Column Chart on a New Sheet

A column chart is useful for depicting changes in data. The first chart that you will create in this chapter is based on data in the PROFFCST.XLS workbook that you modified in Chapter 3. To begin the exercise, open the PROFFCST.XLS workbook.

You will create a chart using the Revenue and Expense values for the five years in the Worksheet Model sheet. When you finish the chart, your screen will look like Figure 5-1.

You will use the five-step ChartWizard to create the chart:

1. Specify the range of cells you want to include in the chart.

2. Select the chart type to include on the worksheet.

3. Select the chart format.

4. Indicate whether the data series are in rows or columns and specify the data series on the worksheet to include as category (X) and value (Y) axis.

5. Specify whether to include a legend, chart title, or axis title information.

Selecting the Chart Data

You specify the data to chart by selecting it before you create the chart. Suppose you want to chart the Revenue and Expense values for the five years. You also need to include the column headings (Year 1 through Year 5) in your selection because they will serve as labels for the x-axis (category axis).

To select the desired cells:

Select   cells A6:F9

Creating the Column Chart

When you create a chart, you can place it on a separate worksheet in the workbook or you can embed it on the same sheet containing the numeric data. In this example, you will place the chart on a separate sheet.

Creating and Printing Charts

To create a chart using the selected data:

Choose	Insert
Choose	Chart
Choose	As New Sheet

The first dialog box associated with the ChartWizard appears.

Notice the command buttons at the bottom of the dialog box. The buttons and the action associated with each one are:

Help	Access the Help feature
Cancel	Cancel the ChartWizard tool and return to the worksheet
< Back	Return to the previous ChartWizard dialog box
Next >	Proceed to the next ChartWizard dialog box
Finish	Create a chart with the options selected at this point and terminate the usage of ChartWizard

The first dialog box is used to specify the data range or ranges to include in the chart.

Since you have already selected the data range for the chart:

Click   the **Next >** command button

The second ChartWizard dialog box appears. Use this dialog box to specify the chart type.

Since you want to create a column chart and the Column chart type is already selected:

Click   the **Next >** command button

The third ChartWizard dialog box appears. This dialog box allows you to select the format for the Column chart.

To accept the default selection format number 6:

Click   the **Next >** command button

The fourth ChartWizard dialog box appears. A sample chart appears in the dialog box. If there is a problem, you can go back to the previous ChartWizard dialog boxes to correct any errors by clicking the <**B**ack command button. If you want to start over, click the Cancel command button or press the ESC key. In this fourth dialog box, you indicate whether the data series are in rows or columns.

To continue:

Click   the **Next >** command button

The fifth ChartWizard dialog box appears. In this dialog box, you indicate whether a legend should be placed on the chart. You can also include a chart title and axis titles to make the chart easier to understand. Excel assumes that you want to include a legend on the column chart. If you do not want a legend to appear on the chart, click the No option button below the Add a Legend question.

To specify the chart title and include a title for the category and value axis:

Click	the Chart Title text box
Type	ACME WHOLESALERS COMPANY
Click	the Value (Y) text box in the Axis Titles group box
Type	Thousands

Notice that the sample chart changes to include the new information. To complete the chart-creation process:

Click the **Finish** command button

The chart is placed on a chart sheet. The Chart toolbar appears near the top of the screen.

Your screen should look similar to Figure 5-2.

> If the Chart toolbar does not appear, choose the Toolbars command on the View menu. Insert an X in the Chart check box in the Toolbars list box and click the OK command button.

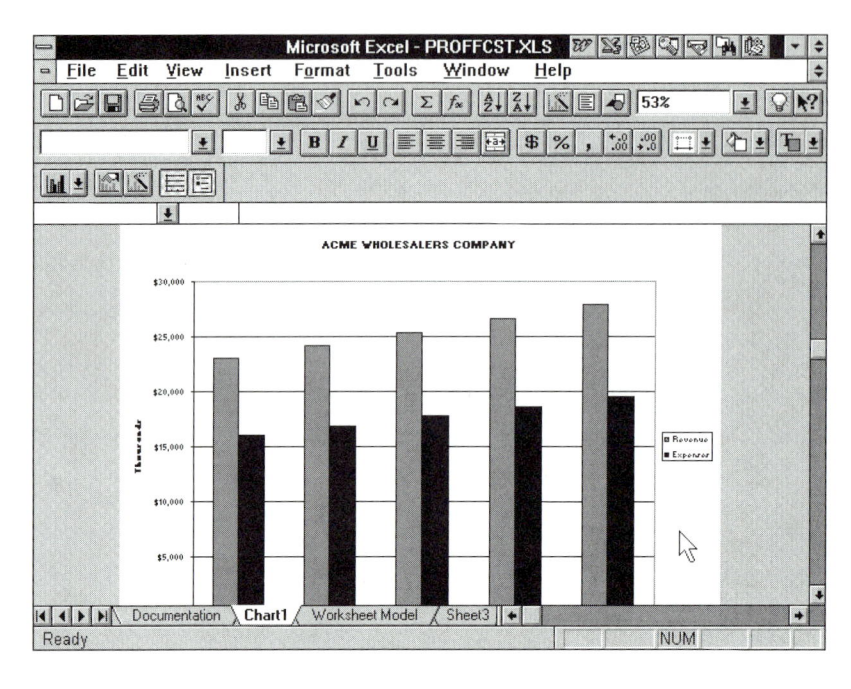

Figure 5-2

If you modify a value or label in the worksheet, the chart is automatically updated.

By default, a new chart sheet is independent of the window size. The default view allows you to see what the chart will look like when it is printed.

- You can use the **Z**oom command on the **V**iew menu to increase the size of the chart to make the labels more readable.
- You can click the down arrow on the Zoom Control button on the Standard toolbar to display different view sizes. You can also type a desired increment in the Zoom Control text box on the Standard toolbar.

Another way to view the entire chart on the screen is to use the Sized with **W**indow command on the **V**iew menu. The chart fills the entire window. This display makes it easier to view and edit the chart but does not show how the chart will print. You cannot use the **Z**oom command on the **V**iew menu when your chart has been sized with the window.

To view the entire chart:

Choose View

Choose Sized with **W**indow

To name the chart sheet:

Double-click the Chart1 tab

The Rename Chart dialog box appears.

> The F11 key can be used to place a chart on a separate sheet. Select the desired range of cells and press F11. By pressing the F11 key, you bypass the ChartWizard, accepting all default choices. A default column chart appears on a separate sheet.

Creating and Printing Charts

Type   `Column Chart`

Click   the OK command button

Your screen should look like Figure 5-3.

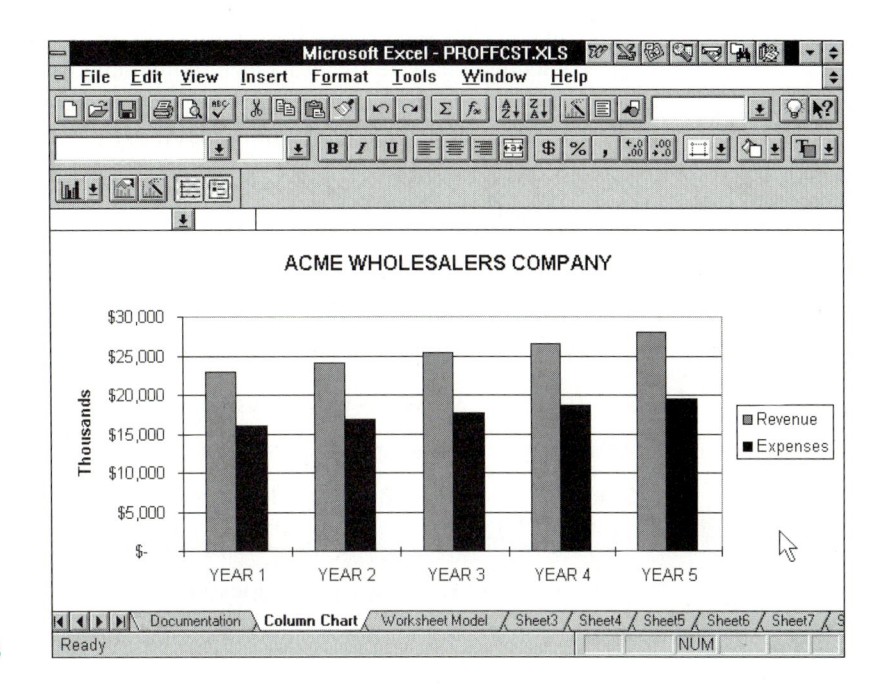

Figure 5-3

Changing the Chart Type

> You can use the AutoFormat command on the Format menu to change chart types and create custom chart appearances.

The column chart is the default appearance. You can change to other chart types.

- You can change the chart type by choosing the Chart **Type** command on the **Format** menu and then selecting the desired appearance.

- You can also change the chart type by clicking the down arrow on the Chart Type button on the Chart toolbar and then clicking the chart type you desire.

To change the column chart to a line chart:

Click   the down arrow on the Chart Type button on the Chart toolbar

Click   the first button on the fourth row

The new chart type replaces the original appearance. Additional enhancements are discussed later in this chapter.

To change the chart back to a column appearance:

Click   the down arrow on the Chart Type button on the Chart toolbar

Click   the first button on the third row

Creating an Embedded Chart

In the last section, you learned to create a chart as a separate sheet in a workbook. In this section, you will use the ChartWizard to embed a chart on the worksheet containing the data.

> You can choose the **On** This Sheet command under the **Ch**art command on the **I**nsert menu to insert an embedded chart on the worksheet containing the data. Follow the instruction at the bottom of the screen to click in the desired location on the worksheet. Then complete the steps of the ChartWizard.

> You can click the ChartWizard button on the Standard toolbar to insert an embedded chart on the worksheet containing the data. Follow the instruction at the bottom of the screen to click in the desired location on the worksheet. Then complete the steps of the ChartWizard.

Suppose you want to prepare a **pie chart** that displays how the revenue is distributed for the first year.

Before creating the pie chart:

Click	the Worksheet Model sheet tab
Select	cells A9:B9 and A11:B12
Scroll	down to view rows 18 through 35

To create a pie chart using the ChartWizard button:

Click	the ChartWizard button on the Standard toolbar

The mouse pointer changes shape and appears as a chart icon.

To place the chart in an appropriate location:

Move	the mouse pointer to the middle of cell A19
Press and hold	the mouse button
Drag	the mouse pointer to the middle of cell G33
Release	the mouse button

When you release the mouse button, the first ChartWizard dialog box appears. Once you have completed the process for creating a chart, the chart appears in the area you designated.

Since you have already selected the data series for the chart:

Click	the **N**ext > command button

The second ChartWizard dialog box appears.

To select the Pie chart type:

Click	the Pie chart type
Click	the **N**ext > command button

The third ChartWizard dialog box appears.

To specify the seventh format for the Pie chart:

Click	format number 7 for the Pie chart
Click	the **N**ext > command button

The fourth ChartWizard dialog box appears. A sample chart appears in the dialog box.

Click	the **N**ext > command button

The fifth ChartWizard dialog box appears. Excel assumes that you do not want to include a legend.

An alternative method for selecting the area for an embedded chart is to simply click the mouse button where you want the top-left corner of the chart to appear. Excel creates a default chart size, which you can later customize. Resizing an embedded chart is discussed later in this chapter.

Creating and Printing Charts

To specify the chart title:

Click the Chart Title text box

Type `Revenue Distribution for Year 1`

Notice that the sample chart changes to include the information.

To complete the chart-creation process:

Click the **Finish** command button

The chart is placed in the area you designate in the worksheet. After you have made row 18 the first row on your screen, your screen should look like Figure 5-4.

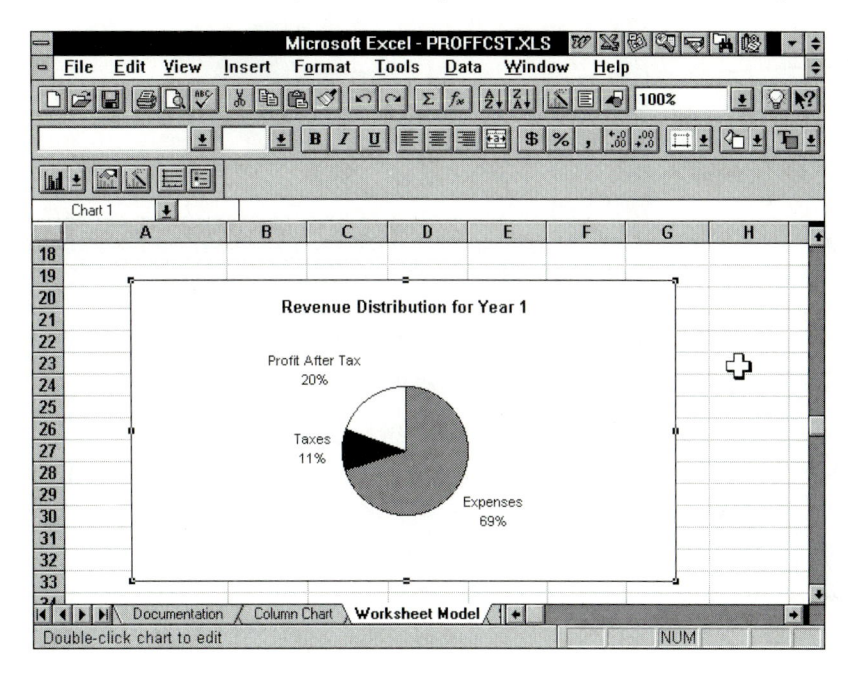

Figure 5-4

Printing an Embedded Chart

You can print an embedded chart by itself or with the chart data.

To activate the embedded chart you created in the last section:

Double-click the chart

In addition to the black selection handles, the chart has small, diagonal lines around its boundaries. Your screen should look like Figure 5-5.

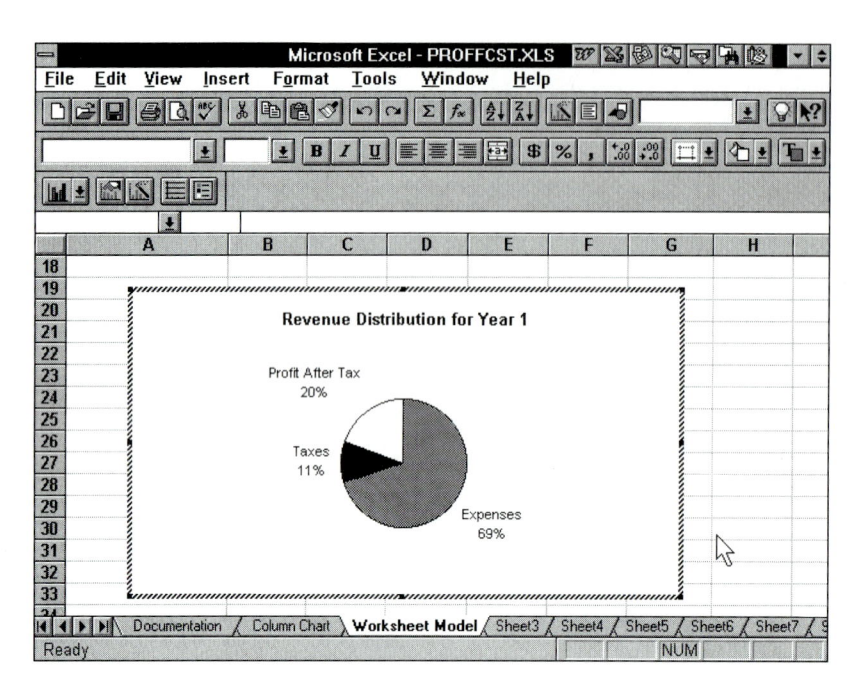

Figure 5-5

To print the embedded chart:

Choose   File

Choose   Print

Notice that the Selected Chart option is selected in the Print What group box of the Print dialog box.

Click   the OK command button

Notice that only the embedded chart is printed. The Worksheet Model tab name appears as the header along with the characters "Chart 1." The default footer is the page number.

Printing an Embedded Chart and Worksheet

If the embedded chart is not active, you can print the worksheet model and chart at the same time by selecting the Selected Sheet(s) option button in the Print What group box within the Print dialog box.

To print the worksheet model and chart:

Double-click   anywhere in the worksheet outside the chart to deactivate and deselect it (the diagonal lines and the selection handles disappear)

Choose   File

Choose   Print

Click   the Selected Sheet(s) option button in the Print What group box (if necessary)

Click   the OK command button

The worksheet model and chart are printed. The Worksheet Model tab name appears as the header. The default footer is the page number.

Deleting an Embedded Chart from a Worksheet

You can delete an embedded chart from a worksheet by selecting the chart and pressing the DELETE key.

To delete the embedded chart from the PROFFCST.XLS Worksheet Model:

Click	anywhere in the embedded chart to select the chart
Press	DELETE

The chart no longer appears on your worksheet.

To restore the embedded chart:

Click	the Undo button on the Standard toolbar

Sizing and Moving an Embedded Chart

Earlier in this chapter, you included an embedded chart on a worksheet. You can also change the size of an embedded chart and move the chart on a worksheet.

Suppose you want to change the size of the embedded pie chart on the Worksheet Model sheet and move the chart to a different location on the worksheet.

To change the size of the embedded chart:

Display	the Worksheet Model of the PROFFCST.XLS workbook (if necessary)
Click	anywhere on the chart to select the chart (if necessary)
Move	the mouse pointer to the sizing handle at the bottom-right corner of the chart until it becomes a double-headed arrow
Press and hold	the mouse button
Drag	the mouse pointer to the left until the pointer is in the middle of column F
Release	the mouse button
Move	the mouse pointer to the sizing handle at the middle-left border of the chart until it becomes a double-headed arrow
Press and hold	the mouse button
Drag	the mouse pointer until the pointer is at the left side of column A
Release	the mouse button

The size of the chart is now changed.

To move the chart to a new location:

Move	the mouse pointer anywhere in the interior of the embedded chart
Press and hold	the mouse button

Drag	the mouse pointer until the top of the chart is positioned in the middle of row 25
Release	the mouse button

Deselect the chart.

After you have made row 25 the first row on your screen, your screen should look similar to Figure 5-6.

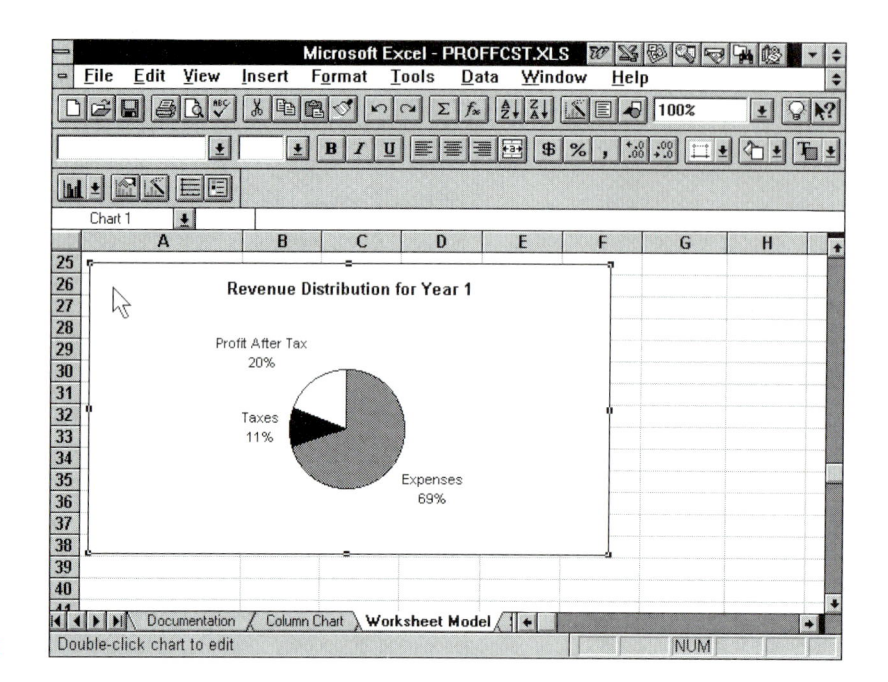

Figure 5-6

Changing the Location of a Legend

The default location of a legend is on the right side of the chart. Sometimes, you may want the legend to appear in a different location on the chart.

> **FYI** The next several sections describe enhancements to a chart on a chart sheet. You can apply all the enhancements to an embedded chart as well. The embedded chart must be active, displaying the selection handles and the gray border around the boundary.

Suppose you wish to place the legend on the column chart at the bottom of the chart.

To select the legend:

Click	the Column Chart sheet tab
Click	the Legend

Selection handles appear around the legend boundaries. Later in this chapter, you will have opportunities to select other parts of the chart. To move the legend:

Choose	Format
Choose	Selected Legend

The Format Legend dialog box appears. Your screen should look like Figure 5-7.

Creating and Printing Charts

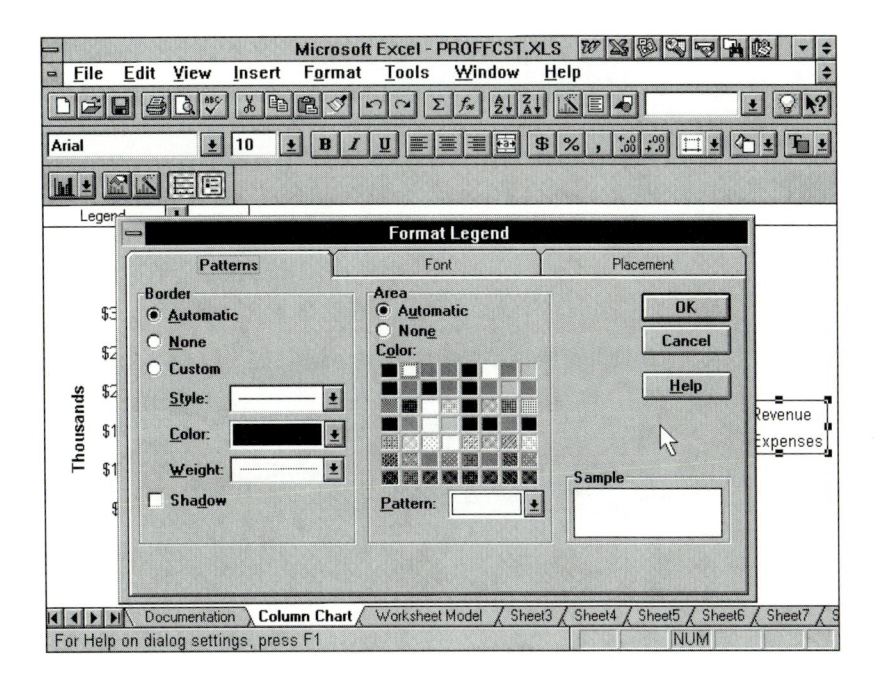

Figure 5-7

To place the legend at the bottom of the chart:

Click the Placement tab

Click the **B**ottom option button in the Type group box

Click the OK command button

The legend appears below the chart. Deselect the legend.

> There are two other ways to edit various chart elements. The Legend is used here as an example. You can position the mouse pointer on some white space on the legend and double-click. The Format Legend Entry dialog box appears. You would edit the legend as needed and click the OK command button. Be careful not to double-click on part of the legend text. If you do so, you will only be editing the text, not the placement or appearance of the legend area.
>
> The other way to edit a portion of a chart is to move the mouse pointer to the desired area and click the alternate mouse button. A shortcut menu appears with commands available for the selected chart element. Use either mouse button to select the desired command. The related dialog box appears.
>
> You can also drag the legend or other selected elements of the chart. However, when you use the drag method, the chart does not resize itself.

Removing and Changing Axes Scales

Excel allows you to remove the category (X) axis or value (Y) axis scales. You can also change the scales of the axes. Suppose you want to remove the value (Y) axis scale from the column chart.

To delete the value (Y) scale:

Choose Insert

Choose Axes

The Axes dialog box appears.

Click the **Value (Y) Axis** check box in the Primary Axis group box to remove the X

Click the OK command button

The values on the Y-axis disappear. Your screen should look like Figure 5-8.

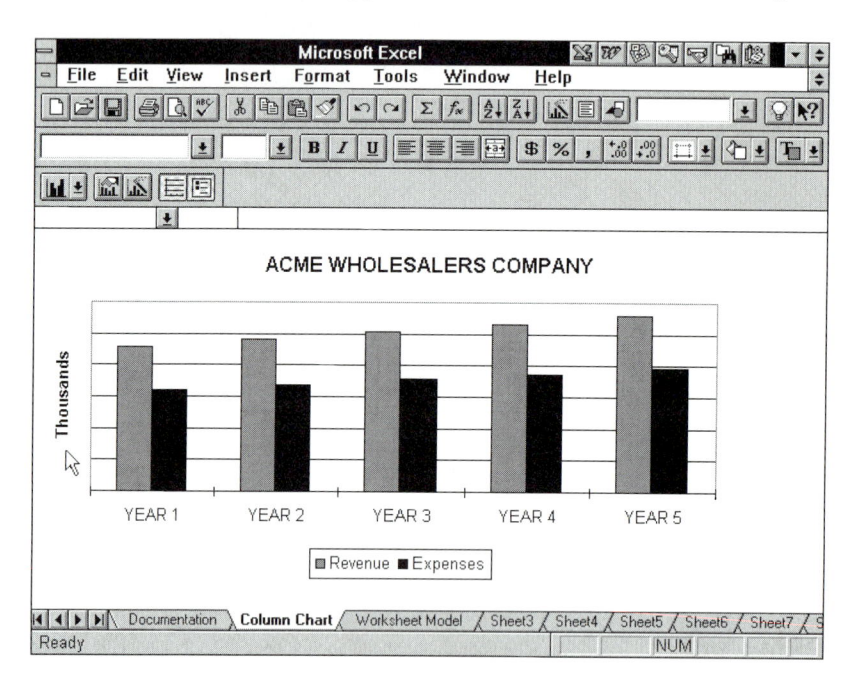

Figure 5-8

To restore the Y-axis values to the chart:

Click the Undo button on the Standard toolbar

Suppose you want to change the scale for the value (Y) axis on the column chart.

Assume you want the value (Y) axis increment to be 10,000 instead of 5,000.

To select the value (Y) axis:

Click on one of the numbers on the Value (Y) axis

or

Click on the vertical line on the left side of the chart

To change the (Y) axis increments:

Choose Format

Choose Selected Axis

The Format Axis dialog box appears. Your screen should look like Figure 5-9.

Creating and Printing Charts

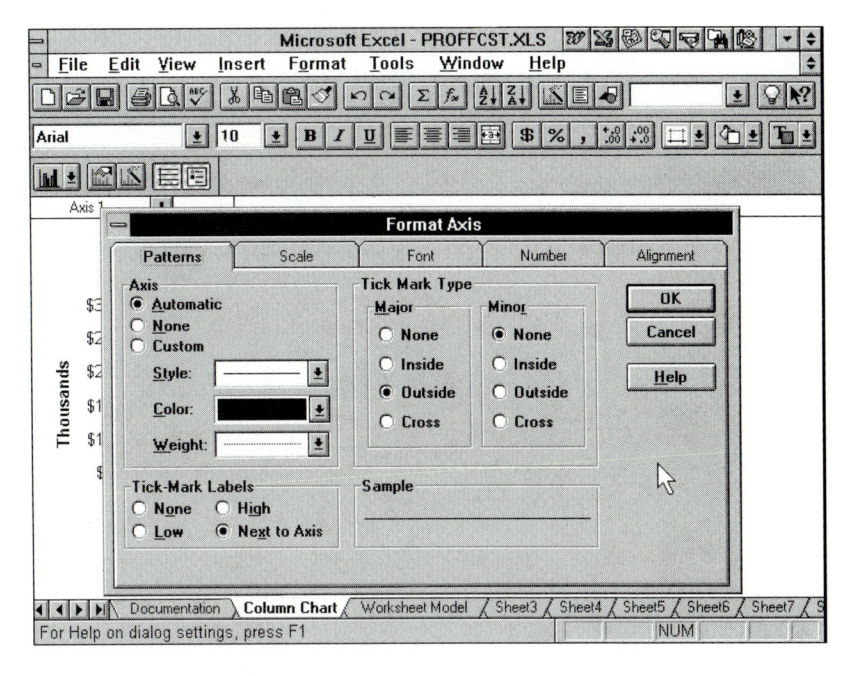

Figure 5-9

Click	the Scale tab
Double-click	the Major Unit text box
Type	10000
Click	the OK command button

The scale for the value (Y) axis is changed. Notice that the maximum value is still $30,000, but there are fewer gridlines. Deselect the value (Y) axis by clicking elsewhere on the chart or by pressing the ESC key. Your screen should look like Figure 5-10.

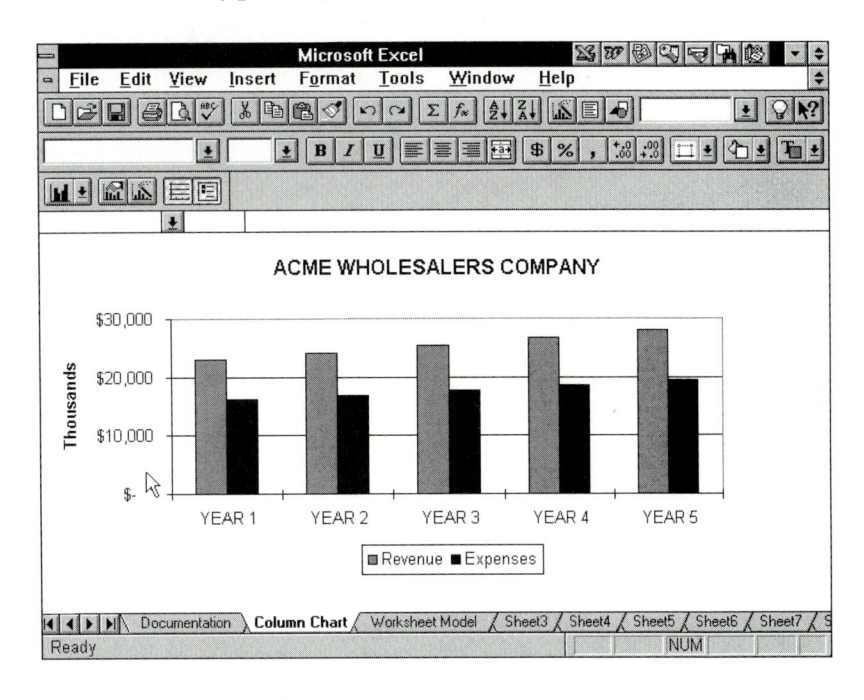

Figure 5-10

Changing the Fonts of Chart Text

You can change or modify the font of the text appearing on a chart, including the actual font, font style, size, and color. You can also underline the selected chart text. Effects such as strikethrough, superscript, and subscript are available. Suppose you need to change the font and size of the title on the column chart in the PROFFCST.XLS workbook. To complete the modifications for the chart title:

Select   the chart title

Choose   Format

Choose   Selected Chart Title

The Format Chart Title dialog box appears. The bottom part of your screen should look like Figure 5-11.

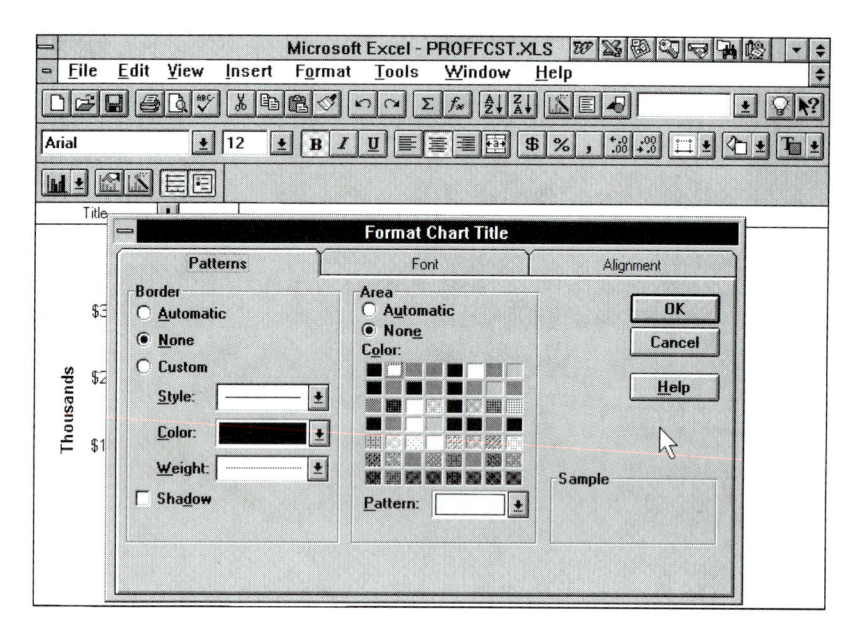

Figure 5-11

Click   the Font tab

Click   Times New Roman in the Font list box

Click   Bold Italic in the Font Style list box

Click   14 in the Size list box

Click   the OK command button

Various font-related items for the chart title have been changed. Deselect the chart title. Your screen should look like Figure 5-12.

Creating and Printing Charts

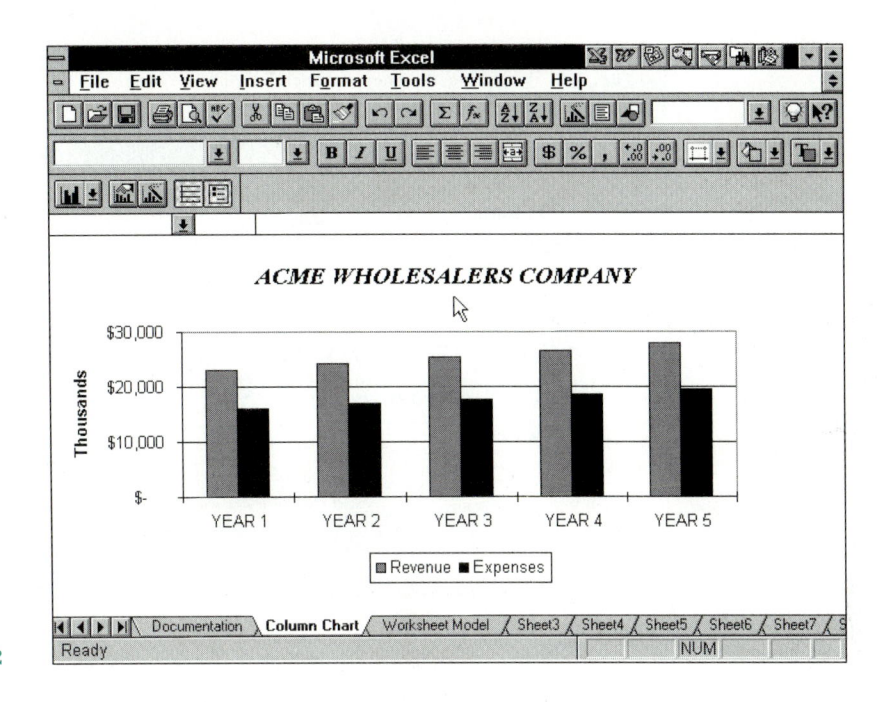

Figure 5-12

Changing Colors and Hatch Patterns

In some situations, you may want to change the color or hatch pattern for a single data marker or all the data markers in a data series. You can modify the border color, area color, and pattern used for a data marker. Suppose you want to use a different color for the Revenue data series in the column chart of the PROFFCST.XLS workbook.

To change the color:

Click   one of the Revenue category data markers

All the Revenue data markers are selected.

Choose   Format

Choose   Selected Data Series

The Format Data Series dialog box appears. The bottom part of your screen should look like Figure 5-13.

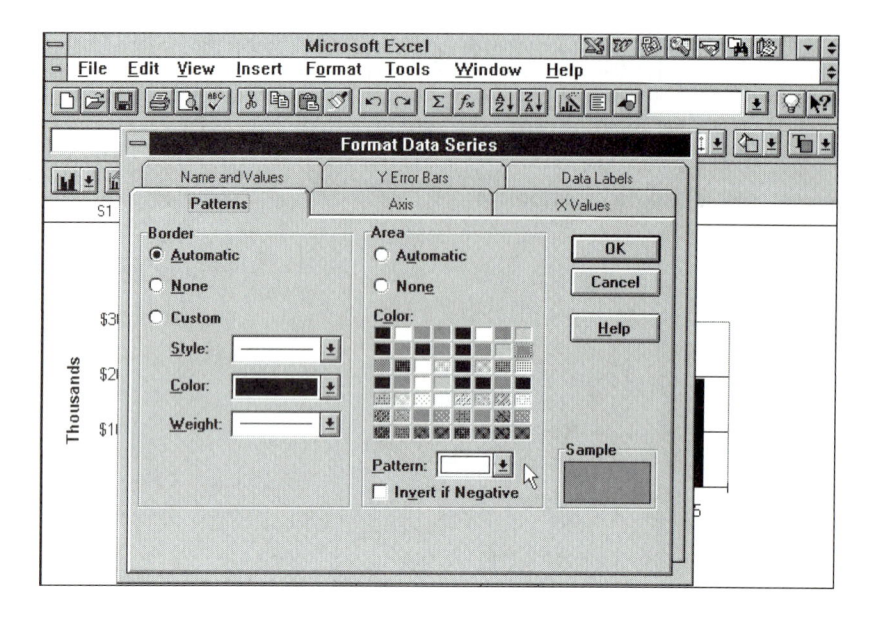

Mastering and Using Microsoft Office Professional

Figure 5-13

To continue:

Click the Red color option in the first row of the Color palette in the Area group box

Click the OK command button

The Revenue category data series is now red. Deselect the data series.

In some instances, you may want to use a hatch pattern rather than a solid color for a data marker.

To illustrate the use of a hatch pattern:

Select one of the Revenue category data markers

Choose Format

Choose Selected Data Series

Click the Black color on the Color palette in the Area group box

Click the drop-down arrow on the Pattern drop-down list box

Click the third pattern on the second row of the pattern palette

Click the OK command button

The red color has changed to black, and a diagonal line pattern appears. Deselect the Revenue data series. Your screen should look like Figure 5-14.

If you wish to change only one data marker in a data series, click once to select the desired data series. Then click once again on the desired data marker. Note: This is not a double-click. The single data marker is selected. Proceed by choosing the Selected Data Point on the Format menu.

Creating and Printing Charts

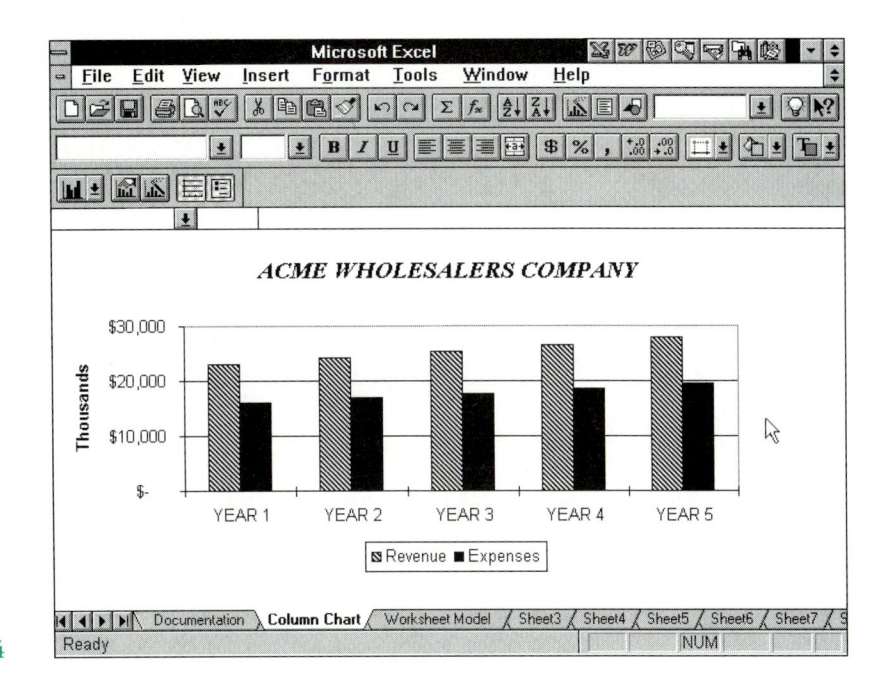

Figure 5-14

Inserting and Removing Gridlines

When you select the format for a chart type, some of the formats include gridlines and some do not. You can insert category (vertical) and/or value (horizontal) gridlines. Also, you can modify the format of existing gridlines. To insert gridlines on the column chart in the PROFFCST.XLS workbook:

| Choose | Insert |
| Choose | Gridlines |

The Gridlines dialog box appears. Notice that you may include gridlines at major and minor units on the X- and Y-axes of the column chart. Your screen should look like Figure 5-15.

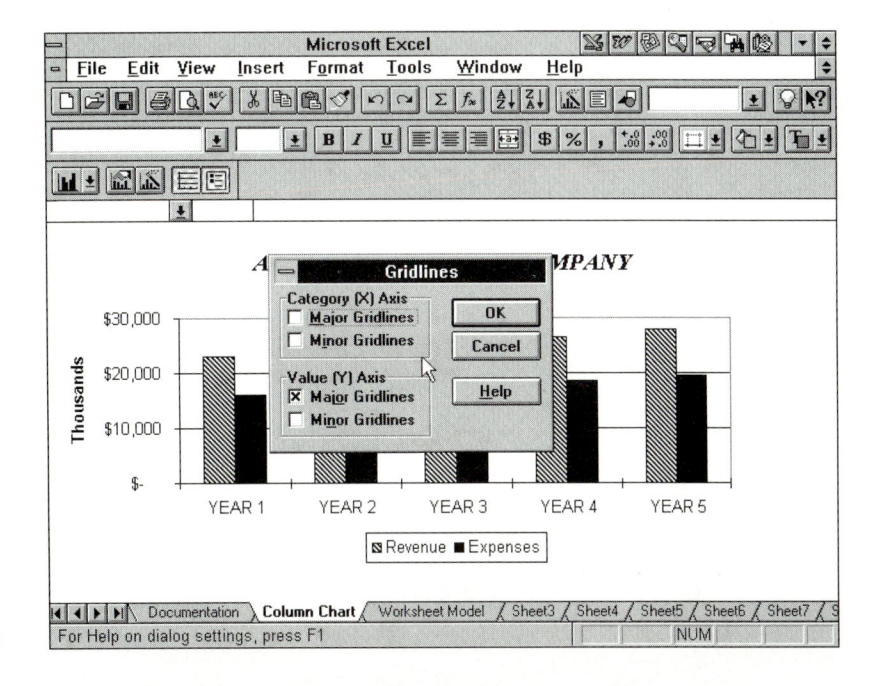

Figure 5-15

To include category (vertical) gridlines at major units on the chart:

Click the **M**ajor Gridlines check box in the Category (X) Axis group box to insert an X

Click the OK command button

Vertical gridlines appear on your screen. Your screen should look like Figure 5-16.

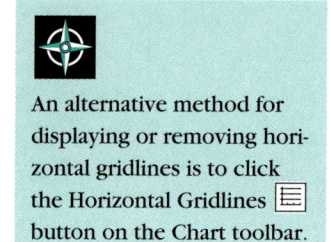

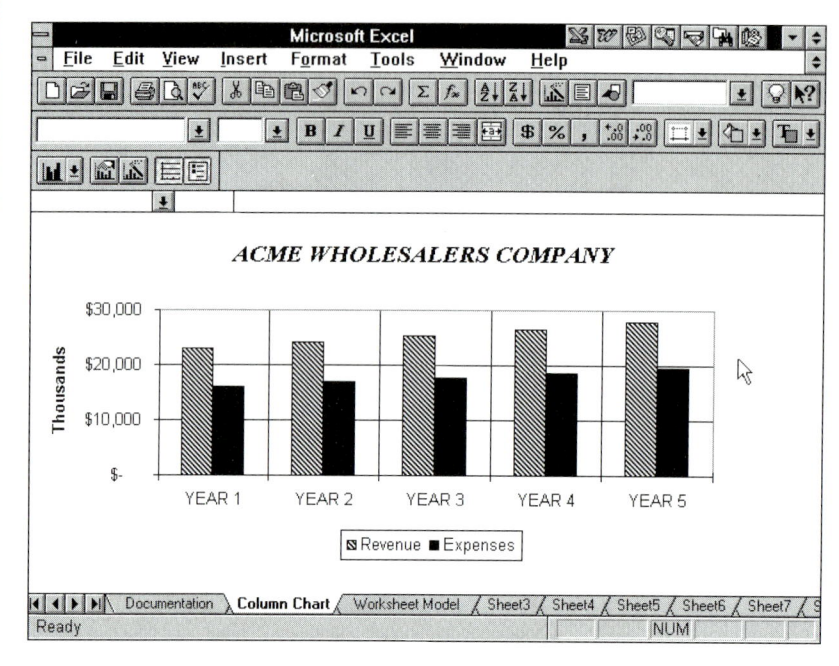

> An alternative method for displaying or removing horizontal gridlines is to click the Horizontal Gridlines button on the Chart toolbar.

Figure 5-16

Vertical gridlines are usually used with line graphs.

To remove the vertical gridlines from the column chart:

Click the Undo button on the Standard toolbar

Adding Unattached Text and Graphic Objects to a Chart

Excel allows you to include additional text on a chart. Such text is sometimes called **unattached text**. You can also place graphic objects such as arrows on a chart. Suppose you want to place the word "Revenue" above the first Revenue data marker and "Expenses" above the first Expenses data marker on the column chart in the PROFFCST.XLS workbook.

To illustrate the process for including text on a chart:

Type Revenue

Click the enter box ✓

or

Press ← ENTER

Creating and Printing Charts

The word "Revenue" appears in the middle of the chart in a text box. Notice the sizing handles. The text box is selected. You can move or size it.

To move the text box:

Move	the mouse pointer to a boundary of the text box (not on a selection handle)
Press and hold	the mouse button
Drag	the text box containing "Revenue" above the first Revenue data marker
Release	the mouse button

The text appears in the proper location. Deselect the text box.

To place additional text above the first Expenses data marker:

Type	Expenses
Click	the enter box ☑
	or
Press	⏎ ENTER
Press and hold	the mouse button
Drag	the text box containing "Expenses" above the first Expenses data marker
Release	the mouse button

The text appears in the proper location. Deselect the text. Your screen should look similar to Figure 5-17.

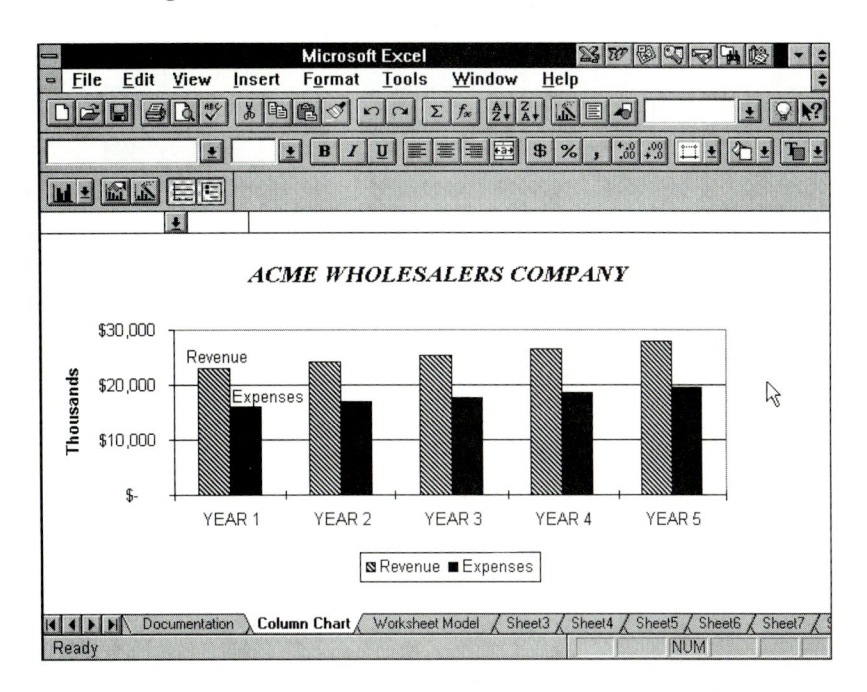

Figure 5-17

> If you wish to copy the text to the other data markers, you can use the Copy and Paste commands to copy the text. Select the text box. Then choose the Copy and Paste buttons on the Standard toolbar. Once the text box appears in the middle of the screen, drag the text box to the appropriate location.

You can place graphic objects on a chart. Suppose that the Revenue for the fifth year will set a record. To indicate this situation, you can place an arrow and some text on the chart.

Before you begin, make sure nothing is selected on your chart.

To add the arrow:

Click the Drawing button on the Standard toolbar

The Drawing toolbar appears on your screen.

Click the Arrow button on the Drawing toolbar

Move the cross-hair pointer to where you want the end of the arrow

Press and hold the mouse button

Drag the cross-hair pointer to where you want the head of the arrow

Release the mouse button

When you release the mouse button, the arrow appears on your chart. Deselect the arrow. Place the unattached text "Anticipated Record" on the chart so your screen looks similar to Figure 5-18.

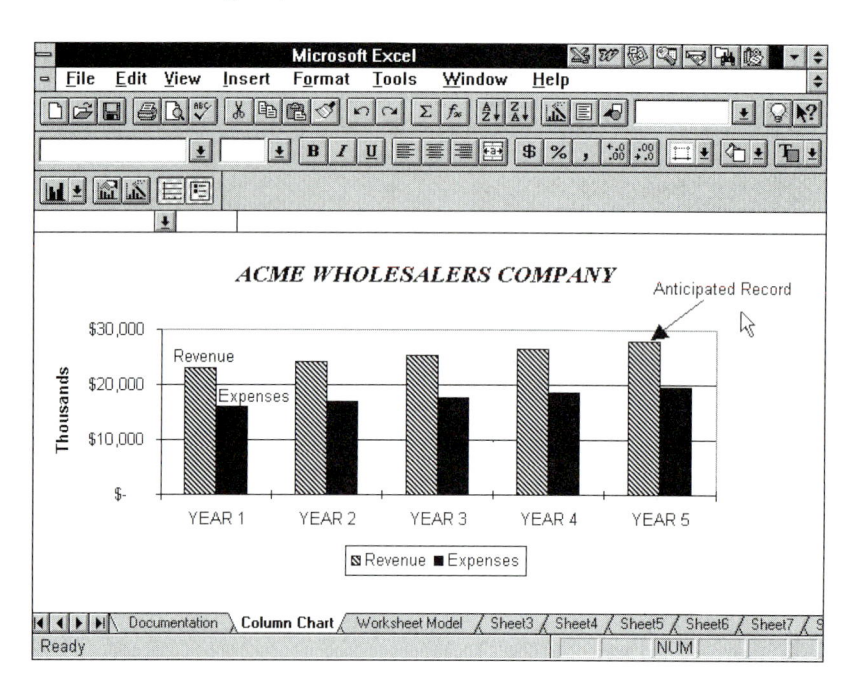

Figure 5-18

Close the Drawing toolbar. For more information about other drawing tools, see your Excel *User's Guide*. Save the workbook in a file using the name CHARTS. Close the workbook.

Summary

Charts can assist you in analyzing data in a worksheet as well as in presenting the data to other individuals. Excel allows you to create a chart on a separate sheet or as an embedded chart on a worksheet document. Creating charts using data series from a worksheet is easy because the data do not need to be entered again before the chart is prepared.

Creating and Printing Charts

The ChartWizard tool leads you through the process for constructing a chart. If the data in the worksheet are recalculated, the chart reflects the modifications in the data the next time the chart is viewed. With Excel, you can enhance the appearance of charts that you create. For example, you can remove or change the axes scales, change the font of chart text, change colors and hatch patterns, and include or exclude gridlines. You can also add unattached text and graphic objects to a chart. Finally, you can change the size of an embedded chart on a worksheet or move a chart to a different location.

Exercise 1

INSTRUCTIONS: Define or explain the following:

1. Chart _____
_____

2. Attached text _____
_____

3. Data label _____
_____

4. Category axis _____
_____

5. Process to embed a chart _____
_____

6. Pie chart _____
_____

7. Unattached text _____
_____

Exercise 2

INSTRUCTIONS: Circle T if the statement is true and F if the statement is false.

T   F   1. Excel offers a total of 11 chart types.
T   F   2. If you change values on the worksheet, you must recreate any charts based on those values.
T   F   3. You can create different charts using data from one worksheet.
T   F   4. A pie chart displays only one range of data.
T   F   5. You may select a range of data before initiating the ChartWizard.
T   F   6. You must save a chart in its own file on a disk.
T   F   7. An embedded chart can be printed only as part of its worksheet.
T   F   8. You can remove an embedded chart from a worksheet.

Exercise 3

INSTRUCTIONS:

1. Open the E03EX03.XLS workbook created in Chapter 3, Exercise 3.
2. Create a default column chart on a new sheet that includes the sales data for each region for the entire week.
3. Include Mon through Fri as the X-axis categories.
4. Place a legend on the chart and include the chart title, "WEEKLY SALES". Include "Dollars" as the Value (Y) axis title.
5. Size the chart within the window.
6. Name the chart sheet "Column Chart."
7. Save the workbook in a file using the name E05EX03.
8. Print the chart.
9. Close the workbook.

Exercise 4

INSTRUCTIONS:

1. Open the E03EX04.XLS workbook created in Chapter 3, Exercise 4.
2. Use the ChartWizard to create an embedded pie chart that includes the yearly totals for each expense category. Place the chart in cells B22:G34.
3. Use pie chart format number 5.
4. Include the title "YEAR TOTALS."
5. Print the chart alone.
6. Save the workbook in a file using the name E05EX04.
7. Print the chart and the data on the same sheet.
8. Close the workbook.

Creating and Using Multiple Worksheets and Workbooks

6

Objectives

In this chapter you will learn to:
- Group worksheets
- Enter data and formulas in multiple worksheets
- Format multiple worksheets
- Insert and format a summary sheet
- Create formulas with 3-D references
- Print multiple worksheets
- Link workbooks together

Chapter Overview

In the previous chapters, you worked with workbooks that included a documentation sheet, worksheet model, and charts. This chapter introduces the process of using worksheet models that include more than one worksheet. You will also learn to create formulas with a 3-D reference that links the worksheets together, and how to link workbooks.

Grouping Worksheets

Suppose the ACME BOATING COMPANY has three divisions and sells two products in each division. Data for projected sales units in the three divisions are noted below:

Division 1:	**Q1**	**Q2**	**Q3**	**Q4**
Boats	105	408	620	90
Motors	83	350	575	70
Division 2:	**Q1**	**Q2**	**Q3**	**Q4**
Boats	107	414	616	110
Motors	75	364	597	83
Division 3:	**Q1**	**Q2**	**Q3**	**Q4**
Boats	106	212	515	88
Motors	71	187	479	69

You need to create a workbook that includes the data for each division on individual worksheets. Also, you need to create a summary worksheet to compute division totals for each quarter and for annual sales units.

Since you already have completed many worksheets as you have progressed through the earlier chapters, the instructions for creating the worksheet for Division 1 are abbreviated. Also, the documentation for proper worksheet design has been omitted.

Figure 6-1 displays the worksheet for Division 1. With the exception of the titles and numeric data, Divisions 2 and 3 display identical information. Excel allows you to group the sheets. When sheets are grouped, any data or formatting entered on one sheet is duplicated to the other grouped sheets.

The SHIFT key allows you to select consecutive sheets.

To group Sheets 1, 2, and 3:

Press and hold	SHIFT
Click	the Sheet3 tab

Notice that the sheet tabs for Sheet1, Sheet2, and Sheet3 are selected. This selection is indicated by the tabs having the same white color. [Group] appears on the title bar.

> If you want to select sheets that are nonadjacent, hold down the CTRL key and click the appropriate sheet tabs.

Create the worksheet and enter all of the labels for each of the quarters. Insert a single-line border as shown in Figure 6-1. All three grouped sheets are identical.

Creating and Using Multiple Worksheets and Workbooks

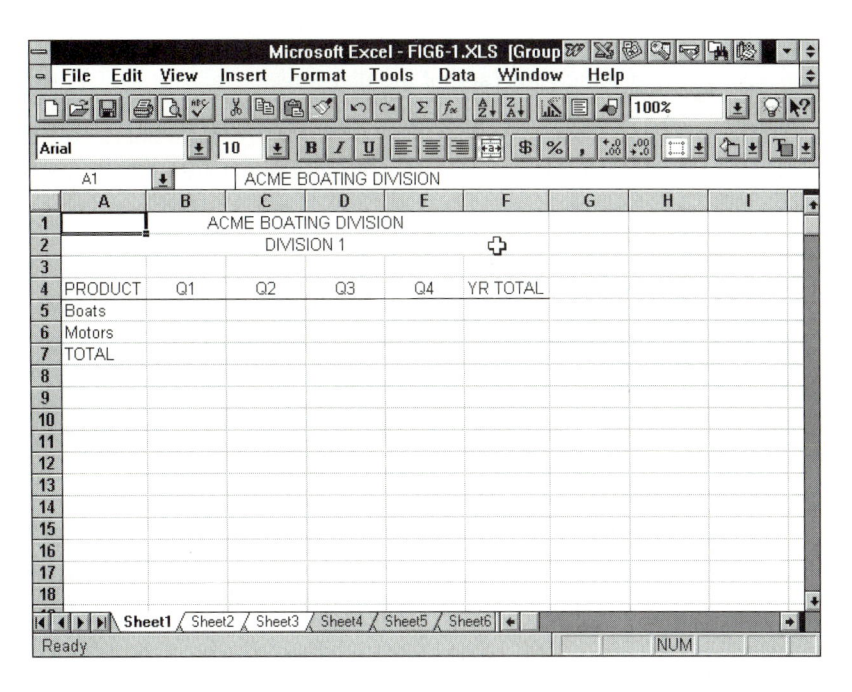

Figure 6-1

Save the workbook in a file using the name BOATSALE.

Entering Data and Formulas in Multiple Worksheets

Since the numeric data are different for each of the divisions, you need to ungroup the sheets before entering the sales units for each sheet. If you do not ungroup the sheets, the data you enter in the Division 1 worksheet is automatically duplicated in the Division 2 and Division 3 worksheets.

To ungroup the sheets:

Move	the mouse pointer to one of the selected tabs
Click	the alternate mouse button to display the shortcut menu
Choose	Ungroup Sheets

> You can also ungroup sheets by clicking a sheet name that is not currently grouped.

Edit the Division titles so that DIVISION 2 appears in cell A2 on Sheet2 and DIVISION 3 appears in cell A2 on Sheet3. Change the sheet tab names to "Division 1," "Division 2," and "Division 3." Enter the quarterly information for each division shown on the first page of this chapter. After you have made cell A1 of the Division 1 worksheet the active cell, the top part of your screen should look like Figure 6-2.

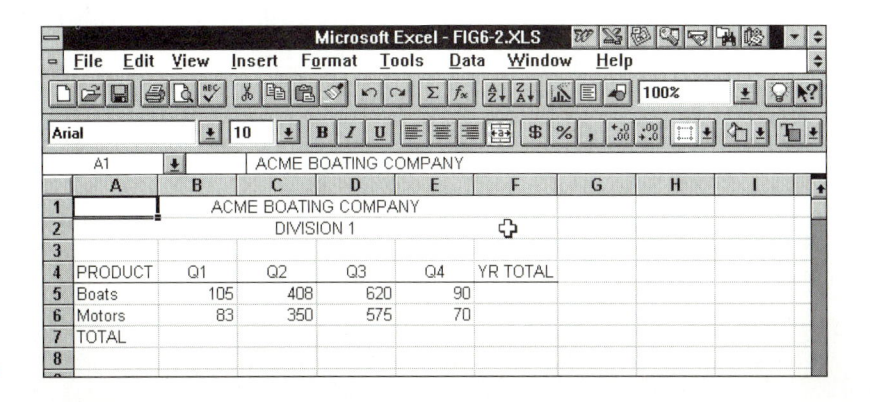

Figure 6-2

You can use Group mode to enter formulas to determine annual sales for each of the products for each of the divisions.

To create a formula for first quarter Boat sales:

Click on cell B7 in the Division 1 worksheet

Group the Division 1, Division 2, and Division 3 worksheets

Double-click the AutoSum Σ button on the Standard toolbar

The formula for computing the first quarter sales units for Boats, =SUM(B5:B6), appears in the formula bar. The sum appears in cell B7. Use the Fill handle to copy the formula in cell B7 to cells C7:E7.

To create a formula for annual Boat sales:

Click on cell F5 in the Division 1 worksheet

Double-click the AutoSum Σ button on the Standard toolbar

Use the Fill handle to copy the formula in cell F5 to cells F6:F7.

The formulas for computing sales units have been duplicated to the Division 2 and Division 3 worksheets and the appropriate values appear in those worksheets.

After you have ungrouped the sheets and made cell B7 on the Division 2 worksheet the active cell, the top part of your screen should look like Figure 6-3.

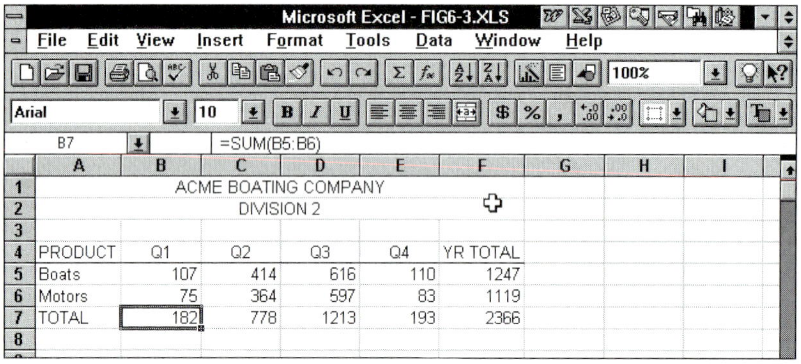

Figure 6-3

Click on the Division 3 tab. After you have made cell A1 the active cell, the top part of your screen should look like Figure 6-4.

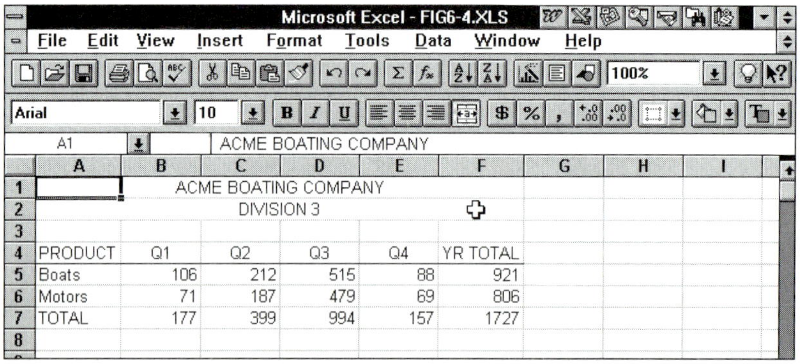

Figure 6-4

Formatting Multiple Worksheets

For this example problem, the format specifications must be the same for all of the worksheets. Rather than format each worksheet individually, you can format all numeric cells at the same time. When you use commands on the menus or buttons on the toolbars, the selected cells are formatted in all the division worksheets.

To group the three division worksheets and apply formatting:

Click	the Division 1 tab
Group	the Division 1, Division 2, and Division 3 sheets
Select	cells B5:F7
Click	the Comma Style button on the Formatting toolbar
Click	the Decrease Decimal button on the Formatting toolbar twice
Select	cells B6:F6 in the Division 1 worksheet
Click	the Underline button on the Formatting toolbar
Select	cells B7:F7 in the Division 1 worksheet
Choose	Format
Choose	Cells
Click	the Font tab
Click	the down arrow on the **U**nderline drop-down list
Click	Double Accounting
Click	the OK command button

Ungroup the worksheet tabs. Click on each division tab to verify that all the division worksheets are formatted the same way.

Save the workbook. Leave the workbook on the screen for the next section.

Inserting and Formatting a Summary Sheet

You may want to summarize the data on one sheet. Typically, a summary sheet appears in front of the individual sheets.

- You can choose the **W**orksheet command on the **I**nsert menu to insert a blank worksheet in the workbook.
- You can also use the shortcut menu and choose Insert to insert a blank worksheet.

To insert a summary worksheet:

Click	the Division 1 tab
Click	the alternate mouse button on the Division 1 tab
Choose	Insert

The Insert dialog box appears. The bottom part of your screen should look like Figure 6-5.

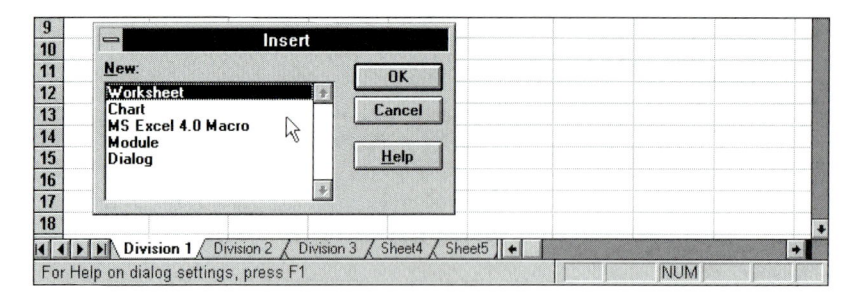

Figure 6-5

Click   Worksheet in the **N**ew group box (if necessary)

Click   the OK command button

The new worksheet appears to the left of the Division 1 worksheet. Change the tab name to "Summary."

Enter the information shown in Figure 6-6 to place the worksheet titles, row headings, column headings, and border. You can also copy the data from one of the divisions and modify the data to appear as it does in Figure 6-6.

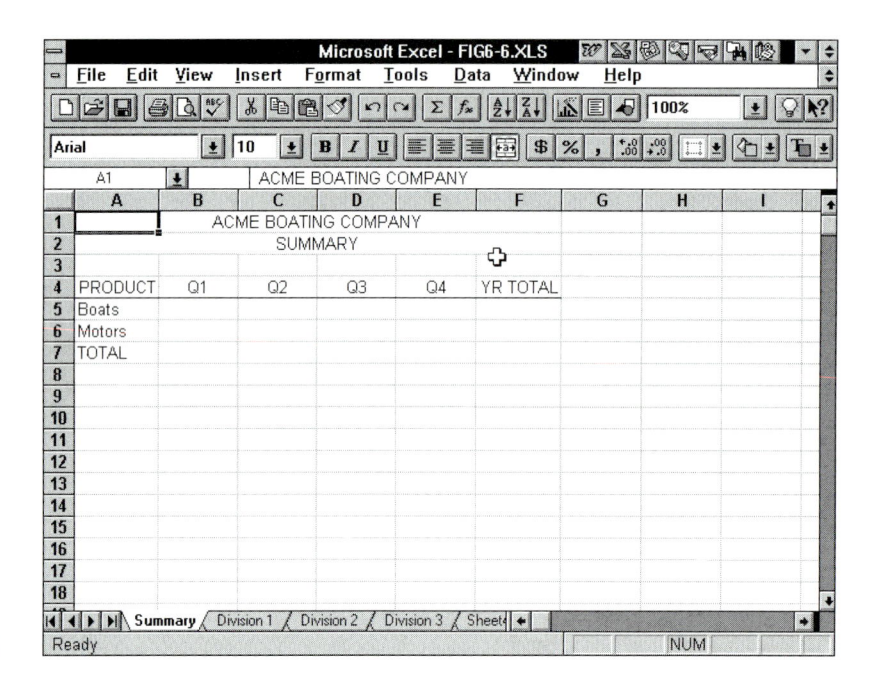

Figure 6-6

Creating Formulas with 3-D References

In Excel 5.0, you can create a formula that will reference cells across several different sheets. This is called a three-dimensional reference.

To create a formula for the first quarter sales units of boats for all three divisions:

Click   on cell B5

Type   =SUM(

Click   on the Division 1 tab

Click   on cell B5

Creating and Using Multiple Worksheets and Workbooks

> Sometimes, you may need a formula that will reference a different cell in different worksheets. Begin the formula as described on the previous page by typing =SUM(. Click on the first desired sheet and then click the first cell to be used in the formula. If you need to use another cell on the same sheet or switch to a different cell on a different sheet, first click at the end of the formula in the formula bar and type a comma. Excel then allows you to click on another cell on the same sheet or switch to a different cell on another sheet. Continue typing a comma to separate each cell reference. When the formula is completed, click the enter box or press the ENTER key.

Notice the formula in the formula bar includes a reference to cell B5 in the Division 1 worksheet.

To create a 3-D reference to the totals for all three divisions:

Press SHIFT

Click on the Division 3 tab

Notice the formula in the formula bar now includes a reference to cell B5 across the range of worksheets Division 1: Division 3.

To complete the formula:

Click the enter box ✓

or

Press ← ENTER

The number in cell B5 is the total sales of boats for the first quarter for all three divisions. Use the AutoFill feature to copy the formula to cells C5:E5.

The top part of your screen should look like Figure 6-7.

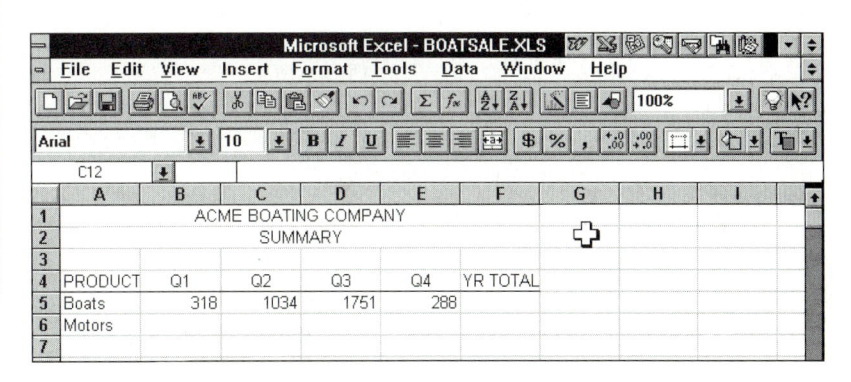

Figure 6-7

Create a formula with a 3-D reference in cell B6 to add the motor sales units for the first quarter for all three divisions. Use the AutoFill feature to copy the formula to cells C6:E6.

Use the AutoSum button on the Standard toolbar to create totals in row 7 and column F. Format the cells containing values to include commas and no decimal places using the Formatting toolbar. Apply accounting single and double underlines to agree with the underlining on the Division 1, 2, and 3 worksheets.

Save the workbook in a file using the name BOATSUM.

Printing Multiple Worksheets

Just as it is convenient to format multiple worksheets at one time, you may want to print multiple worksheets at one time. If you want to print the information appearing in the Division 1, Division 2, and Division 3 worksheets, you can group the sheets and then choose the Select**ed** Sheet(s) option button in the Print dialog box. If you want to print the entire workbook, you can choose the **E**ntire Workbook option button in the Print menu.

To print only the Division 1, Division 2, and Division 3 worksheets:

Group	the Division 1, Division 2, and Division 3 worksheets
Choose	**F**ile
Choose	**P**rint
Click	the Selec**t**ed Sheet(s) option button in the Print What group box (if necessary)
Click	the OK command button

The three division worksheets are printed, but the Summary sheet is not printed. Close the workbook.

Linking Workbooks Together

With Excel, you can link workbooks. Suppose you want to use the Total Revenue information appearing in the REVENUE.XLS workbook for the Revenue for Year 1 in the PROFFCST.XLS workbook. The REVENUE.XLS workbook may be found on the diskette at the back of this book and is illustrated in Figure 6-8.

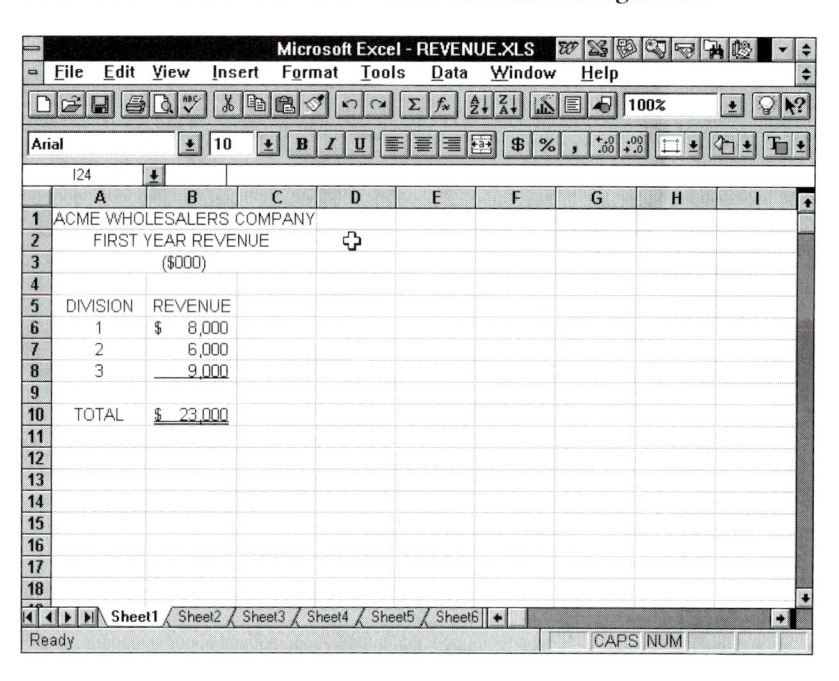

Figure 6-8

To illustrate the process of linking two workbook files:

Open	the PROFFCST.XLS workbook
Click	on cell B8 on the Worksheet Model worksheet (the Year 1 Revenue value)
Delete	the contents of cell B8

Since all the other values are based on the contents of cell B8, most of the cells no longer display values.

Open	the REVENUE.XLS workbook
Click	on cell B10
Click	the Copy button

Creating and Using Multiple Worksheets and Workbooks

Switch to	the PROFFCST.XLS workbook
Click	on cell B8 on the Worksheet Model worksheet (if necessary)
Choose	**E**dit
Choose	Paste **S**pecial

The Paste Special dialog box appears. The bottom part of your screen should look similar to Figure 6-9.

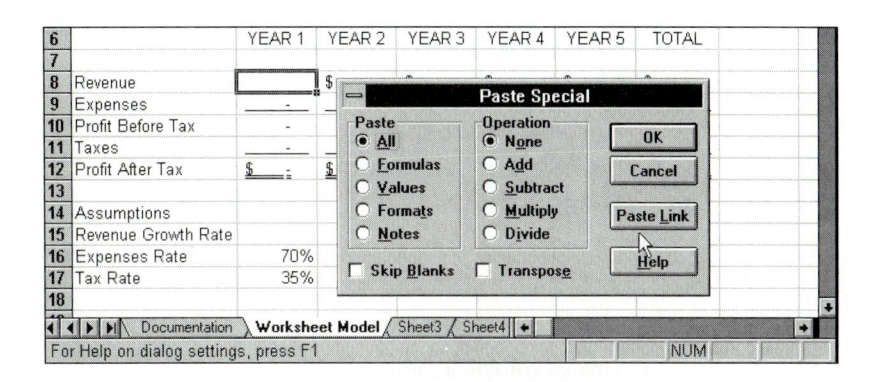

Figure 6-9

Click the Paste **L**ink command button

The Revenue Total from the REVENUE.XLS workbook now appears on the Worksheet Model worksheet in the PROFFCST.XLS workbook.

After you have made cell B8 the active cell, the top part of your screen should look similar to Figure 6-10.

Figure 6-10

Notice the link that appears in the formula bar. If the revenue in one of the divisions changes in the REVENUE.XLS workbook, the Revenue for Year 1 will also change in the PROFFCST.XLS workbook. If the PROFFCST.XLS workbook is closed when the REVENUE.XLS workbook is changed, the link is not updated until you open the PROFFCST.XLS workbook. When you open the PROFFCST.XLS workbook, a confirmation box displays and asks if you want to update the links. Usually, you will click the **Y**es command button.

Close the PROFFCST.XLS workbook. Do not save any changes. Close the REVENUE.XLS workbook. Do not save any changes.

Summary

Using multiple worksheets provides flexibility in creating worksheet applications that have similar structures and formats. You can print entire workbooks or selected worksheets. You can create formulas with 3-D references in several worksheets. You can link workbooks.

Exercise 1

INSTRUCTIONS: Define or explain the following:

1. Grouping worksheets _____
   _____

2. Inserting a worksheet _____
   _____

3. 3-D formulas _____
   _____

4. Linking workbooks together _____
   _____

Exercise 2

INSTRUCTIONS: Circle T if the statement is true and F if the statement is false.

T   F   1. You can only group three worksheets at a time.
T   F   2. You can copy information from one sheet to another.
T   F   3. To select adjacent sheets, hold down the SHIFT key and click the appropriate tab names.
T   F   4. Excel always automatically updates changes in linked workbooks.
T   F   5. You can have more than one workbook open at a time.

Exercise 3

INSTRUCTIONS:

1. Open the BOATSUM.XLS workbook created in this chapter.
2. Select the Summary sheet and the Division 1 sheet.
3. Print the selected worksheets.
4. Close the BOATSUM.XLS workbook.

Exercise 4

INSTRUCTIONS:

1. Open the BOATSUM.XLS workbook created in this chapter.
2. On the Summary sheet, enter the word "AVERAGE" in cell G4.
3. Using the AVERAGE function, calculate the average sales for each product in column G.
4. Format the cells in column G so that they match their corresponding cells in columns A through F.
5. Save the workbook in a file using the name E06EX04.
6. Print all the worksheets in the workbook.
7. Close the workbook.

Introduction to Lists, Sorting, and Filtering

7

Objectives

In this chapter you will learn to:
- Identify basic terms and guidelines
- Enter data in a list
- Sort data in a list
- Edit data in a list
- Find data using the Form command
- Use AutoFilter to filter data in a list
- Use Advanced Filter
- Use the Subtotals command

Chapter Overview

You can use worksheets in Excel workbooks to store information. Such worksheets are called **lists**. One example of a list you can store on a worksheet might be the names and salaries for employees in a small company or department of a large organization. Sometimes, such lists are referred to as **databases**.

Once you have prepared a list, you can sort the information in the list by a particular category such as an identification number, total salary, or last name. You can find a specific item in a list, such as a particular invoice or a certain individual's salary, that satisfies a particular condition. For example, you can determine all those individuals in a particular division of a company who have a total annual salary greater than $40,000. This chapter demonstrates how to accomplish each of these tasks. This chapter also shows how to create subtotals in a list.

Identifying Basic Terms and Guidelines

Three basic terms used when you create lists in Excel include field, record, and header row.

A **field** is a collection of characters that are grouped together. In Excel, each field is contained in a separate column within the list. An example would be a person's last name. A **field name** is the term used to describe each field. You include a field name on a list by specifying a unique **column label**. For example, you can use the column label LAST NAME as a field name. In Excel, the field names must be in the cell immediately above the data.

A **record** is a group of data fields that are combined in some logical pattern. For example, the personnel record for individuals in a company might include the individual's social security number, last name, first name, middle initial, or department in which the individual works. All the information about one person would be considered a record. When you combine a set of records together, you have a list.

The **header row** is the top row in the list. The header row contains the column labels (field names) for each of the fields.

In Excel, you can create a list for a variety of applications, including invoices, salary information, grade sheets, and personal budgets.

Some suggestions to use when you create a list include:

- Create only one list on a worksheet.
- If other information is included on a worksheet, leave at least one blank row and one blank column between the list and the other parts of the worksheet.
- If your worksheet includes other data, you may want to specify a range name for your list using the **Name** command on the **Insert** menu.
- Place column labels in the initial row in your list.
- Each of the column labels must be unique text.
- You must format the column label text differently from other text by using a different font, capitalizing, underlining, or boldfacing the text. You may also wish to add borders around the column headings.
- Do not include any blank rows below the column labels or between rows in the list.
- Make sure the rows all have similar data in each column.
- Format all data in a specific column consistently. For example, do not make some records **boldfaced** and others *italic*.

Entering Data in a List

To create a list, use Sheet1 of a blank workbook to enter appropriate documentation for your workbook. Recall from Chapter 2 that documentation should include company name; owner of the workbook; user(s) of the workbook; relevant dates; workbook filename; and description, assumptions, and parameters about the worksheet model. Change the name of Sheet1 to Documentation.

Introduction to Lists, Sorting, and Filtering

Select Sheet2. Rename Sheet2 as List. On the List sheet, you will prepare the worksheet shown in Figure 7-1.

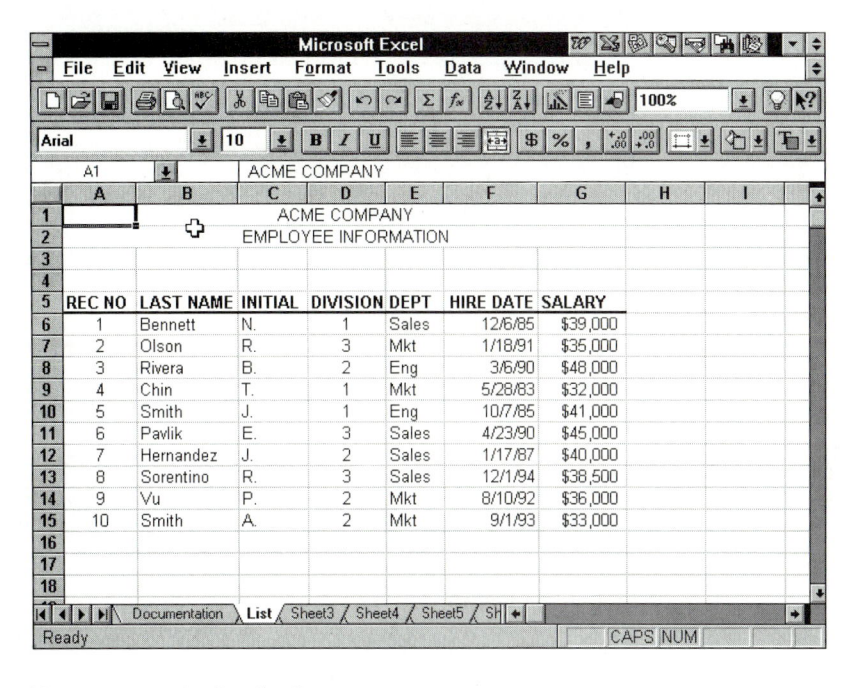

Figure 7-1

To create a title for the list:

Enter the title information in cells A1 and A2

Center the title information across cells A1:G2

To create the column headings:

Enter the column headings in cells A5:G5

To make the column headings appear different from the rest of the list:

Select cells A5:G5

Click the Bold **B** button on the Formatting toolbar

Click the down arrow on the Borders button on the Formatting toolbar

Click the Single Underline option on the second row

To identify row 5 as the header row of the list:

Click on any cell in the range A5:G5

To use the **F**orm command on the **D**ata menu to enter data in the list:

Choose **D**ata

Choose Form

A confirmation dialog box appears on your screen asking if you want to use the current row as the header row for the list.

Click the OK command button

The Data Form dialog box appears, and your screen should look like Figure 7-2. Notice that the name on the dialog box title bar is the name of the current worksheet. In this case, the name is "List."

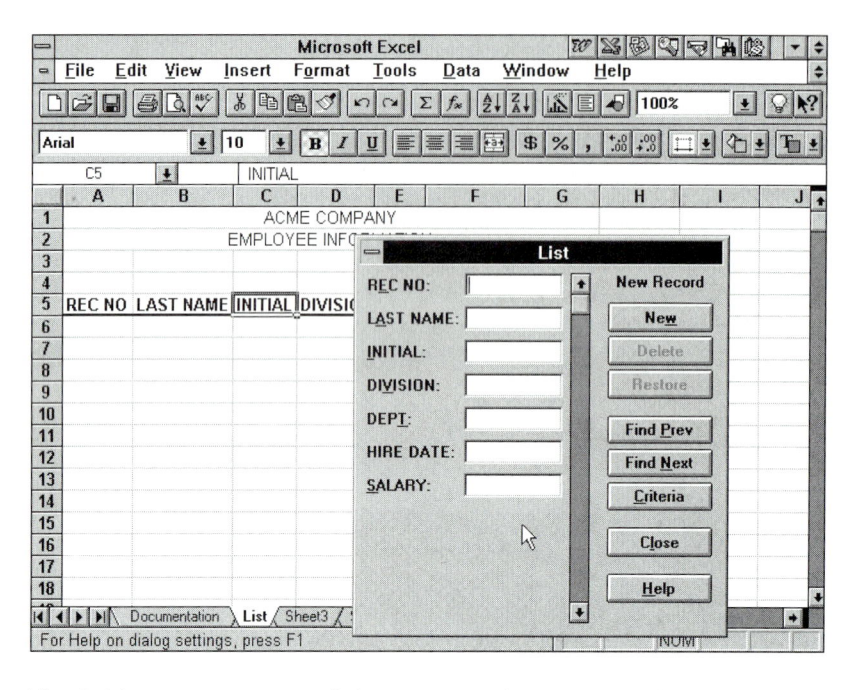

Figure 7-2

The field names appear, and there is a text box to enter the information for each field in a record. After you have entered all of the information for a record in the various text boxes, press the ENTER key to place the information in the worksheet. *Note:* If you do not know particular information for a record, such as the hire date, you may leave individual fields blank.

To enter the data for the first employee:

Type   1 in the REC NO text box

To advance to the next text box, you can click the text box or press the TAB key. Do not press the ENTER key until all the fields for a record are completed. If you accidentally press the ENTER key, the Data Form creates a new record. To return to the incomplete record, click the Find **P**rev command button in the Data Form dialog box.

Press	TAB
Type	Bennett in the LAST NAME text box
Press	TAB
Type	N. in the INITIAL text box
Press	TAB
Type	1 in the DIVISION text box
Press	TAB
Type	Sales in the DEPT text box
Press	TAB
Type	12/6/85 in the HIRE DATE text box
Press	TAB
Type	39000 in the SALARY text box

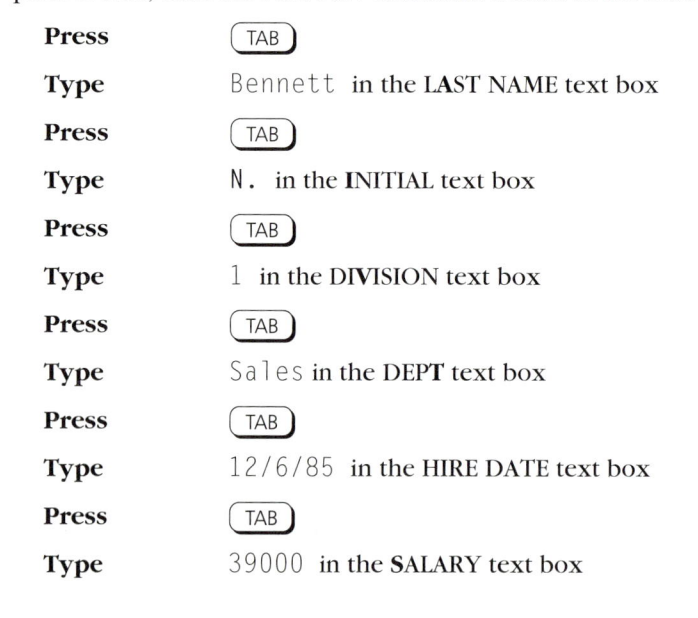

> If a field in the record contains a formula, the field name and calculated value appear in the Data Form dialog box. However, you may not alter a field entry containing a formula from the Data Form dialog box.

Introduction to Lists, Sorting, and Filtering

To create the next record:

Press   ⏎ ENTER

or

Click   the New command button

Your screen should look like Figure 7-3.

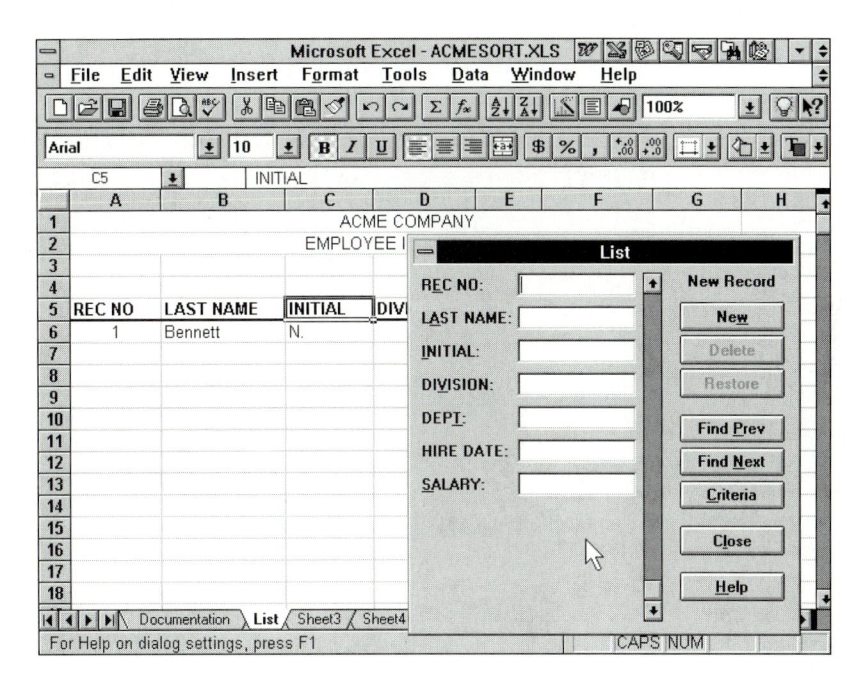

Figure 7-3

Notice that the data for the first employee appear in the list. The Data Form dialog box remains on your screen, so that you can enter additional employee records, if desired.

To enter the data record for the second employee into the list:

Type	2 in the REC NO text box
Press	TAB
Type	Olson in the LAST NAME text box
Press	TAB
Type	R. in the INITIAL text box
Press	TAB
Type	3 in the DIVISION text box
Press	TAB
Type	Mkt in the DEPT text box
Press	TAB
Type	1/18/91 in the HIRE DATE text box
Press	TAB
Type	35000 in the SALARY text box
Click	the New command button

Press   ⏎ ENTER

or

The second record now appears in the list.

Enter the remaining data from Figure 7-1 until your screen looks like Figure 7-4. After you have entered the data, click the Close command button to close the Data Form dialog box. Format the cells containing the salary values to include dollar signs, commas, and no decimal places. Center the data in columns A and D. You should also widen the columns as needed to accommodate the column headings and data.

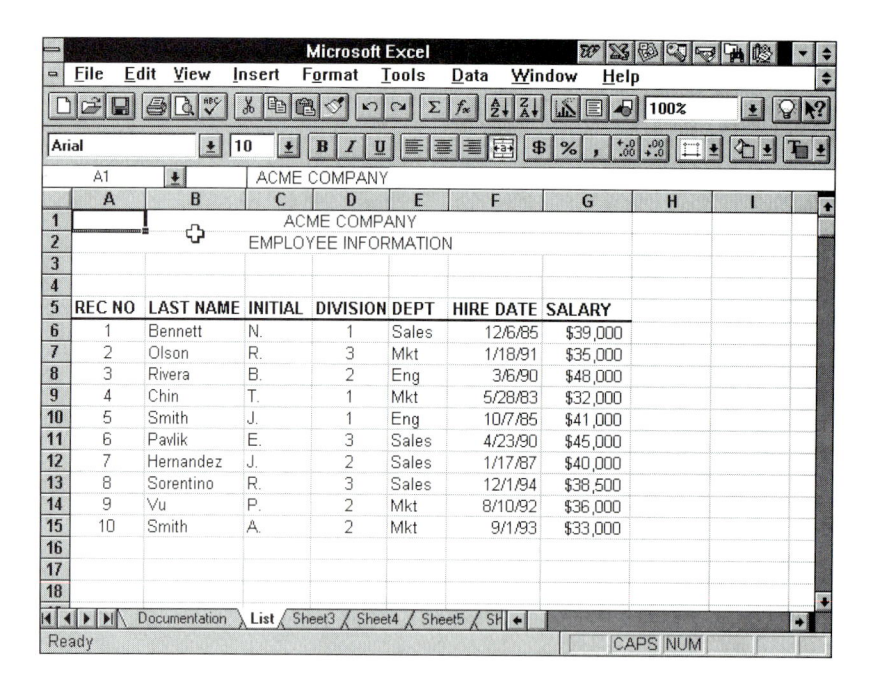

Figure 7-4

Save the workbook in a file using the name ACME-EMP.

Sorting Data in a List

Sometimes you may need to sort list data in a particular order. For example, you may want to sort sales transactions in order by type of transaction such as cash or credit sale. Excel allows you to sort one, two, or three columns at one time. You can sort more than three columns by doing multiple sorts.

The two options for sorting are **Ascending** and **Descending**. Ascending order can refer to alphabetical order (from A to Z) or numerical order (from the smallest number to the largest number). Descending order can refer to reverse alphabetical order (from Z to A) or to reverse numerical order (from largest number to the smallest number).

Sorting by One Column

- You can sort data in a list by choosing the **S**ort command on the **D**ata menu.
- You can click the Sort Ascending or Sort Descending buttons on the Standard toolbar to sort data in one column at a time.

Introduction to Lists, Sorting, and Filtering

Suppose you need to sort the data contained in the List worksheet of the ACME-EMP.XLS workbook by division number.

To sort the data:

Verify the active cell is within the list anywhere in column D (the DIVISION column)

Click the Sort Ascending button on the Standard toolbar

The employee records in the list are sorted by division number. After you have made cell A1 the active cell, your screen should look like Figure 7-5.

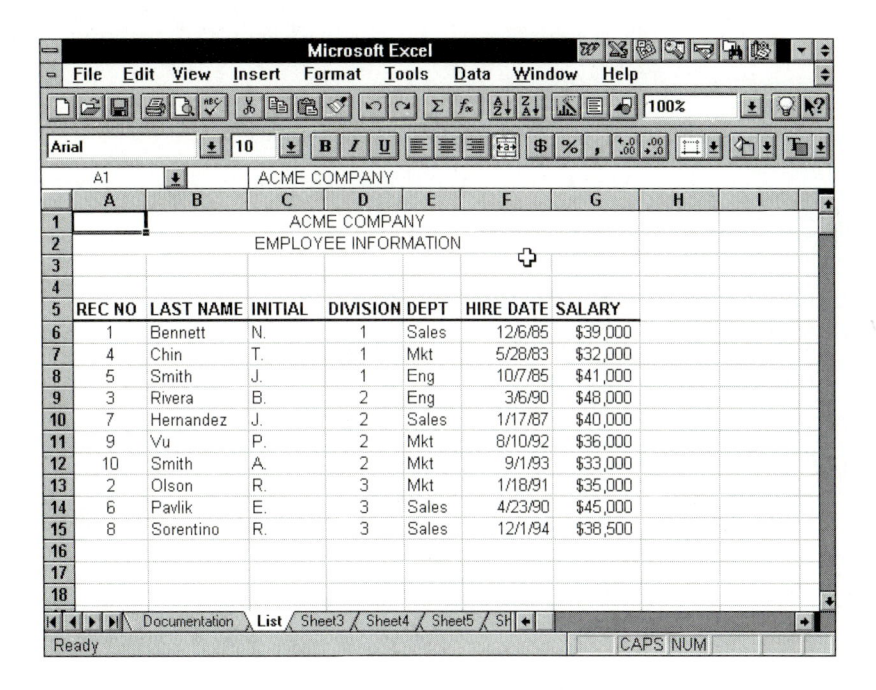

	A	B	C	D	E	F	G
1				ACME COMPANY			
2				EMPLOYEE INFORMATION			
3							
4							
5	REC NO	LAST NAME	INITIAL	DIVISION	DEPT	HIRE DATE	SALARY
6	1	Bennett	N.	1	Sales	12/6/85	$39,000
7	4	Chin	T.	1	Mkt	5/28/83	$32,000
8	5	Smith	J.	1	Eng	10/7/85	$41,000
9	3	Rivera	B.	2	Eng	3/6/90	$48,000
10	7	Hernandez	J.	2	Sales	1/17/87	$40,000
11	9	Vu	P.	2	Mkt	8/10/92	$36,000
12	10	Smith	A.	2	Mkt	9/1/93	$33,000
13	2	Olson	R.	3	Mkt	1/18/91	$35,000
14	6	Pavlik	E.	3	Sales	4/23/90	$45,000
15	8	Sorentino	R.	3	Sales	12/1/94	$38,500

Figure 7-5

Sorting by Two or Three Columns

Please note that employees' names in Figure 7-5 are not in alphabetical order. If you had a large number of employees in each division, you would need to place the data in alphabetical order. You might also wish to sort the employees by their hire date.

> You can use the **S**ort command on the **D**ata menu to sort by more than one column at a time.

To sort the information in Figure 7-5 in alphabetical order by last name and by hire date:

Verify the active cell is in the list

Choose **D**ata

Choose **S**ort

The list is selected and the Sort dialog box appears. The bottom part of your screen should look like Figure 7-6.

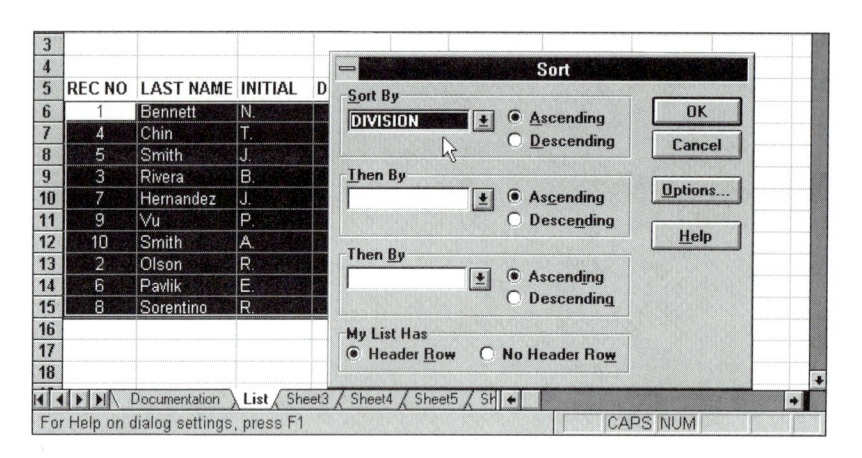

Figure 7-6

You may sometimes need to perform a sort on more than three columns. You should sort the data first by the least important criteria, and then by the more important criteria. Excel maintains a previous sort order as much as possible.

To specify the columns to sort by:

Click	the down arrow in the **S**ort By group box to display the drop-down list
Click	DIVISION (if necessary)
Click	the **A**scending option button in the **S**ort By group box (if necessary)
Click	the down arrow in the first **T**hen By group box to display the drop-down list
Click	LAST NAME
Click	the A**s**cending option button in the first **T**hen By group box (if necessary)
Click	the down arrow in the second Then **B**y group box to display the drop-down list
Click	INITIAL
Click	the A**s**cending option button in the second Then **B**y group box (if necessary)
Click	the OK command button

The data are now in alphabetical order by last name and initial within each division.

Save the workbook in a file using the name ACMESORT. Leave the workbook open for the next section.

Editing Data in a List

Suppose you need to include an additional person in the List worksheet of the ACMESORT.XLS workbook. The information to add is shown below:

REC NO.	LAST NAME	INITIAL	DIVISION	DEPT	HIRE DATE	SALARY
11	Jones	C.	3	Eng	1/24/91	53000

Inserting a New Record in a List

> You can use the **F**orm command on the **D**ata menu to enter additional data or edit data that already exist in a list.

To enter the new data in the List worksheet:

Introduction to Lists, Sorting, and Filtering

Verify	the active cell is in the list
Choose	**D**ata
Choose	**F**orm

The Data Form dialog box appears. Notice that the first record is displayed and the field names and data appear for this record.

Click	the Ne**w** command button
Enter	the data for the Jones employee

To stop entering additional information:

Click	the **C**lose command button

The record for the new employee appears in row 16 at the bottom of the list.

> You can also create new records by simply typing the data in the row below the last entry. Excel automatically includes the new data in the list.

Deleting a Record from a List

You can delete a record from a list by deleting the row in which it appears or by using the **F**orm command on the **D**ata menu.

To remove the record you just entered using the **F**orm command on the **D**ata menu:

Verify	the active cell is in the list
Choose	**D**ata
Choose	**F**orm
Click	the down arrow on the scroll bar until the information for Jones appears

Notice that the record number indicator is "11 of 11."

To remove the record:

Click	the **D**elete command button

A confirmation dialog box indicating that the record displayed in the dialog box will be permanently deleted appears.

To complete the process:

Click	the OK command button
Click	the **C**lose command button

The record is deleted from the list.

To return the records to the original record number order:

Verify	the active cell is within the list anywhere in column A (the REC NO column)
Click	the Sort Ascending [A↓Z] button on the Standard toolbar

The records appear in record number order. Leave the workbook open for the next section.

Finding Data Using the Form Command

▤ You can use the **F**orm command on the **D**ata menu to locate data in a list.

Suppose you want to examine the records in the ACMESORT.XLS workbook that have a salary greater than $40,000.

To find the records for employees who have a salary greater than $40,000:

Verify	the active cell is in the list
Choose	**D**ata
Choose	**F**orm
Click	the **C**riteria command button

A blank record appears.

To search for records for individuals who have a salary greater than $40,000:

Click	the **S**ALARY text box
Type	`>40,000`
Click	the Find **N**ext command button

Excel searches the list from top to bottom until it finds a record with a salary greater than $40,000. The information associated with the record is then displayed. In this case, the record for Rivera is the first record encountered with a salary greater than $40,000. The bottom part of your screen should look like Figure 7-7.

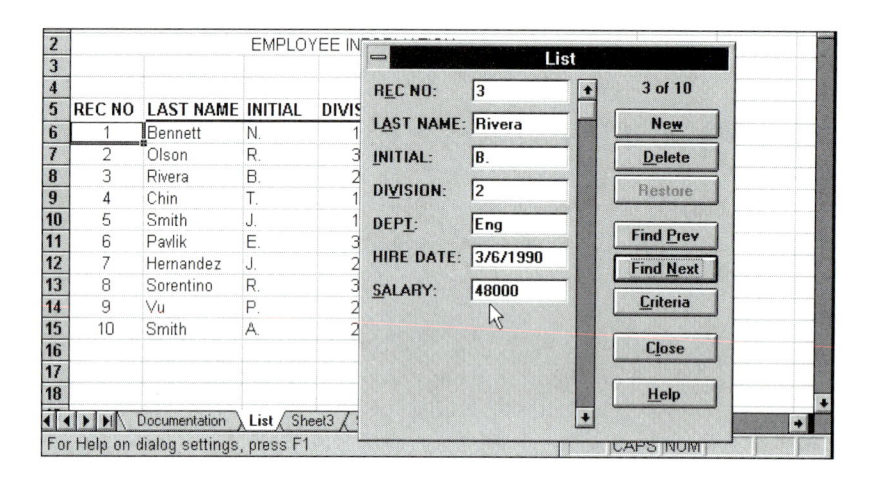

Figure 7-7

> You can use the Find **P**rev command button to examine records containing the specified criteria that precede the current record.

To find the next record matching the criteria:

Click	the Find **N**ext command button

The fifth record is displayed. Continue clicking the Find **N**ext command button until the last record containing a total salary greater than $40,000 appears. In this case, the sixth record is the last record containing a salary greater than $40,000.

To close the Data Form dialog box:

Click	the **C**lose command button

Leave the workbook open for the next section.

Using AutoFilter to Filter Data in a List

Excel allows you to find and work with subsets of data in a list. This process is called **filtering**. Whenever you filter a list, you must specify a set of search conditions called **criteria**. Excel displays only those rows that satisfy the criteria conditions. Once the subset of data are displayed, you can format, edit, chart, and print your subset list without moving or rearranging it.

Introduction to Lists, Sorting, and Filtering

Excel provides two ways to filter a list. You can use the AutoFilter command to match cell contents using simple criteria. For example, using the ACMESORT.XLS workbook, you can use AutoFilter to examine all rows containing total salaries greater than $40,000 or those rows containing employees in Division 2.

For more complex criteria, you can use the Advanced Filter command in Excel. Advanced Filter is discussed later in this chapter.

Using AutoFilter to Filter One Column

You can filter a list by selecting the AutoFilter command under the **F**ilter command on the **D**ata menu.

Drop-down arrows appear on each column heading. You can specify a subset of your list by selecting a column and indicating specific criteria. Only a subset of the list appears on your screen.

Suppose you want to display only the individual employees in Division 2 on the List worksheet of the ACMESORT.XLS workbook file.

To filter the list and only show the rows associated with employees in Division 2:

Verify	the active cell is in the list
Choose	Data
Choose	Filter
Choose	AutoFilter

A drop-down arrow is placed on each of the columns in the header row of the list. Your screen should look like Figure 7-8.

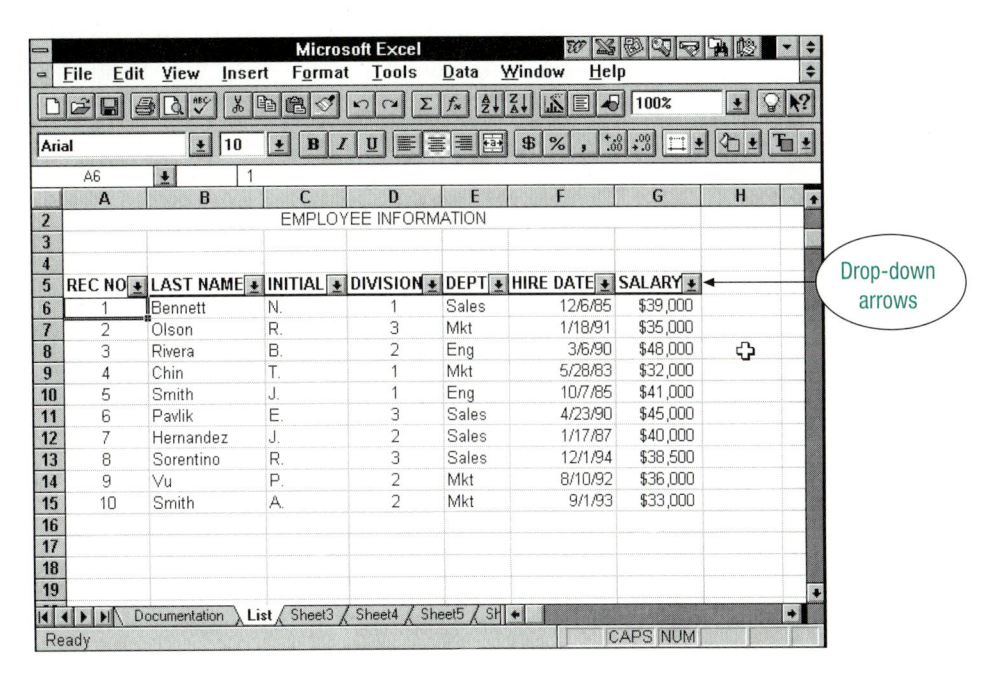

Figure 7-8

When you click one of the drop-down arrows, a drop-down list of the unique items in the column appears. If you click an item in the drop-down list of items, all rows containing the item are listed. All other rows are hidden.

To display only the Division 2 employees:

Click   the drop-down arrow on the DIVISION column

Click   2

Only the Division 2 employees are now listed. After you have made cell A1 the active cell, the bottom part of your screen should look like Figure 7-9.

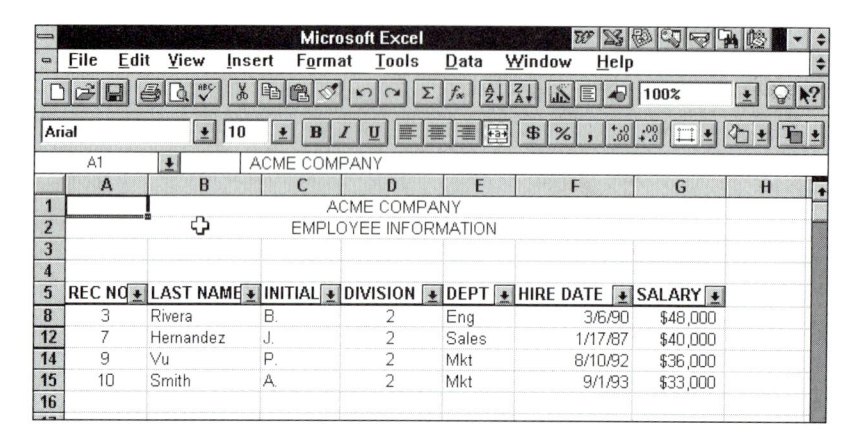

Figure 7-9

Notice that some of the row heading numbers are hidden, indicating that those records are not associated with a Division 2 employee. Notice also that the drop-down arrow in the DIVISION column and the visible row heading numbers are displayed in a different color. You can now sort, edit, print, or format the filtered data.

- You can display all the rows in the list again by choosing the **S**how All command under the **F**ilter command on the **D**ata menu.

- You can display all the rows in the list again by clicking the down arrow in the filtered column and clicking All. *Note:* If more than one column is filtered, the **S**how All command under the **F**ilter command on the **D**ata menu is faster.

To place the entire list on your screen again:

Click   the drop-down arrow on the DIVISION column

Click   (All)

The complete employee list appears.

When you use the AutoFilter command, you can create custom filter criteria. For example, suppose you want to examine the list of employees who have a total salary greater than $40,000.

To indicate that you want to use custom criteria:

Click   the drop-down arrow on the SALARY column

Click   (Custom...)

The Custom AutoFilter dialog box appears. The bottom part of your screen should look like Figure 7-10.

Introduction to Lists, Sorting, and Filtering

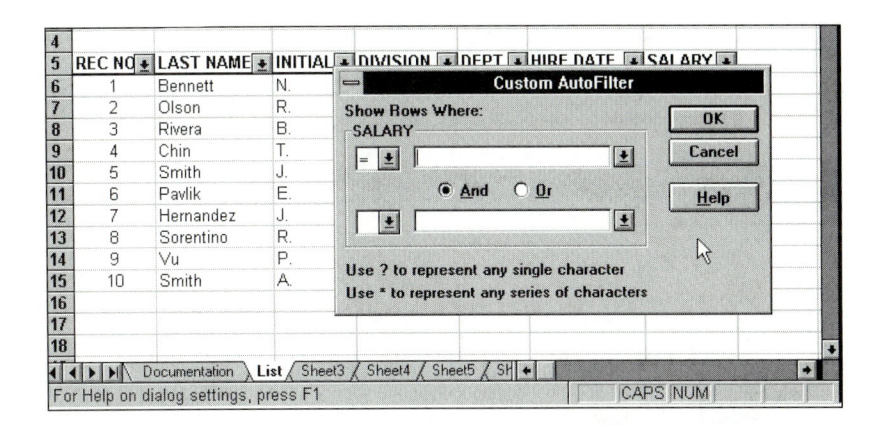

Figure 7-10

You can enter filter criteria to specify an operator and which rows in the list to display. Because you are filtering the SALARY column, the word "SALARY" appears as the group box title.

To indicate that you want to use the ">" operator instead of "=":

Click	the down arrow on the first operator drop-down list box
Click	>

To specify the value to use in the criteria:

Click	the text box in the first criteria line
Type	40,000

If you want to use one of the values in the SALARY column, you can click the drop-down arrow on the text box and choose one of the values from the drop-down list.

To complete the process:

Click	the OK command button

Only employees who have an annual salary greater than $40,000 are displayed. After you have made cell A1 the active cell, the top part of your screen should look like Figure 7-11.

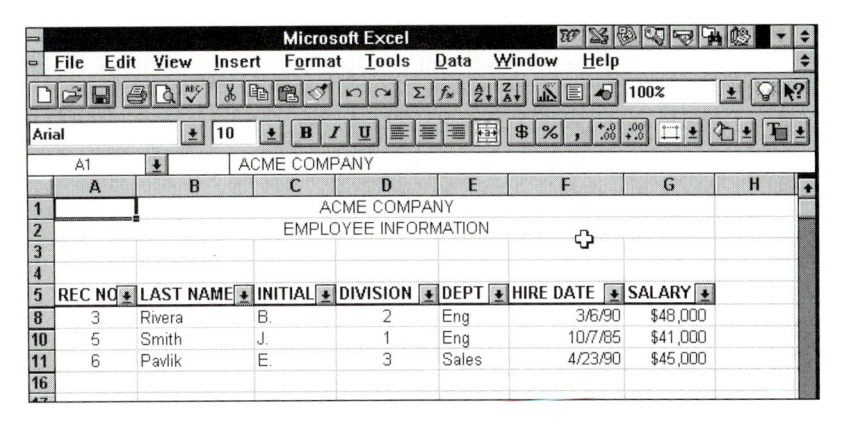

Figure 7-11

To redisplay all the data:

Choose	Data
Choose	Filter
Choose	Show All

Filtering a List Containing Multiple Criteria Using AutoFilter

Excel allows you to use two type of criteria: **comparison criteria** and **computed criteria**. You should use comparison criteria to display rows that fall within a range of values. A comparison criteria can be a series of characters to match, or it can contain a logical comparison.

For the ACMESORT.XLS workbook example, you might want to see Division 2 employees in the Sales department or Division 3 employees in the Marketing department whose salaries fall in a particular range.

> You can also use computed criteria. For this type of criteria, you can evaluate items in a selected column in a list against values that do not appear in the list. For example, you might want to select the personnel in the ACMESORT.XLS workbook who have a salary greater than the average salary for all employees. For more information about computed criteria, see your Excel *User's Guide*.

In this exercise, you will use AutoFilter to filter the List worksheet of the ACMESORT.XLS workbook to display the records for individuals who have a total salary less than $40,000 and who are in Division 3.

To show the rows containing employees with a total salary less than $40,000:

Click	the drop-down arrow on the SALARY column
Click	(Custom...)
Click	the down arrow on the first operator drop-down list
Click	<
Click	the text box in the first criteria line
Type	40,000
Click	the OK command button

The records containing a total salary less than $40,000 are displayed.

To display only the records having a total salary less than $40,000 and in Division 3:

Click	the drop-down arrow on the DIVISION column
Click	3

The appropriate records are displayed. After you have made cell A1 the active cell, the top part of your screen should look like Figure 7-12.

Figure 7-12

Introduction to Lists, Sorting, and Filtering

Redisplay all the records by choosing the **S**how All command under the **F**ilter command on the **D**ata menu.

In some cases, you may want to specify criteria within a range. For example, suppose you want to display the records for individuals who have a salary less than or equal to $32,500 or greater than $40,000.

To show the records for those individuals with salaries satisfying the criteria:

Click	the drop-down arrow on the SALARY column
Click	(Custom...)
Click	the drop-down arrow on the first operator list box
Click	<=
Click	the text box in the first criteria line
Type	32,500
Click	the **O**r option button
Click	the drop-down arrow in the second operator box
Click	the > operator
Click	the text box in the second criteria line
Type	40,000

The bottom part of your screen should look like Figure 7-13.

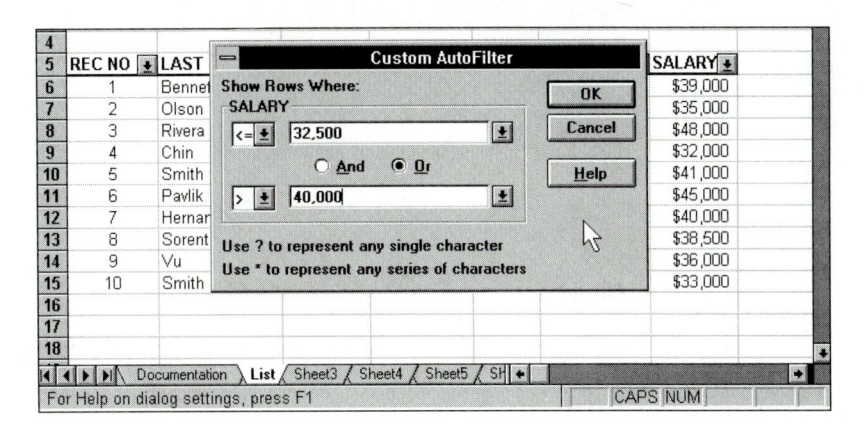

Figure 7-13

To complete the process:

Click	the OK command button

The appropriate records in the list are displayed. After you have made cell A1 the active cell, the top part of your screen should look like Figure 7-14.

Mastering and Using Microsoft Office Professional

Figure 7-14

Redisplay all the records by choosing the **S**how All command under the **F**ilter command on the **D**ata menu.

Using Wildcard Characters to Filter a List

In some situations, you may need to find all individuals in a list whose last name begins with the same first letter or display a list based on a single character in the same position. To create such a list, use wildcard characters. Use an asterisk (*) to find any number of characters in the exact same position as the asterisk. Use a question mark (?) to find any single character in the same position as the question mark.

Suppose you want a list of all individuals in the List worksheet of the ACMESORT.XLS workbook who have a last name beginning with the letter "S."

To specify the criteria:

Click   the drop-down arrow on the LAST NAME column

Click   (Custom...)

> Use a tilde (~) before a question mark, asterisk, or tilde when you are actually searching for a question mark, asterisk, or a tilde on the worksheet.

To enter the criteria for finding all last names that start with an "S":

Type   S* in the first criteria text box

Click   the OK command button

Only the records for employees having a last name beginning with "S" are displayed.

After you have made cell A1 the active cell, the top part of your screen should look like Figure 7-15.

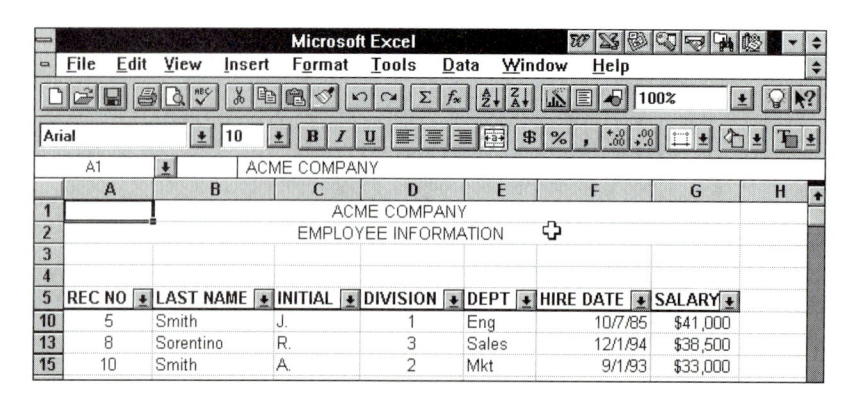

Figure 7-15

Introduction to Lists, Sorting, and Filtering

To display all rows in the list and stop using the AutoFilter:

Choose Data

Choose Filter

Choose AutoFilter

Leave the workbook open for the next section.

Using Advanced Filter

If you only have one or two comparison criteria, you should use the Custom option available in the drop-down lists provided when you use AutoFilter. When you cannot obtain the desired subset using the AutoFilter drop-down lists, you will need to use the Advanced Filter command in which a criteria range is created.

> You can filter a list by choosing **Advanced Filter** under the **Filter** command on the **Data** menu.

These are some guidelines for entering comparison criteria on your worksheet:

- Place all criteria in the same row to determine the records that satisfy all the criteria in that row. For example, part of your criteria identifies those individuals who have a salary in excess of $40,000 *and* are in Division 3.

- Enter criteria in different rows when you need to determine those rows that meet all criteria in the first row *or* the second row. For example, part of your criteria is to find records that contain salary information for those individuals who are in Division 2 *or* who have a total salary greater than $28,000.

- Enter a column heading more than once if there are multiple criteria associated with one column. For example, part of your criteria is to identify those individuals who have a salary greater than $20,000 and less than or equal to $30,000.

A good location for the criteria range is above and to the right of the columns in the list.

Suppose you want to find individuals in the List worksheet of the ACMESORT.XLS workbook who:

> have salaries greater than $35,000 and who are in the Sales department of Division 1, or

> have salaries less than $40,000 and who are in the Marketing department of Division 2.

Enter the criteria range information in cells H1:J3 as shown in Figure 7-16.

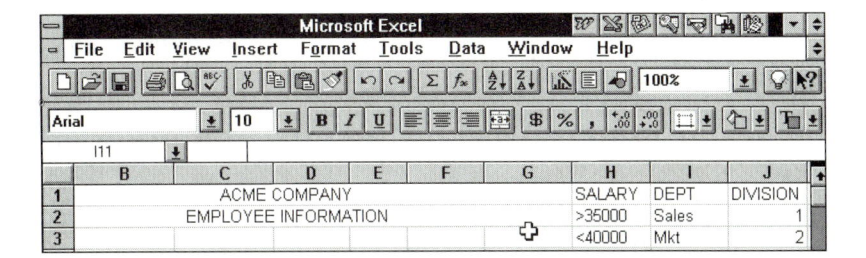

Figure 7-16

	B	C	D	E	F	G	H	I	J
1		ACME COMPANY					SALARY	DEPT	DIVISION
2		EMPLOYEE INFORMATION					>35000	Sales	1
3							<40000	Mkt	2

Case does not matter when you type the column headings. However, the spelling must match the column label in the header row. You may wish to copy the column headings instead of retyping them.

To continue the process:

Verify	the active cell is in the list
Choose	**D**ata
Choose	Filter
Choose	Advanced Filter

The Advanced Filter dialog box appears. After you have scrolled to view row 1, your screen should look like Figure 7-17.

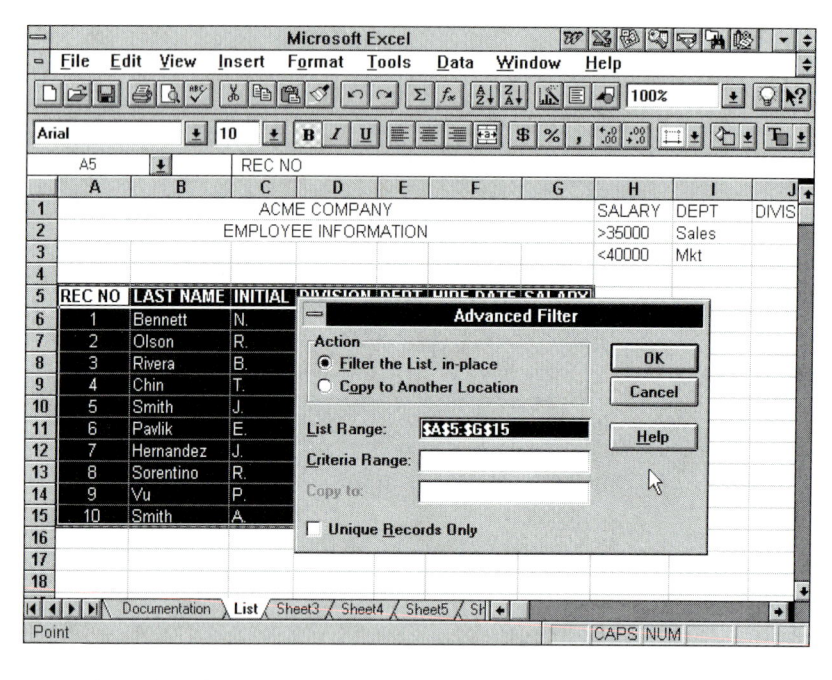

Figure 7-17

Since the **F**ilter the List, in-place option button is selected in the Action group box, the resulting list appears beginning in cell A6, the first row below the header row. In this exercise, the resulting list is allowed to appear in cell A6.

If you want to place the results in a different location, you must specify the location of the results in the Copy **t**o text box. This method is demonstrated later in this chapter.

Since the default **L**ist Range is already displayed, it is not necessary to enter or alter it.

To specify the location of the **C**riteria Range:

Click	the **C**riteria Range text box
Scroll	to view column J
Move	the dialog box, if necessary, to display the range H1:J3
Select	cells H1:J3

Notice that the sheet tab name and the absolute location are included in the Criteria Range.

To complete the process:

Click	the OK command button

After you have made cell A1 the active cell, the top part of your screen should look like Figure 7-18.

Introduction to Lists, Sorting, and Filtering

Figure 7-18

Notice that two individuals in the Marketing department and one in the Sales department meet the salary and division criteria.

Redisplay all the records by choosing the **S**how All command under the **F**ilter command on the **D**ata menu.

Placing Results in a Different Area

Suppose you want to place the results at a different location on the worksheet.

To specify the location for the results and the criteria range:

Verify	the active cell is in the list
Choose	**D**ata
Choose	**F**ilter
Choose	Advanced Filter
Verify	the **L**ist Range and **C**riteria Range are still correct from the previous exercise
Click	the **C**opy to Another Location option button in the Action group box
Click	the Copy **t**o text box
Select	cell A20 (scroll to view the row)

To complete the process:

Click	the OK command button

After you have made row 20 the first row appearing on your screen and cell A20 the active cell, the top part of your screen should look like Figure 7-19.

When you filter to a different location, any calculated fields filter as values. There is no link to the original data. Thus, if you change a value in the list, the fields in the original list will recalculate. The filtered records in a different location will not change.

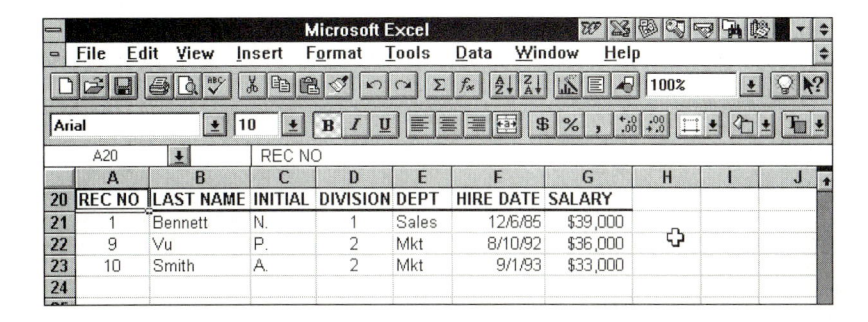

Figure 7-19

Select the range A20:G23 and delete it. Make cell A1 the active cell. Leave the ACMESORT.XLS workbook open for the next section.

Using the Subtotals Command

Sometimes you may need to calculate subtotals in a list. For example, you may need to compute the subtotals of salaries by division.

Excel can insert automatic subtotals to assist you in summarizing data that appear in the list. Grand totals are also computed.

> You can use the Subtotals command on the Data menu to calculate subtotals and a grand total.

The data in the list must be sorted in the order in which you want to calculate subtotals. In the ACMESORT.XLS workbook, you need to sort the data in order by division before you use the Subtotals command.

Sort the data in the List worksheet by division and then by last name, both in ascending order. Once you complete the sort and make cell A1 the active cell, the bottom part of your screen should look like Figure 7-20.

Figure 7-20

REC NO	LAST NAME	INITIAL	DIVISION	DEPT	HIRE DATE	SALARY
1	Bennett	N.	1	Sales	12/6/85	$39,000
4	Chin	T.	1	Mkt	5/28/83	$32,000
5	Smith	J.	1	Eng	10/7/85	$41,000
7	Hernandez	J.	2	Sales	1/17/87	$40,000
3	Rivera	B.	2	Eng	3/6/90	$48,000
10	Smith	A.	2	Mkt	9/1/93	$33,000
9	Vu	P.	2	Mkt	8/10/92	$36,000
2	Olson	R.	3	Mkt	1/18/91	$35,000
6	Pavlik	E.	3	Sales	4/23/90	$45,000
8	Sorentino	R.	3	Sales	12/1/94	$38,500

To calculate the subtotals for the salaries by division and the grand total for salaries:

Verify	the active cell is in the list
Choose	Data
Choose	Subtotals

The Subtotal dialog box appears. Your screen should look like Figure 7-21.

Introduction to Lists, Sorting, and Filtering

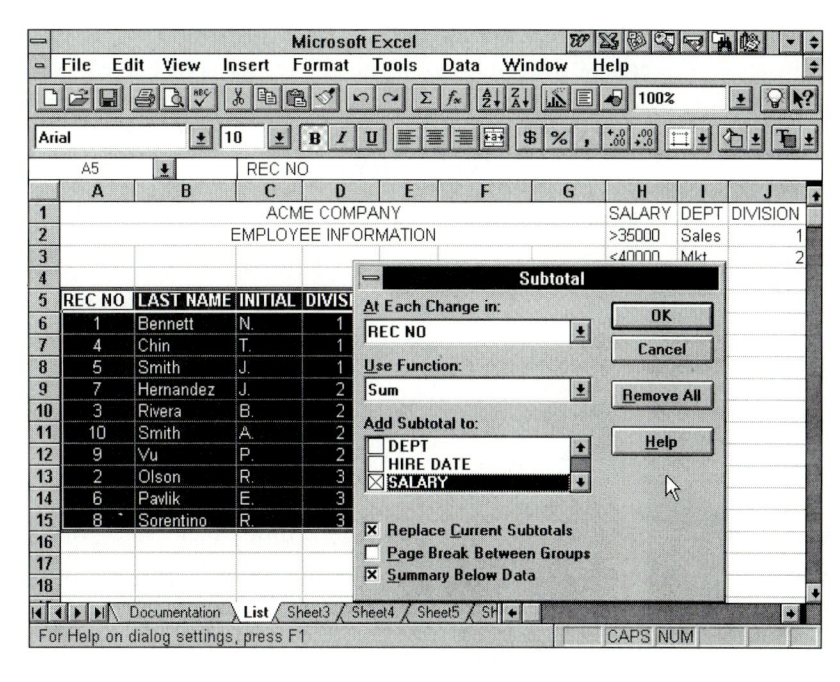

Figure 7-21

Click	the down arrow on the **At** Each Change in list box
Click	DIVISION
Verify	SUM is displayed in the **U**se Function list box
Verify	the SALARY check box in the **Ad**d Subtotal to: list box contains an X
Click	the OK command button

The subtotals and grand total are calculated. Adjust the width of the SALARY column, if necessary. After you have scrolled to view rows 4 through 20, your screen should look similar to Figure 7-22.

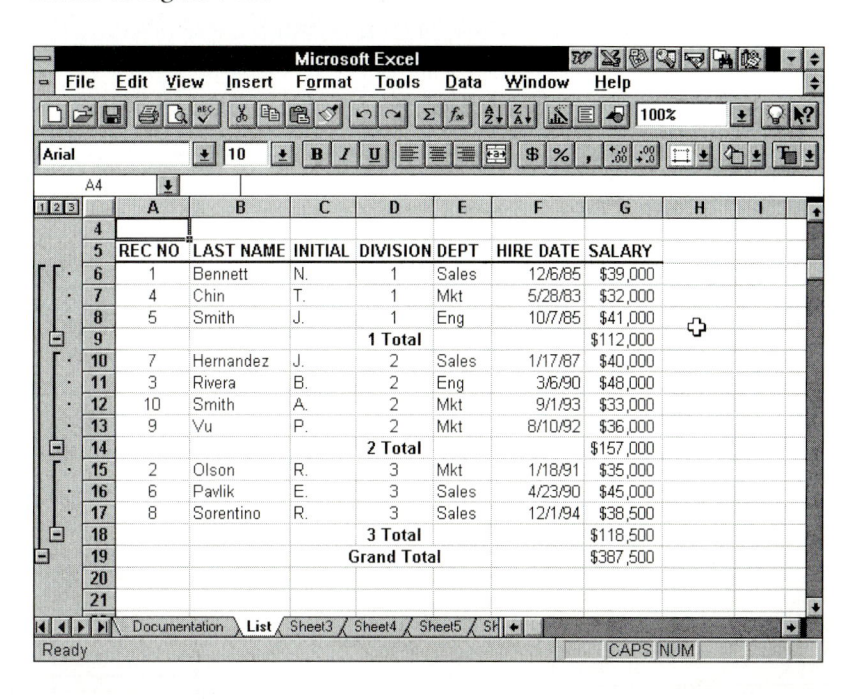

Figure 7-22

When you click the outline symbol 1, which is near the column headings in the left area of the screen, only the grand total is displayed. When you click the outline symbol 2, the subtotals for each division are displayed. When you click the outline symbol 3, all the data, subtotals, and grand total for the list are displayed. Once you display the desired level, you can format, print, or create a chart from the displayed data.

Save the workbook in a file using the name ACME-SUB.

To remove the display of subtotals:

Verify	the active cell is in the list
Choose	**D**ata
Choose	Su**b**totals
Click	the **R**emove All command button

The subtotals and grand total are removed from the worksheet. For more information about the Subtotals feature, see your Excel *User's Guide*.

Close the workbook. Do not save any changes.

Summary

In Excel, you can group data together into a list. Sometimes, a list is referred to as a database and the rows are called records. A list contains a top row of unique column labels called row headers. You can create or modify a list using the **F**orm command on the **D**ata menu. After you have created a list, you can sort it. You can identify specific records in a list using criteria and either **A**utoFilter or **A**dvanced AutoFilter. With the Su**b**totals command on the **D**ata menu, you can automatically calculate subtotals and a grand total for a worksheet.

Exercise 1

INSTRUCTIONS: Define or explain the following:

1. Database _____
   _____

2. List _____
   _____

3. Data Sort command _____
   _____

4. Ascending order _____
   _____

5. Descending order _____
   _____

6. Data Form command _____
   _____

7. Field _____
   _____

8. Record _____

Introduction to Lists, Sorting, and Filtering

9. Criteria _____
_____
_____

10. AutoFilter command _____
_____

11. Advanced Filter command _____
_____

12. Subtotals command _____
_____
_____

13. Header row _____
_____

14. Column label _____
_____

Exercise 2

INSTRUCTIONS: Circle T if the statement is true and F if the statement is false.

T   F   1. Before sorting a list in Excel, you must select the entire range of the list.

T   F   2. There should not be a blank row between column names and the first row of data in a list.

T   F   3. It is appropriate to have two-row column names.

T   F   4. You can filter complex criteria using the AutoFilter command.

T   F   5. You can place the results of a filter in a new location in the workbook.

T   F   6. You cannot sort more than three columns in a list.

Exercise 3

INSTRUCTIONS: Create the worksheet shown in Figure 7-23. Save the workbook in a file using the name E07EX03.

1. Column A has a width of 7.
2. Column B has a width of 15.
3. Column C has a width of 14.
4. Column D has a width of 7.
5. Sort the data in the E07EX03.XLS workbook alphabetically by city.
6. Save the workbook.
7. Print the worksheet with the sorted data.
8. Close the workbook.

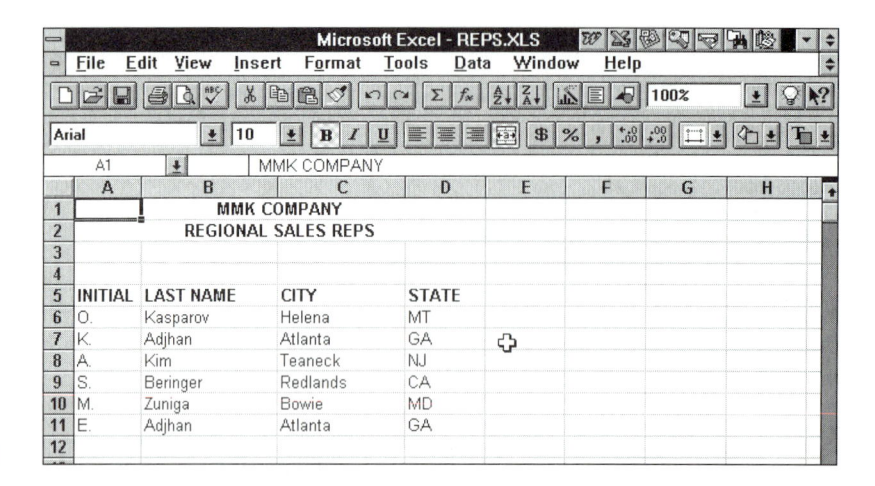

Figure 7-23

Exercise 4

INSTRUCTIONS:

1. Open the E07EX03.XLS workbook created in Exercise 3.
2. Filter the records to show only those people living in Georgia.
3. Save the workbook in a file using the name E07EX04.
4. Print the filtered list.
5. Close the workbook.

Introduction to Macros

8

Objectives

In this chapter you will learn to:

→ Create a macro
→ Execute a macro
→ Edit a macro
→ Record additional steps into an existing macro
→ Create a macro in the Personal Macro Workbook
→ Remove a macro from the Personal Macro Workbook
→ Use a shortcut key to execute a macro

Chapter Overview

A **macro** is a set of instructions to automatically execute a series of Excel commands. Macros are especially useful when performing detailed, repetitive routines. Macros may include steps to consolidate worksheets, perform special edit routines, or print reports and charts. The Visual Basic programming language is used to create macros in Excel 5.0. Macros created using Visual Basic are very different from macros prepared in earlier versions of Excel.

The simplest way to create a macro in Excel is to record your actions while performing a task. For example, you might record the steps for performing a sort, creating a customized header and footer, or printing named ranges. By placing the Excel commands in a macro, you can automate the process rather than repeat the commands each time they are needed. You can save macros in the same workbook in which the macro will be used, in the Personal Macro Workbook, or in a separate workbook.

Creating a Macro

In some situations, you may only want to use a macro with a specific workbook. In this case, you can save the macro in a **module sheet** or separate sheet within the workbook. In Chapter 6, you created a worksheet containing sales of boats and motors. Suppose you need to create a macro that will create a 3-D column chart of boat and motor sales for the four quarters for Division 1. First, open the BOATSALE.XLS workbook.

A range name is used to select the cells to be used in the chart. Creating a range name is not required. However, range names are recommended so that if additional rows or columns are inserted, the same cells are always selected for the chart data.

To create a range name for the Boat and Motor sales for Division 1:

Select	cells A4:E6
Click	in the Name Box
Type	CHART_DATA
Press	← ENTER
Deselect	the range

The range A4:E6 is now named CHART_DATA. This range name is used in the macro to select the cells for the chart.

To create the macro:

Choose	Tools
Choose	Record Macro
Choose	Record New Macro

The Record New Macro dialog box appears. The bottom part of your screen should look like Figure 8-1.

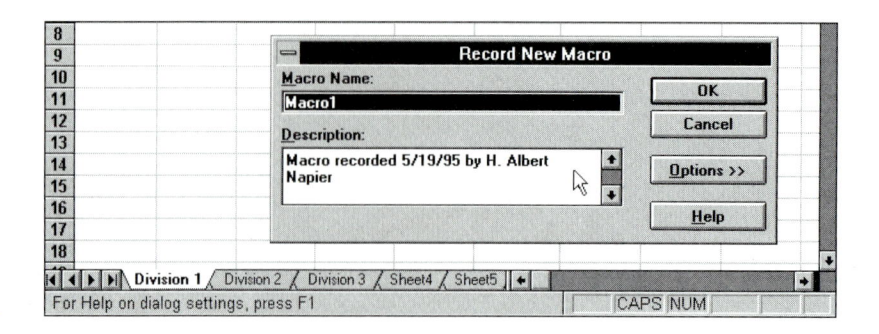

Figure 8-1

Type	CHART in the **Macro Name** text box
Click	at the end of the entry in the **Description** text box
Type	. This macro creates a column chart to illustrate boat and motor sales for the year.
Click	the **Options** command button
Click	the This **Workbook** option button in the Store in group box (if necessary)
Click	the OK command button

Introduction to Macros

You are now in Record mode. The word Recording appears in the lower-left corner of the status bar. The Macro toolbar appears on the screen. When you have finished recording the Excel commands, click the Stop Macro button on the Macro toolbar. Complete the following steps:

Click	the down arrow on the Name Box
Click	CHART_DATA

The range A4:E6 is selected.

To create a chart on a new sheet:

Choose	Insert
Choose	Chart
Choose	As New Sheet

The ChartWizard appears on the screen.

To use the ChartWizard to create a chart:

Verify	the correct range A4:E6 in the **R**ange text box
Click	the **N**ext command button
Click	the 3-D C**o**lumn type
Click	the **N**ext command button
Click	format 1
Click	the **N**ext command button
Verify	the options in step 4 of the ChartWizard (**R**ows option should be selected for Data Series, Row 1 is to be used as X-axis labels, and Column 1 is to be used as Legend text)
Click	the **N**ext command button
Click	in the Chart Title text box
Type	ACME BOATING COMPANY

A sample chart displays in the ChartWizard. To complete the process:

Click	the **F**inish command button

The column chart appears on the Chart1 sheet. To stop recording macro commands:

Click	the Stop Macro button on the Macro toolbar
	or
Choose	**T**ools
Choose	**R**ecord Macro
Choose	**S**top Recording

The macro commands appear on the Module1 sheet to the right of Sheet16.

To view the Module1 sheet:

Click	the ▶| scroll arrow to view the last group of sheet tabs
Click	the Module1 sheet tab

Your screen should look like Figure 8-2.

```
' CHART Macro
' Macro recorded 5/8/96 by Al Napier.  This macro creates a column chart to i

Sub CHART()
    Application.Goto Reference:="CHART_DATA"
    Charts.Add
    ActiveChart.ChartWizard Source:=Sheets("Division 1").Range("A4:E6"), _
        Gallery:=xl3DColumn, Format:=1, PlotBy:=xlRows, CategoryLabels _
        :=1, SeriesLabels:=1, HasLegend:=1, Title:= _
        "ACME BOATING COMPANY", CategoryTitle:="", ValueTitle:="", _
        ExtraTitle:=""
End Sub
```

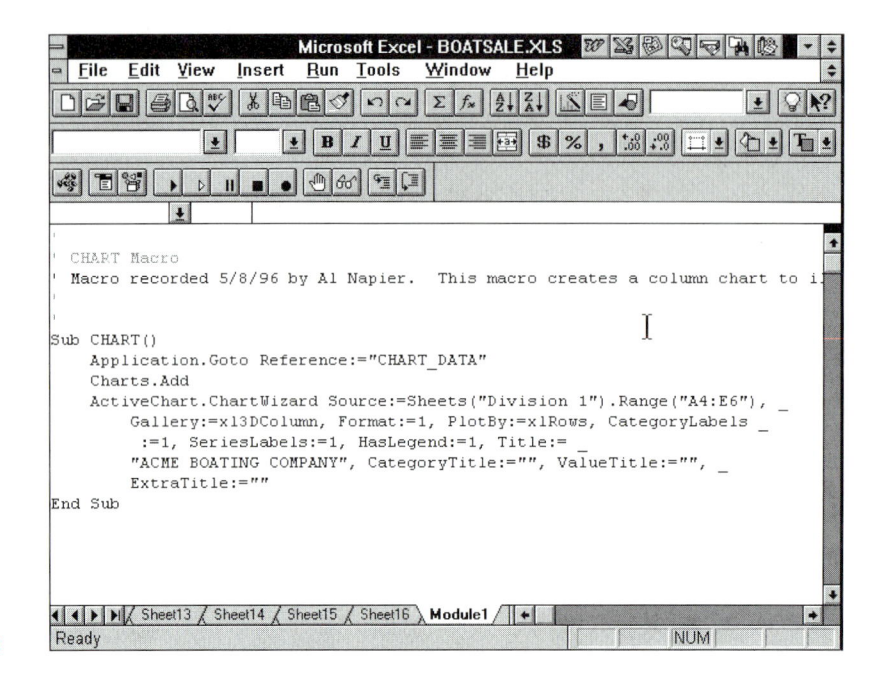

Figure 8-2

The Visual Basic instructions on the Module1 sheet create a 3-D column chart with the ACME BOATING COMPANY title.

The information below describes the various lines in the macro:

Top few lines appearing in a unique color	These lines identify the macro name, the date of creation, the author, and a description of the macro.
Sub CHART( )	Initial line of the macro. Sub marks the beginning of a macro.
Application.Goto Reference: ="CHART _DATA"	Specifies the selection of the range.
Charts.Add ActiveChart.ChartWizard Source: =Sheets("Division1").Range("A4:E6"), _Gallery:=xl3DColumn, Format:=1, PlotBy:=xlRows, CategoryLabels _:=1, SeriesLabels:=1, HasLegend:=1, Title:= _"ACME BOATING COMPANY", CategoryTitle:=" ", ValueTitle:=" ", _ ExtraTitle:=" "	Displays the choices made in the ChartWizard steps. Even if you do not choose to alter particular settings, some of them are noted.
End Sub	Marks the end of a macro.

Introduction to Macros

To return the workbook to its original state before the chart was created:

Click the Chart1 sheet (use scroll arrows to view the tab name)

Choose **E**dit

Choose De**l**ete Sheet

Click the OK command button in the confirmation dialog box

Click on cell A1 to deselect the range and position the active cell in the Home position. Save the workbook in a file using the name CHARTMAC.

Executing a Macro

Suppose you want to execute, or use, the CHART macro you just completed.

- You can execute a macro by choosing the **M**acro command on the **T**ools menu.

To execute the macro:

Verify the CHARTMAC.XLS workbook is open

Choose **T**ools

Choose **M**acro

The Macro dialog box appears.

Click CHART in the **M**acro Name/Reference list box (if necessary)

Click the **R**un command button

The CHART macro is executed and the 3-D column chart is created on a chart sheet. Your screen should look like Figure 8-3.

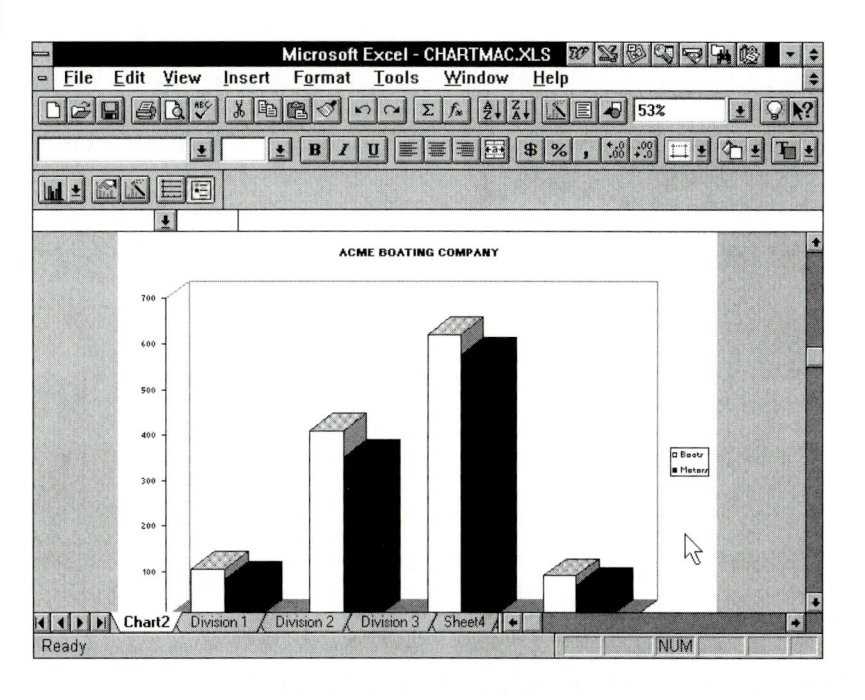

> Macros can be assigned to the Tools menu, or you can use keyboard shortcut keys to execute a macro. These topics are discussed later in this chapter. You can also place a button on the worksheet or place a button on a toolbar to execute the macro.

Figure 8-3

Close the workbook and do not save any changes.

Editing a Macro

When you use the recording process to create a macro, Excel copies every task you perform. Therefore, mistakes as well as extra, unnecessary activities may be included in the macro. You also may wish to change some of the text in the macro. In the example you completed earlier, the macro created a chart and placed the company name in the title. Suppose you want to include the text ",INC." in the chart title and wish to add the word "UNITS" as a title for the value axis. Rather than create the macro again, you can edit the existing macro.

To edit the CHART macro:

Open	the CHARTMAC.XLS workbook
Click	the Module1 sheet tab (use scroll arrows to view this sheet tab)

To place additional text in the macro:

Click	between the y and the quote mark at the end of the text "Company"
Type	`, INC.`
Click	between the quote marks in the phrase ValueTitle:=" "
Type	`UNITS`
Click	the Division 1 tab (use scroll arrows to view this sheet tab)

Make cell A1 the active cell. Save the workbook in a file using the name CHARTEDT. Execute the macro. The chart title has changed and the Value axis has a title. Leave the file open for the next section.

Recording Additional Steps into an Existing Macro

Suppose you also want to print the chart after it is created. You can place additional steps or instructions into an existing macro.

> You can manually type the instructions into the macro or record the instructions using the **R**ecord Macro command on the **T**ools menu.

The basic steps are:

1. Move the insertion point to the location in the macro module sheet where you want to place the additional instructions.

2. Choose the **R**ecord Macro command on the **T**ools menu. Then choose **M**ark Position for Recording.

3. Switch to the worksheet from which you will record new activities.

4. Choose the **R**ecord Macro command on the **T**ools menu. Then choose **R**ecord at Mark.

5. Complete the tasks you want to add to the macro.

6. Click the Stop Macro button.

Suppose you want to include instructions for printing the chart sheet in the CHARTEDT.XLS workbook in the CHART macro you created earlier in this chapter.

To illustrate the process for including additional instructions in a macro:

Verify	the CHARTEDT.XLS workbook is open
Click	the Module1 sheet tab (use scroll arrows to view this sheet tab)
Click	at the beginning of the last line in the macro (End Sub) in the Module1 sheet
Choose	Tools
Choose	Record Macro
Choose	Mark Position for Recording

You are now ready to record the additional instructions to include in the macro:

Click	the Chart1 sheet tab (use scroll arrows to view this sheet tab)
Choose	Tools
Choose	Record Macro
Choose	Record at Mark

At this point, you are in Record mode. Notice that the word "Recording" appears in the status bar and the Macro toolbar appears again.

To record the instructions for printing the current worksheet:

Choose	File
Choose	Print
Verify	the Selected Sheet(s) option button is selected in the Print What group box
Click	the OK command button
Click	the Stop Macro button on the Macro toolbar

The 3-D Column Chart in the CHARTEDT.XLS workbook is printed. Click the Module1 sheet tab. Notice the additional instruction that appears at the end of the macro for printing the active worksheet. Your screen should look like Figure 8-4.

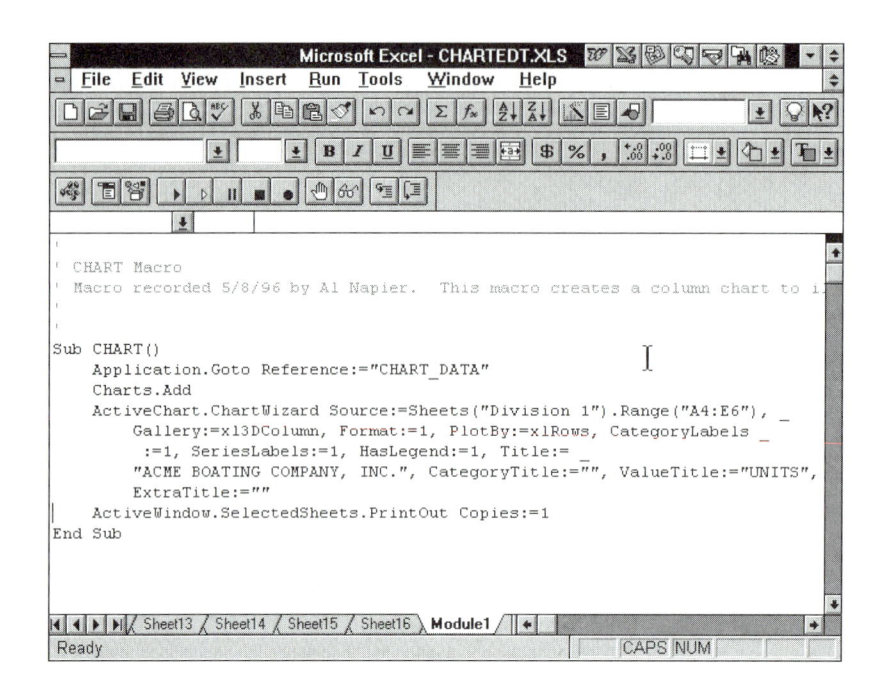

Mastering and Using Microsoft Office Professional

```
' CHART Macro
' Macro recorded 5/8/96 by Al Napier.  This macro creates a column chart to i
'
Sub CHART()
    Application.Goto Reference:="CHART_DATA"
    Charts.Add
    ActiveChart.ChartWizard Source:=Sheets("Division 1").Range("A4:E6"), _
        Gallery:=xl3DColumn, Format:=1, PlotBy:=xlRows, CategoryLabels _
        :=1, SeriesLabels:=1, HasLegend:=1, Title:= _
        "ACME BOATING COMPANY, INC.", CategoryTitle:="", ValueTitle:="UNITS", _
        ExtraTitle:=""
    ActiveWindow.SelectedSheets.PrintOut Copies:=1
End Sub
```

Figure 8-4

To return the workbook to its appearance before the macro was created:

Click	the Chart1 sheet tab
Choose	**E**dit
Choose	**D**elete Sheet
Click	the OK command button to confirm deleting the sheet
Deselect	the range in the worksheet

Save the workbook in a file using the name CHARTPRT. To execute the modified macro:

Verify	the CHARTPRT.XLS workbook is open
Choose	**T**ools
Choose	**M**acro
Click	CHART in the **M**acro Name/Reference list box
Click	the **R**un command button

The macro executes. After the chart is created, it is printed.

Save the workbook. Close the workbook.

Creating a Macro in the Personal Macro Workbook

In some situations, you may want access to a macro when you are using any workbook. For example, you may want to create a macro that will design a custom header and footer to be used on many of your workbooks. A macro that you want to have available all the time should be placed in the Personal Macro Workbook. The Personal Macro Workbook does not exist until you create a macro and place it in the Personal Macro Workbook. You can save as many macros as you wish in the Personal Macro Workbook.

Introduction to Macros

To create the macro in a blank workbook:

Create	a blank workbook
Choose	**T**ools
Choose	**R**ecord Macro
Choose	**R**ecord New Macro

With the Record New Macro dialog box on your screen:

Type	`HEADER_FOOTER` in the **M**acro Name text box
Click	at the end of the entry in the **D**escription text box
Type	`. This macro creates a custom header with company name and a custom footer with the time and page number.`

To place the macro in the Personal Macro Workbook:

Click	the **O**ptions command button
Click	the **P**ersonal Macro Workbook option button in the Store in group box
Click	the OK command button

You are now in Recording mode.

To create a custom header and footer to be used on any specified worksheet:

Choose	**F**ile
Choose	Page Set**u**p
Click	the Header/Footer tab
Click	the **C**ustom Header command button
Delete	the current contents in the Center Section
Type	`ACME COMPANY` in the **C**enter Section
Click	the OK command button
Click	the C**u**stom Footer command button
Verify	the insertion point is in the **L**eft Section
Click	the Time button to place the current time in the **L**eft Section of the footer
Click	the OK command button to close the Footer dialog box
Click	the OK command button to close the Page Setup dialog box

To stop recording macro steps:

Click	the Stop Macro button on the Macro toolbar

Viewing the Personal Macro Workbook

Once you place a macro in the Personal Macro Workbook, the Personal Macro Workbook always opens when you open the Excel application. However, it is hidden from view.

To view the Personal Macro Workbook:

Choose **W**indow

Choose **U**nhide

The Unhide dialog box appears. The bottom part of your screen should look like Figure 8-5.

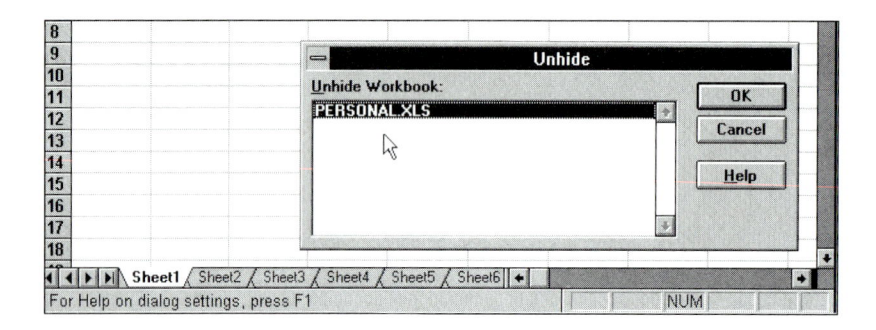

Figure 8-5

Notice that PERSONAL.XLS appears in the **U**nhide Workbook list box. This is the Personal Macro Workbook.

To view the PERSONAL.XLS workbook:

Click PERSONAL.XLS in the **U**nhide Workbook list box (if necessary)

Click the OK command button

The PERSONAL.XLS workbook appears with the macro you created. When you scroll up to view the top part of the macro, your screen should look like Figure 8-6.

> If someone else has used the Excel application previously, more Module sheets may appear in the PERSONAL.XLS workbook. All the macros you create in one session in the Personal Macro Workbook are stored on one Module sheet. When you record additional macros in the Personal Macro Workbook during other sessions, they are placed on additional Module sheets.

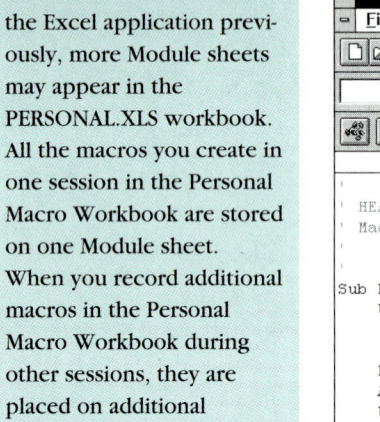

Figure 8-6

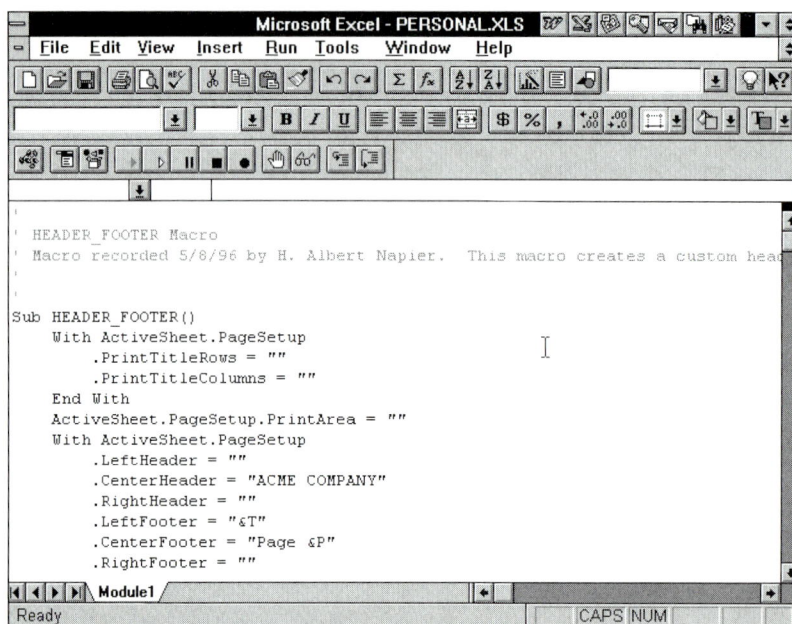

In addition to your changes in the header and footer, the commands in the HEADER_FOOTER macro indicate several page setup settings. The macro records the default settings even if you do not specify new settings.

Introduction to Macros

To hide the PERSONAL.XLS workbook:

Choose	**W**indow
Choose	**H**ide

Close the workbook. Do not save any changes.

Using a Macro Stored in the Personal Macro Workbook

> When you exit Excel after changing the Personal Macro Workbook, you are asked whether or not to save the changes. Respond to the confirmation dialog box appropriately for your situation. In most situations, you will want to save the changes you have made.

To illustrate the use of the HEADER_FOOTER macro you saved in the Personal Macro Workbook:

Open	the CHARTMAC.XLS workbook
Click	the Division 1 tab (if necessary)
Choose	**T**ools
Choose	**M**acro

The Macro dialog box appears. Notice that the PERSONAL.XLS workbook name is listed with the macro name HEADER_FOOTER in the **M**acro Name/Reference list box. If other macros are stored in the PERSONAL.XLS workbook or in the current workbook, the names of these macros also appear.

To run the macro:

Click	PERSONAL.XLS!HEADER_FOOTER in the **M**acro Name/Reference list box
Click	the **R**un command button

The macro takes several seconds to execute. *Note:* This macro does not change the default header or footer on the chart sheet or any of the other worksheets. If you want to make changes to the header and footer on other worksheets in the workbook, you need to activate the worksheet and run the macro. To make changes to the header or footer on the chart sheet, select the chart sheet and choose the Page Setup commands just as you would on a worksheet.

Close the workbook. Do not save any changes.

Removing a Macro from the Personal Macro Workbook

Sometimes, you may need to remove a macro from the Personal Macro Workbook. Suppose you need to delete the HEADER_FOOTER macro you created earlier in this chapter.

To view the HEADER_FOOTER macro:

Open	an existing or new workbook
Choose	**W**indow
Choose	**U**nhide
Click	PERSONAL.XLS workbook in the **U**nhide Workbook list box (if necessary)
Click	the OK command button

To delete the macro:

| **Select** | all the text pertaining to the HEADER_FOOTER macro |
| **Press** | DELETE |

The HEADER_FOOTER macro is deleted from the Personal Macro Workbook.

To hide the Personal Macro Workbook:

| **Choose** | **W**indow |
| **Choose** | **H**ide |

You can save a macro again to the Personal Macro Workbook at any time by choosing the **P**ersonal Macro Workbook option button in the **R**ecord New Macro dialog box.

Close the workbook and do not save any changes.

Using a Shortcut Key to Execute a Macro

Excel allows you to assign a shortcut key to execute a macro. You can then use a combination of keys to execute the macro rather than select the macro name from the **M**acro command on the **T**ools menu. The shortcut key can be either a lowercase or uppercase letter. If you use a lowercase letter, you execute the macro by pressing down the CTRL key and then the letter. If the macro is assigned to a capital letter, you must press down the CTRL plus the SHIFT keys and then the letter.

As noted earlier in this book, Excel has numerous keyboard shortcut keys that are used to execute commands. For example, you can press the CTRL key and the letter "c" to execute the **C**opy command on the **E**dit menu. Thus, you should not assign a macro to the lowercase letter "c." If you want to assign a macro to the letter "c," make sure you use an uppercase "C." The best rule to follow is: Always assign a macro to a shortcut key that is a capital letter.

Suppose you want to assign the CHART macro to the uppercase letter "C."

Open	the CHARTMAC.XLS workbook
Choose	**T**ools
Choose	**M**acro
Click	CHART in the **M**acro Name/Reference list box
Click	the **O**ptions command button

The Macro Options dialog box appears. Your screen should look like Figure 8-7.

Introduction to Macros

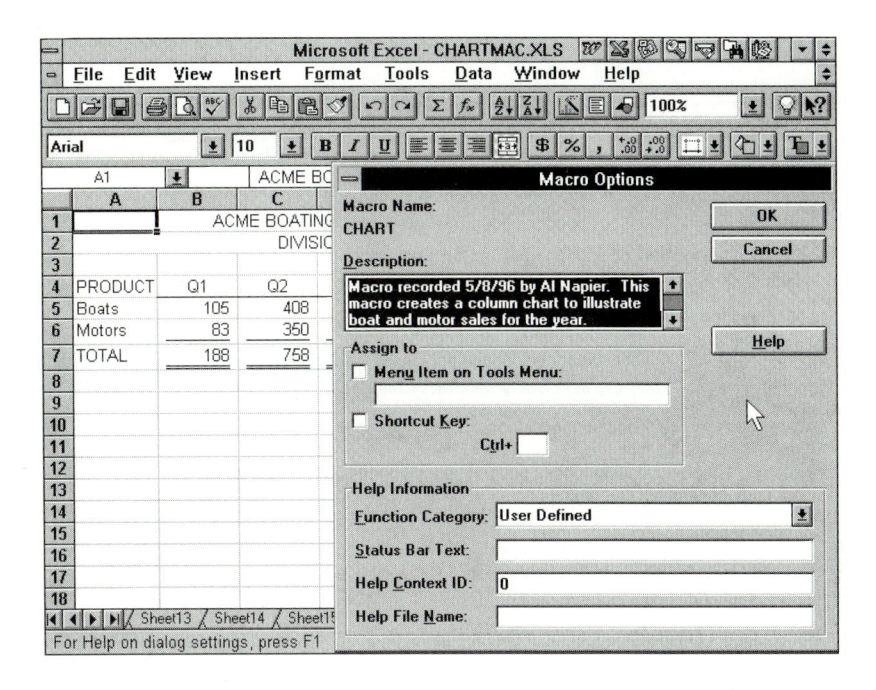

Figure 8-7

To assign the macro to a shortcut key:

Click	the Shortcut **K**ey check box to insert an X
Click	the Ctrl+ text box
Type	an uppercase C
Click	the OK command button
Click	the Close command button

To execute the macro using the shortcut key method:

Click	the Division 1 tab
Press	CTRL + SHIFT + C

The CHART macro executes, and a column chart is created.

> Similarly, you can assign a macro to the **T**ools menu. Open the workbook containing the macro. Choose the **M**acro command on the **T**ools menu. Select the desired macro name in the **M**acro Name/Reference list box. Click the **O**ptions command button to display the Macro Options dialog box. Click in the Men**u** Item on Tools Menu check box to insert an X. In the text box below the check box, type the text to be displayed on the **T**ools menu. Then click the OK command button and then the Close command button. When you click the **T**ools menu, the descriptive text for the macro appears at the bottom of the menu commands. When you click the descriptive text for the macro, the macro is executed.

Close the workbook and do not save any changes.

For additional information about macros, see your Excel Visual Basic *User's Guide*.

Summary

A macro is a set of instructions used to automatically execute a series of Excel commands. This capability allows you to save time when you complete repetitive processes. Excel uses the Visual Basic programming language to create macros. Excel allows you to create macros in the same workbook on which the macro will be used, in the Personal Macro Workbook, or in a separate workbook.

Exercise 1

INSTRUCTIONS: Define or explain the following:

1. Macro _____
   _____

2. Module _____
   _____

3. Visual Basic _____
   _____

4. Recording a macro _____
   _____

5. Location of a macro _____
   _____

6. Personal Macro Workbook _____
   _____

Exercise 2

INSTRUCTIONS: Circle T if the statement is true and F if the statement is false.

T   F   1. Macros are useful tools that automate repetitive procedures.

T   F   2. You can save a macro only on a module sheet in the workbook in which it was written or recorded.

T   F   3. To execute a macro named AVALON, you must hold down the CTRL key and type the letter A.

T   F   4. You cannot specify which macros reside in the Personal Macro Workbook.

T   F   5. You can execute a macro by selecting the macro name from the list in the Macro Name/Reference list box.

Introduction to Macros

Exercise 3

INSTRUCTIONS:

1. Open the NATSALES.XLS workbook. It can be found on the diskette located at the back of this book.
2. Record a macro that will print only the worksheet data with the following settings:

    Centered vertically and horizontally on the page

    No header

    No gridlines
3. Name the macro PRINTMAC and create a description of your own choice.
4. The macro should be placed in a module sheet in the NATSALES.XLS workbook.
5. Save the workbook in a file using the name E08EX03.
6. Print the module sheet.
7. Close the workbook.

Exercise 4

INSTRUCTIONS:

1. Open the E07EX03.XLS workbook created in Chapter 7, Exercise 3.
2. Record a macro that sorts the list by state.
3. Create a name and description of your own choice for the macro.
4. Place the sort macro in a module sheet in the E07EX03.XLS workbook.
5. Save the workbook in a file using the name E08EX04.
6. Print the module sheet.
7. Close the workbook.

Integrating Word and Excel Data

9

Objectives

In this chapter you will learn to:

→ Insert a copy of Excel worksheet data into a Word document
→ Embed Excel worksheet data in a Word document
→ Link Excel worksheet data to a Word document
→ Link an Excel chart to a Word document

Chapter Overview

This chapter discusses inserting a copy of data from an Excel workbook into a Word document using the insert file and copy/paste methods. Creating an embedded Excel worksheet object in a Word document using the Word Standard toolbar, the copy/paste method, and the drag-and-drop method are demonstrated. Linking Excel workbook data and a chart to a Word document is illustrated.

Inserting a Copy of Excel Worksheet Data into a Word Document

Sharing data between a Word document and an Excel workbook can increase flexibility and productivity. Suppose you need to distribute information summarized in an Excel worksheet together with an analysis or instructions regarding the information. You can create an interoffice memo containing the analysis or instructions and attach a copy of the Excel worksheet. This entails distributing two pages. Alternatively, you can easily place a *copy* of the Excel worksheet data in your memo, thereby eliminating the need to copy and attach an additional page.

- You can insert a copy of Excel worksheet data into a Word document with the **File** command on the **Insert** menu. You can copy the Excel worksheet data to the Clipboard and then paste the data into the Word document with the **Copy** and **Paste** commands on the **Edit** menu.

- You can also copy the Excel worksheet data to the Clipboard and then paste the data into the Word document using the Copy and Paste buttons on the Standard toolbar.

Using these methods, the Excel worksheet data is inserted in the Word document as a Word table. You can then edit and format the table using the commands on the **Table** menu and the formatting buttons on the toolbars.

Create the interoffice memo in Figure 9-1. Use the MEMO1 template. Add a blank line after the last paragraph.

```
Memorandum

DATE:    February 19, 1996

TO:      All Regional Managers

FROM:    D. H. Rice
         National Sales Manager

RE:      Sales Information for Week Beginning
         February 11

CC:      J. B. Doolin
         R. L. Whitte

Congratulations to all the sales representatives
in the South Region!

The weekly sales figures by region are displayed
below. These sales figures indicate the South
Region continues to lead other regions in total
sales effort. Notice that Thursday's sales were
well above projections. Because of these
outstanding results, Nations Lumber Company will
continue the "Spring into '96" sales campaign
until further notice.
```

Figure 9-1

Save the document in a file using the name MEMO.

Integrating Word and Excel Data

Inserting an Excel File into a Word Document

One way to place a copy of Excel worksheet data in a Word document is to insert the Excel worksheet into the Word document. Verify that MEMO.DOC is active and the insertion point is at the bottom of the document. You now want to insert a copy of the Feb 11 worksheet in the NATSALES.XLS Excel workbook at the end of the MEMO.DOC document. The NATSALES.XLS workbook can be found on the diskette at the back of this book.

To insert the Excel worksheet:

| **Choose** | Insert |
| **Choose** | File |

The File dialog box appears. Switch to the appropriate disk drive and directory. The top part of your screen should look similar to Figure 9-2.

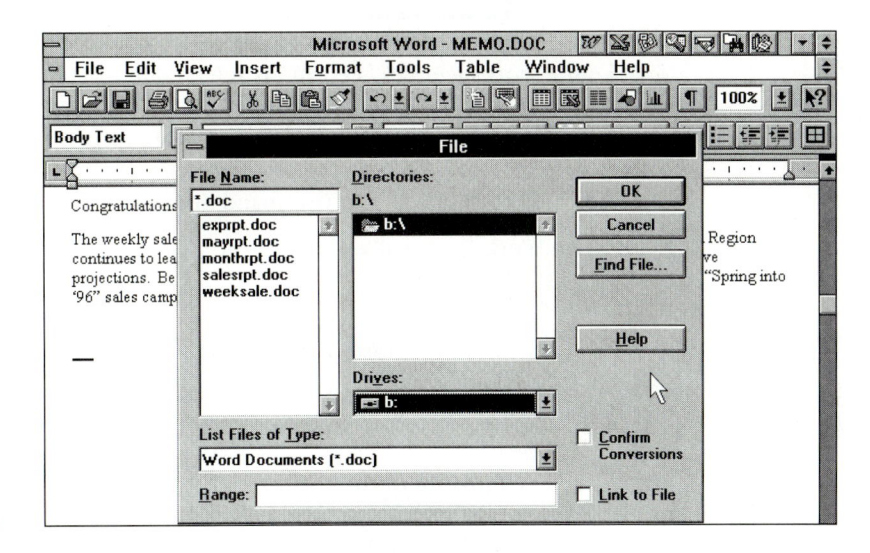

Figure 9-2

Notice that the File **N**ame list box contains only .DOC files created in Word. You will need to change the list to include all files, including .XLS files created in Excel.

To select the NATSALES.XLS file:

Verify	the appropriate directory is open
Click	the down arrow on the List Files of **T**ype drop-down list box
Click	All Files (*.*)
Double-click	NATSALES.XLS in the File **N**ame list box (scroll to view this file name, if necessary)

The Open Workbook dialog box appears. The top part of your screen should look like Figure 9-3.

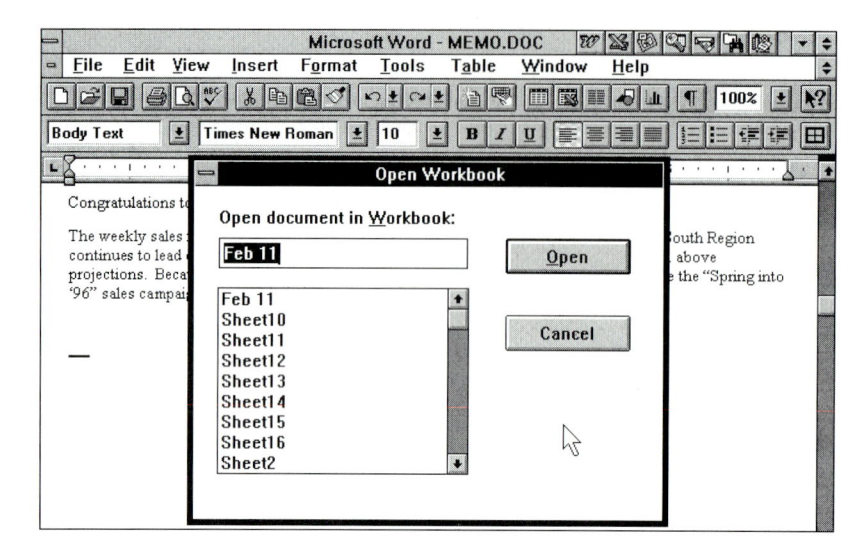

Figure 9-3

Notice the worksheet tab "Feb 11" is selected in the Open Document in **W**orkbook text box. This is the first worksheet tab in the workbook.

To open this worksheet:

Click   the **O**pen command button

The Open Worksheet dialog box appears. The top part of your screen should look like Figure 9-4.

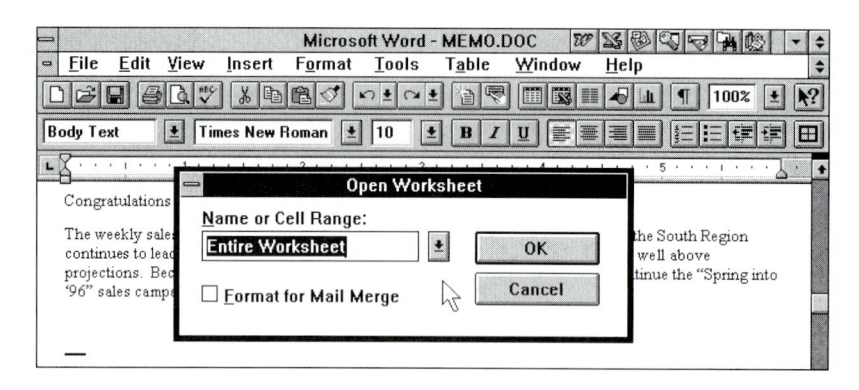

Figure 9-4

Notice that "Entire Worksheet" is selected in the **N**ame or Cell Range text box.

To insert the entire worksheet:

Click   the OK command button

The Feb 11 worksheet in the NATSALES.XLS workbook is inserted in the MEMO.DOC document as a Word table. After you have scrolled, your screen should look similar to Figure 9-5.

You can now format the table. You want to merge the cells in rows 1-4, center-align the text in rows 1-4, and remove the extra hard returns in rows 1-4.

To format the table:

Select   Rows 1-4

Choose   Table

Integrating Word and Excel Data

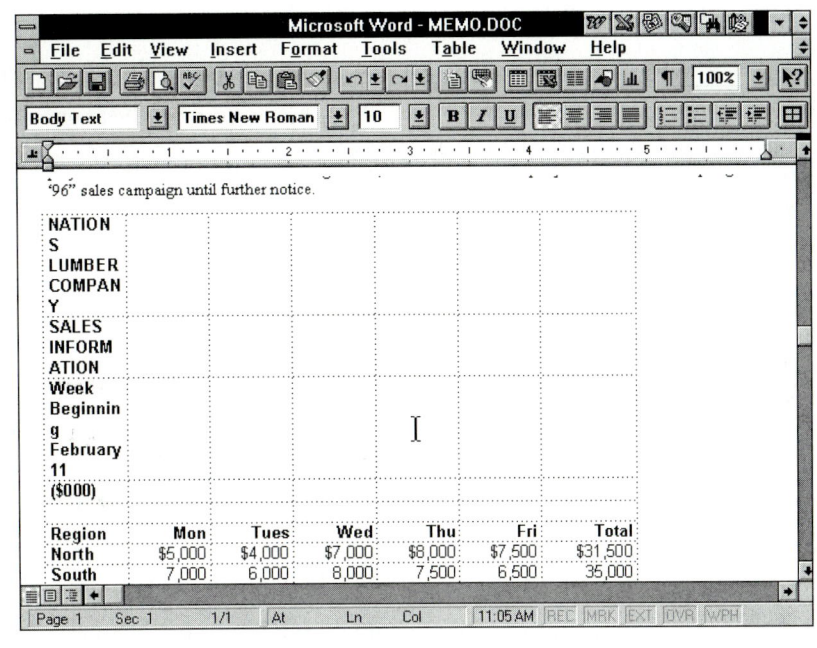

Figure 9-5

Choose	**Merge Cells**
Click	the Center button on the Formatting toolbar
Deselect	rows 1-4
Delete	the extra hard returns at the end of each line in rows 1-4 (display nonprinting characters, if necessary)

Print Preview the document. Notice that the Word table grid does not display or print. For more information on adding a border grid that will display and print, see Word unit Chapter 11 or your Word *User's Guide*. Close Print Preview. You now want to return the MEMO.DOC document to its original form.

To delete the table:

Select	all the rows of the table
Choose	**Table**
Choose	**Delete Rows**

The MEMO.DOC document returns to its original form.

Copying an Excel File to a Word Document

An alternate method of inserting a copy of Excel worksheet data into a Word document is to copy the data to the Clipboard, switch to the Word application, and then paste the data into the Word document.

Verify that MEMO.DOC is active. Open the Excel application, if necessary, and open the NATSALES.XLS workbook. The Feb 11 worksheet tab should be selected.

To copy the worksheet data:

Select	the range A1:G11
Click	the Copy button on the Standard toolbar

> You can switch to another application by clicking the appropriate button on the MOM toolbar. You can also switch between application windows by pressing `ALT`+`TAB`, by choosing the **S**witch To command on the Control menu, or by pressing `CTRL`+`ESC`.

Switch	to the Word application window
Verify	the insertion point is at the bottom of the document
Click	the Paste button on the Standard toolbar

The Excel worksheet data is pasted into the MEMO.DOC document as a Word table. Notice that the formatting for rows 1-4 is also pasted. Suppose you now want to center the table.

To center the table:

Move	the insertion point to any cell in the table (Do not select a cell.)
Choose	Table
Choose	Cell Height and **W**idth
Click	the **R**ow tab (if necessary)
Click	the Center option button in the Alignment group box
Click	the OK command button

The table is centered between the left and right margins.

Save the document in a file using the name MEMO1. Close the document.

Embedding Excel Worksheet Data in a Word Document

Sometimes you want to share data between Excel and Word but still be able to edit the data with the Excel menus and toolbars. You can *embed* an Excel worksheet object in a Word document. Embedding leaves the data in its original Excel format and the data must be edited with Excel features.

When you embed or link data between Excel and Word, the Excel worksheet is usually the *source* or *server*. The Word document is usually the *destination* or *client*. When you save a destination file with an embedded object, the source file that contains all the information needed to print, display, and edit the embedded object is also saved with the destination file. You may want to link rather than embed the Excel data to save disk space. Linking data files between Word and Excel is discussed later in this chapter.

> You can embed Excel worksheet data in a Word document with the **O**bject command on the **I**nsert menu. You can also use the Paste **S**pecial command on the **E**dit menu.

> You can embed Excel worksheet data in a Word document with the Insert Microsoft Excel Worksheet button on the Standard toolbar. You can also use drag-and-drop to embed Excel worksheet data by dragging the selected data across application boundaries from the Excel application window into the Word application window.

Suppose you want to embed the Feb 11 worksheet data in the NATSALES.XLS workbook in the MEMO.DOC document. First, open the original MEMO.DOC document you created earlier in this chapter.

Using the Word Standard Toolbar to Embed Excel Worksheet Data

To create an embedded Excel worksheet object:

Move	the insertion point to the bottom of the document

Integrating Word and Excel Data

Click	the Insert Microsoft Excel Worksheet button on the Standard toolbar
Move	the mouse pointer to the top-left box on the worksheet grid
Press and hold	the mouse button
Drag	down to select 4 rows and across to select 3 columns
Release	the mouse button

An Excel worksheet object is inserted in the MEMO.DOC document. The top part of your screen should look like Figure 9-6.

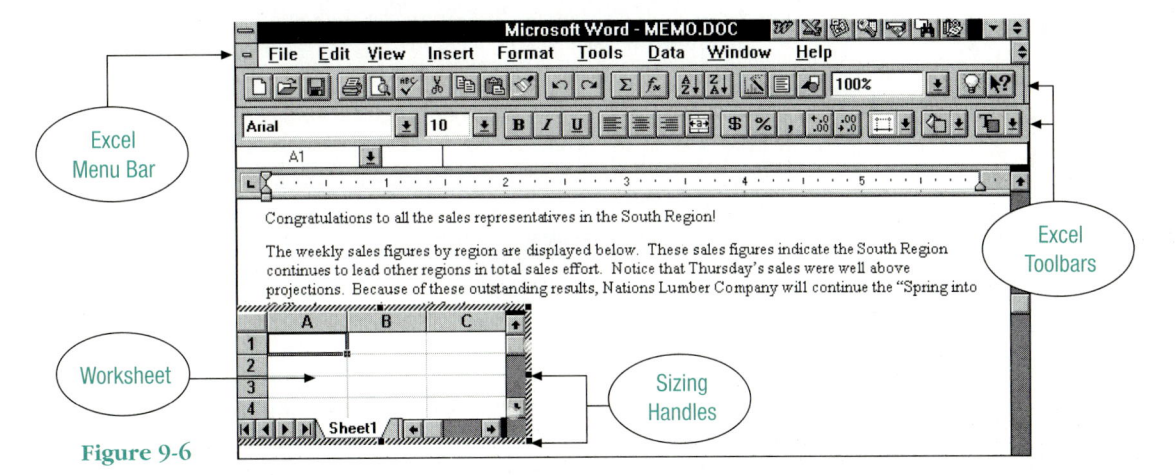

Figure 9-6

Notice the sizing handles on the boundaries of the object. Also notice that the Excel menu bar and toolbars are displayed. For the following exercise, enter and format only a portion of the data.

You can use the sizing handles to increase the size of the worksheet object. When the mouse pointer is placed on a sizing handle it changes shape to become a black, double-headed arrow. You can drag the boundary of the object with the mouse pointer to resize the object.

To display columns A:G in the worksheet object:

Move	the mouse pointer to the middle sizing handle on the right boundary of the worksheet object
Press and hold	the mouse button
Drag	the object boundary to the right 4 columns
Release	the mouse button

Columns A:G are displayed. You can now enter the worksheet headings.

To enter and format the headings:

Enter	NATIONS LUMBER COMPANY in cell A1
Enter	SALES INFORMATION in cell A2
Enter	Week Beginning February 11 in cell A3

Enter	`'($000)` in cell A4
Select	the range of cells A1:A4
Click	the Bold **B** button on the Formatting toolbar
Select	the range of cells A1:G4
Click	the Center Across Columns button on the Formatting toolbar

Deselect the worksheet object by double-clicking anywhere in the MEMO.DOC document outside the object. The top part of your screen should look like Figure 9-7.

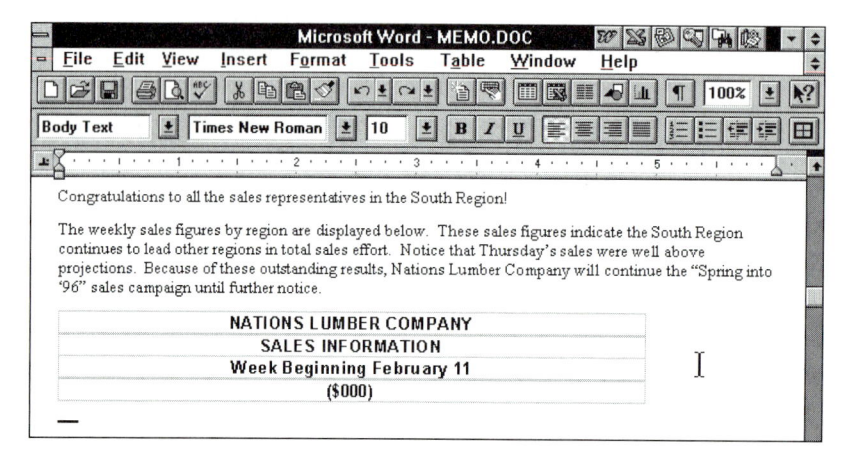

Figure 9-7

You cannot edit the worksheet object using Word editing features. To edit the object, you must redisplay the Excel menu bar, toolbars, and worksheet grid. Clicking the object once selects it. Double-clicking the object redisplays the Excel worksheet grid, menu bar, and toolbars.

To display the Excel worksheet grid, menu bar, and toolbars:

Double-click	the worksheet object

The Excel worksheet grid, menu bar, and toolbars are displayed. Now you can edit the object.

To edit the worksheet object:

Move	the insertion point to the middle sizing handle on the bottom boundary of the worksheet object
Press and hold	the mouse button
Drag	downward to display rows 1–12
Release	the mouse button
Select	the range of cells A6:G6
Enter	`Region` in A6
Enter	`Mon` in B6
Enter	`Tues` in C6
Enter	`Wed` in D6
Enter	`Thur` in E6

Integrating Word and Excel Data

Enter	`Fri` in F6
Enter	`Total` in G6
Click	the Bold **B** button on the Formatting toolbar
Select	the range B6:G6
Click	the Align Right button on the Formatting toolbar

Deselect the range by clicking outside the range but in the worksheet area. Notice the Excel worksheet object includes gridlines. Suppose you do not want to print the gridlines. You must turn off the display of the gridlines before you deselect the Excel object and return to the Word document window.

To display the Options dialog box:

Choose	**T**ools
Choose	**O**ptions

The Options dialog box appears. Click the View tab, if necessary.

To turn off the display of gridlines:

Click	the **G**ridlines check box in the Window Options group box to remove the X
Click	the OK command button

Double-click outside the object to deselect it. Print Preview the document. The gridlines do not display or print. Close Print Preview.

Suppose you now want to delete the partially completed worksheet object.

> You can delete a selected object with the Cle**a**r command on the **E**dit menu.

You can also delete a selected object by pressing the DELETE key.

To delete the worksheet object:

Click	the worksheet object to select it
Press	(DELETE)

The MEMO.DOC returns to its original form.

Using the Paste Special Command to Embed Excel Worksheet Data

> An alternate method of embedding Excel worksheet data is to copy the data to the Clipboard, switch to the Word application, and paste the data into a Word document using the Paste **S**pecial command on the **E**dit menu.

Verify that MEMO.DOC is displayed. Switch to the Excel application and verify that NATSALES.XLS is open or, open the Excel application, if necessary, and open the NATSALES.XLS file. The Feb 11 sheet tab should be selected.

To copy the worksheet data:

Select	the range A1:G11 (if necessary)
Click	the Copy button on the Standard toolbar

Switch to the Word application window and move the insertion point to the bottom of the document, if necessary.

To display the Paste Special dialog box:

Choose   Edit

Choose   Paste **S**pecial

The Paste Special dialog box appears. The top part of your screen should look like Figure 9-8.

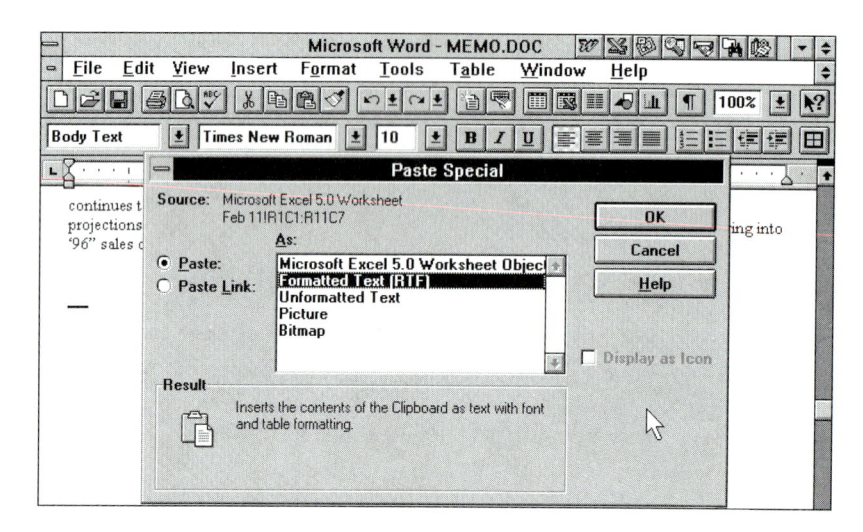

Figure 9-8

Notice the five data types listed in the **As** list box.

Data Type	Description
Microsoft Excel 5.0 Worksheet Object	Embeds Excel worksheet data
Formatted text (RTF)	Pastes data and formats into a Word table
Unformatted text	Pastes values and text separated by tab characters
Picture	Embeds a graphic image that can be sized or edited and requires less space than a bitmap graphic
Bitmap	Embeds a bitmap graphic that cannot effectively be sized or scaled

For more information on these five data types, see your Word or Excel *User's Guide*.

> The **D**isplay as Icon check box in the Paste Special dialog box allows you to insert an icon representing the worksheet data. Double-clicking on the icon in the destination document displays the worksheet data.

To embed the Excel worksheet data:

Click   the **P**aste option button (if necessary)

Click   Microsoft Excel 5.0 Worksheet Object in the **As** list box

Click   the OK command button

The Excel worksheet data is embedded in the MEMO.DOC document. Your screen should look like Figure 9-9.

Integrating Word and Excel Data

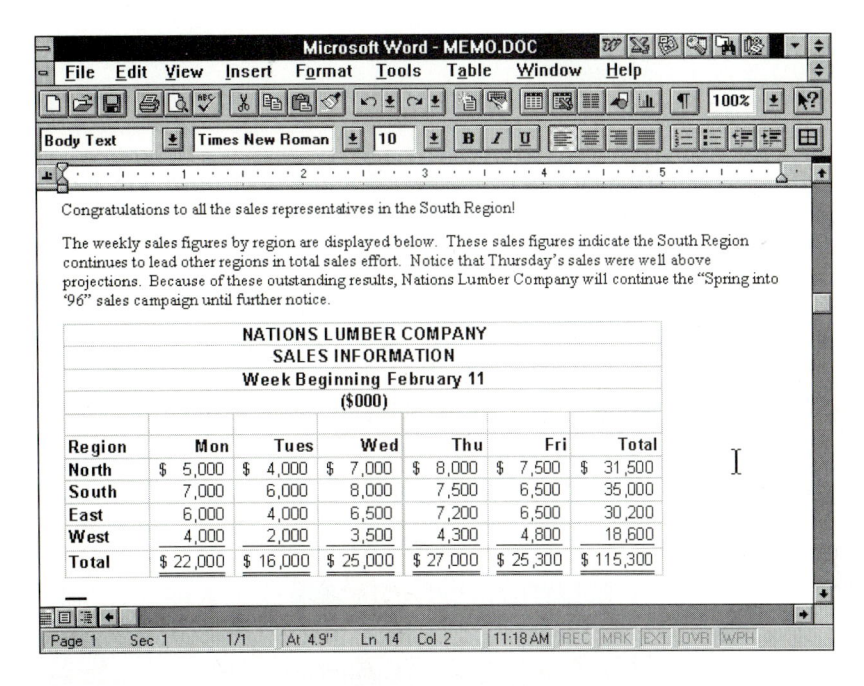

Figure 9-9

Print preview the document. Notice the gridlines that display will also print. *Note:* To avoid printing the gridlines, you must turn off the display of gridlines in the Excel worksheet before you copy the worksheet data to the Clipboard. Close Print Preview.

You can edit the embedded worksheet object by first displaying the Excel menu bar, toolbars, and worksheet grid. When you edit an embedded object, you are changing the data in the destination file only. You are not changing the data in the source file.

You can now edit the worksheet object in the MEMO.DOC document (the destination file) and see that no changes are made to the data in the Feb 11 worksheet in the NATSALES.XLS workbook (the source file).

To edit the worksheet object:

Double-click	the worksheet object
Turn off	display of gridlines
Click	on cell B7
Enter	4000
Double-click	outside the worksheet object

The gridlines are removed and the data in the worksheet object have changed. Switch to the Excel application window and observe that the gridlines are displayed and there is no change to the data.

Switch to the Word application window. Save the document in a file using the name MEMO2. Close the document.

Using Drag-and-Drop to Embed Excel Worksheet Data

You can also use the drag-and-drop method to embed Excel worksheet data in a Word document.

First, open the original MEMO.DOC document created earlier in this chapter. Then restore the Word application and file window to a smaller window.

If the Excel application and NATSALES.XLS workbook are open, restore their window to a smaller window. If the Excel application is not open, open it and open the NATSALES.XLS workbook. Then restore the application and file window to a smaller window.

Minimize all other application windows. Then size and move the Word and Excel application windows until your screen resembles Figure 9-10.

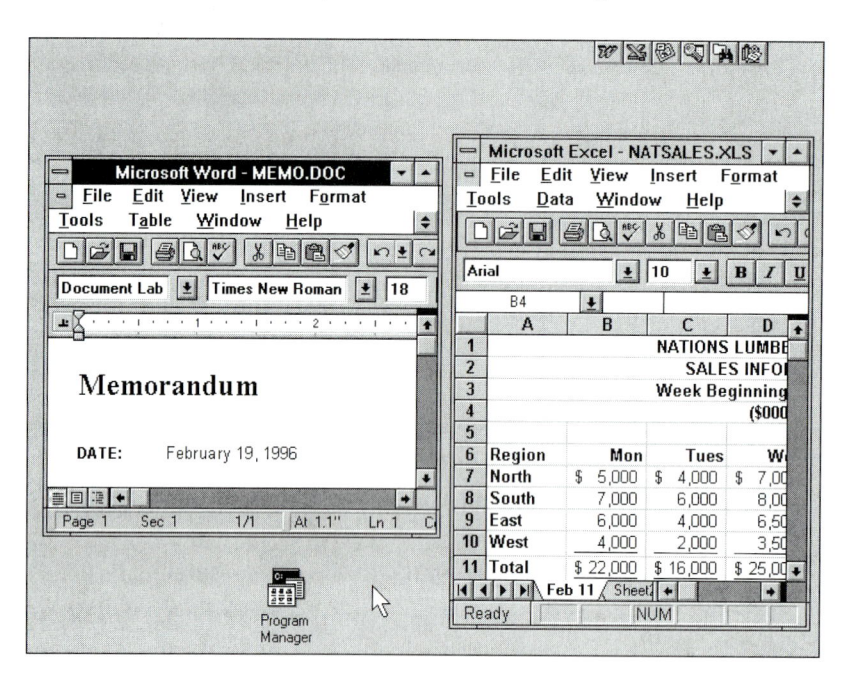

Figure 9-10

Activate the Word application window, if necessary, and scroll to see the bottom of the document. Activate the Excel application window.

To copy the worksheet data to the Clipboard:

Turn off	display of the gridlines
Select	the range of cells A1:G11 (if necessary)
Move	the mouse pointer to a boundary of the selected range
Press and hold	the mouse button
Press	CTRL
Drag	the selected range to the left across the Excel application window boundary and into the Word application window
Verify	the insertion point is at the left margin of the blank line above the end-of-file marker
Release	the mouse button
Release	CTRL

You can display two application windows on the desktop using the MOM toolbar. Open the first application. Then press and hold the SHIFT key and click on the second application's button on the MOM toolbar. The two application windows will be tiled.

Integrating Word and Excel Data

The Excel worksheet data is embedded in the MEMO.DOC document. *Note:* Remember, if you do not want to print gridlines in the Word document, you must turn off the display of gridlines in the NATSALES.XLS workbook before embedding the data.

Maximize the Excel application window. Switch to the Word application window and maximize it. Close the MEMO.DOC document without saving any changes.

Linking Excel Worksheet Data to a Word Document

Excel and Word can also share data by linking. When you link data between an Excel workbook and a Word document, the destination file contains only a reference or pointer to the source file. The data exist only in the source file. When you edit linked data, you actually open the source application and file. All editing must be done in the source file. When you change data in the source file, the representation of the data in the destination file is updated.

You should link data between files when you do not need a copy of the data in the destination file. While this saves disk space when saving the destination file, the source file must be available at all times to provide the data for the destination file. If you move or rename the source file, you will break the link to the destination file. For more information on breaking, modifying, and reestablishing links, see your Word or Excel *User's Guide*.

Open the original MEMO.DOC document you created earlier in this chapter. Switch to the Excel application window and verify that the NATSALES.XLS workbook is open. If necessary, open the Excel application and the NATSALES.XLS file. The Feb 11 worksheet tab should be selected.

To copy the worksheet data:

Turn off	display of gridlines (if necessary)
Select	the range A1:G11 (if necessary)
Click	the Copy button on the Standard toolbar

Switch to the Word application window and move the insertion point to the bottom of the document.

To link the worksheet data:

Choose	**E**dit
Choose	Paste **S**pecial
Click	the Paste **L**ink option button
Click	Microsoft Excel 5.0 Worksheet Object in the **A**s list box
Click	the OK command button

The Excel worksheet object appears in the MEMO.DOC document.

This object is a reference or pointer to the NATSALES.XLS source file. The data do not exist in the MEMO.DOC document and cannot be edited in the MEMO.DOC document. Switch to the Excel application window and close the application and the NATSALES.XLS workbook. Do not save any changes.

Suppose you now want to edit data to change the South region sales for Monday to $10,000.

To edit the data:

Double-click   the worksheet object

The Excel application and NATSALES.XLS workbook open. The Feb 11 worksheet should be selected. Maximize the workbook, if necessary.

To edit the data:

Turn off	display of the gridlines (if necessary)
Click	on cell B8
Enter	10000
Click	the Save button on the Standard toolbar

Notice the data in the worksheet have changed. Close the Excel application and the NATSALES.XLS workbook. Observe the changes to Monday sales for the South region in the worksheet object in the MEMO.DOC document. Your screen should look like Figure 9-11.

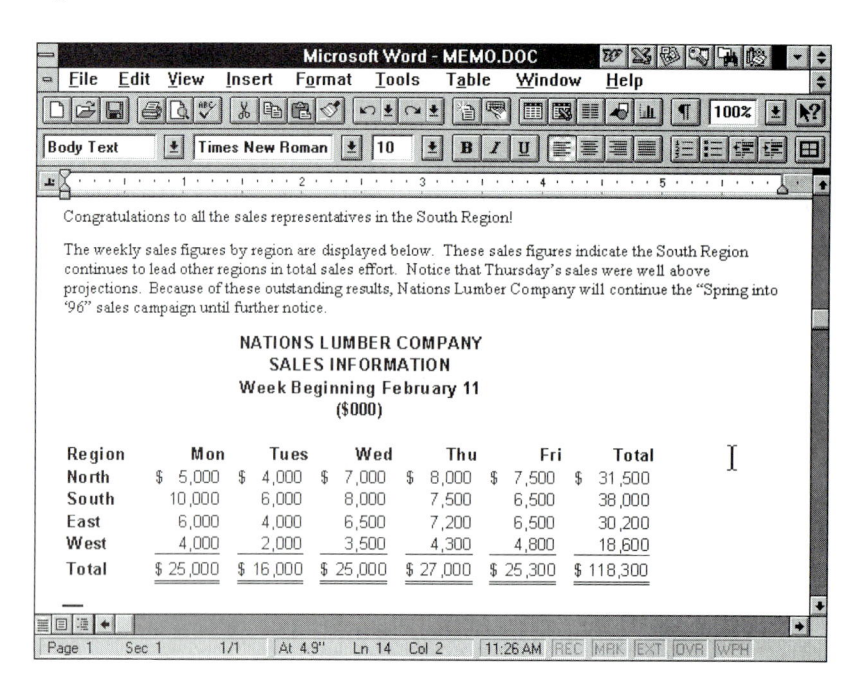

Figure 9-11

Changing the data in a source file automatically changes the data in the linked worksheet object in the destination file. By default, links are updated automatically. For more information on establishing manual updating of links, see your Word or Excel *User's Guide*.

Integrating Word and Excel Data 163

> You can link and embed Excel charts in a Word document. Copy the chart to the Clipboard, choose the Paste Special command on the Edit menu, click the Paste or Paste Link option button, and click Microsoft 5.0 Chart Object in the As list box. You can also use the drag-and-drop method to embed an Excel chart in a Word document.

Save the document in a file using the name MEMO3. Leave the document open for the next section.

Linking an Excel Chart to a Word Document

You can also link Excel charts to a Word document. Move the insertion point to the bottom of the document, if necessary, and press the ENTER key twice to insert two blank lines. Suppose you want to add the embedded chart in the NATSALES.XLS workbook to the MEMO3.DOC. Open the Excel application and the NATSALES.XLS workbook. Verify that the Feb 11 worksheet tab is selected. Scroll to view the embedded chart. You will copy the chart to the Clipboard and then Paste Link the chart into the Word document.

To copy the embedded chart to the Clipboard:

| **Click** | the embedded chart to select it |
| **Click** | the Copy button on the Standard toolbar |

Switch to the Word application. Verify that the insertion point is at the bottom of the document.

To link the chart data:

Choose	Edit
Choose	Paste Special
Click	the Paste Link option button
Verify	Microsoft Excel 5.0 Chart Object is selected in the As list box
Click	the OK command button

The embedded chart is inserted into the MEMO3.DOC as a linked object. To select the chart object, click once on the object. To deselect the chart object, click in the document outside the object.

Because the chart object is linked to the NATSALES.XLS workbook, any changes made to the chart data or the chart in the NATSALES.XLS workbook are automatically made to the chart in the MEMO3.DOC document. You can edit the chart from Word by double-clicking on the chart object to open or switch to the Excel application and the NATSALES.XLS workbook.

Sizing and Moving an Object in Word

You can size a selected object in Word by moving the mouse pointer to a sizing handle and dragging the sizing handle in the desired direction.

To size the chart object:

Select   the chart object

Move   the insertion point to the middle sizing handle on the bottom boundary of the frame

The mouse pointer changes shape to become a black, double-headed arrow.

Drag   the sizing handle downward approximately 1"

The size of the chart object changes. To return the object to its original size, click the Undo button on the Standard toolbar.

You can move a selected object using the drag-and drop method. You also can reposition a selected object with the Align Left, Center, and Align Right buttons on the Formatting toolbar.

However, it is sometimes easier to move an object in Word by first inserting a **frame** around the object and then moving the frame. A frame is a box or container that you can place around text, tables, or objects to easily reposition them in a Word document. When you insert a frame around an object, Word switches the display of the document to Page Layout view.

To insert a frame around the chart object:

Select   the chart object (if necessary)

Choose   Insert

Choose   Frame

Click   the **Yes** command button to display the document in Page Layout view

A frame is placed around the object.

You can reposition the chart object on the document by dragging the frame with the mouse pointer or by setting the position of the frame with the **Frame** command on the Format menu.

To reposition the chart object:

Move   the mouse pointer to the left boundary of the frame

The mouse pointer changes shape to add two double-headed arrows.

To continue:

Press and hold   the mouse button

Drag   the chart object approximately 2" to the right

Release   the mouse button

The chart object is repositioned. Deselect the chart object.

Deleting an Object in a Word Document

You can easily delete an object that has been inserted into a Word document.

To delete the chart object:

Integrating Word and Excel Data

Select   the chart object

Press   ⌈DELETE⌉

The chart object is deleted from the MEMO3.DOC document.

Close the document without saving any changes. Close the Word and Excel applications.

> Excel is usually the source application and Word is usually the destination application when sharing data between Excel and Word. Word can, however, be the source application and Excel can be the destination application. You can embed and link Word text into an Excel worksheet. For example, you can paste Word text such as a date into the Excel formula bar; or, you can paste link long text from a Word document into a cell on a worksheet or into a text box on a worksheet. For more information on embedding or linking text from a Word document to a worksheet, see your Word or Excel *User's Guide*.

Summary

You can insert an Excel file into a Word document. You can also copy and paste Excel worksheet data into a Word document. With both of these methods, the worksheet data pastes into a Word table. You can edit these data with commands on the T**a**ble menu or buttons on the toolbars.

You can share data between Word and Excel by embedding the data or by linking the data. When you embed data, you are placing a copy of the data in the destination file. When you link data, you are placing a representation of the data in the destination file, but the data exist only in the source file. Data that have been copied or linked must be edited in the source application.

Pasting, Embedding, and Linking		
	What does it do?	**When should I do it?**
Paste	Places an independent copy of the source data into the current file. No connection exists between the copy and the original. If copied to a new application, the data may alter in form to fit the new application. Modifications to the copied data are made using the tools of the new application.	If you need a "snapshot" of the copied data. That is, you do not foresee changing the data. In addition, you want the data in the format of the new application. For example, if you copy a range in Excel and paste it into Word, it will be pasted as a Word table.
Embed	Places a copy of the source data into the current file. It is not linked to the original data, that is, changes to the original data will not affect the copy or vice versa. However, these data, unlike pasted data, do "remember" where they came from. The data look the same as they did in the original application and changes to the data are made using the tools of the original application. To edit the data, double-click on the embedded object.	If you want to be able to modify the data using the tools of the original application. For example, double-clicking an Excel range embedded in a Word document will change the Word menus and toolbars to the Excel menus and toolbars, giving you access to all Excel commands and shortcuts as you modify your data. Unlike linked files (see below) a file with embedded data contains the data and can be transferred to any computer with both the "copied from" and "copied to" applications.
Link	Places a representation in the current application that notes the source application and file of the linked data. The linked data are displayed in the new, or *destination*, application but still "reside" in the original, or *source*, application. Any changes made to the original data are reflected in the linked file. If the linked file is open, the changes are made immediately; if the file is closed, the changes will be made when it is next opened. In the destination application, the data are displayed in their original form. The data can be modified from the destination application by double-clicking on the linked object. The source application and file are opened and displayed. Any changes made should be saved before closing the source file.	If you would like the data in the destination application to automatically reflect changes made in the source application. In addition, since the destination file does not actually contain the data (but, rather, just a reference to it), the file's size is smaller than if the data had been embedded.

Integrating Word and Excel Data

Exercise 1

INSTRUCTIONS: Define or explain the following:

1. Embed _____
   _____

2. Source or server _____
   _____

3. Destination or client _____
   _____

4. Paste Special command _____
   _____

5. Link _____
   _____

6. Paste _____
   _____

Exercise 2

INSTRUCTIONS: Circle T if the statement is true and F if the statement is false.

T   F   1. When you embed an Excel worksheet object in a Word document, the data remain in their original Excel format and the data must be edited with Excel features.
T   F   2. When you paste data into an application, the data are linked to the original data.
T   F   3. If you want to be able to modify the data using the tools of the original application, you should embed the data.
T   F   4. If you would like the data in the destination application to automatically reflect changes made in the source application, you should paste the data.
T   F   5. If you need a "snapshot" of the copied data, you should link the data.
T   F   6. When you link data, any changes made to the original data are reflected in the linked file.

Exercise 3

INSTRUCTIONS:

1. Create the following interoffice memo. Use the MEMO1 template. Add a blank line after the last paragraph. Save the document in a file using the name E09E03A.

2. Open the Excel application and open the E03EX03.XLS workbook created in Chapter 3, Exercise 3.

> **Memorandum**
>
> DATE: current date
>
> TO: All Sales Managers
>
> FROM: Steve White
>   Regional Sales Manager
>
> RE: Weekly Sales Report
>
> CC: Jim Walker
>   Matthew Gray
>
> The weekly sales figures by region are displayed below. I was very pleased with the figures. They exceeded the sales projections. Keep up the good work!

3. Copy the Worksheet Model worksheet data in the range A1:G9 and paste the data below the last paragraph of the E09E03A.DOC document.
4. Save the document in a file using the name E09E03B.
5. Print the document.
6. Close the document.
7. Open the original E09E03A.DOC document.
8. Use the Paste Special command on the Edit menu to embed the E03EX03.XLS workbook to the bottom of the document.
9. Edit the worksheet object so the gridlines are turned off and center the column headings in cells B4:F4.
10. Save the document in a file using the name E09E03C.
11. Print the document.
12. Close the document.

Exercise 4

INSTRUCTIONS:

1. Open the original E09E03A.DOC document created in Exercise 3.
2. Link the worksheet data in the E03EX03.XLS workbook below the last paragraph of the document.
3. Close the E03EX03.XLS workbook and the Excel application. Do not save any changes.
4. Edit the worksheet object so the gridlines are turned off, center the column headings in cells B4:F4, and change the sales figures for the North Region to 1,000 for Mon, 800 for Tues, 1,300 for Wed, 1,025 for Thurs, and 1,200 for Fri.
5. Save the workbook in a file using the name E09E04A. Close the Excel application.
6. Save the document in a file using the name E09E04B.
7. Print the document.
8. Close the Word application.

Business Simulation: Part One

CTI Business Simulation

Introduction

CTI, located in Cambridge, MA, is a division of Course Technology. CTI is a publisher of Information Systems products, such as the New Perspectives and Illustrated series of books for the college and university market.

CTI is organized into editorial teams with each team focusing on one major section of the information technology book market, as follows:

→ The Illustrated Team and New Perspectives Team each focus entirely on maximizing the performance of these two book series.

→ The Management Information Systems (MIS) Team focuses on introductory and upper-division courses in the Management Information Systems curriculum as well as texts on computer concepts addressing the impact of information technology on society.

→ The Applied Technology (AT) Team publishes highly technical materials on programming, networking, operating systems, office technology, and client/server systems development for the two-year, four-year, and career college Information Systems curriculums.

→ The Interactive Technology (IT) Team develops and markets technology products for alternative markets, such as retail and corporate.

The CTI editorial offices are located in Kendall Square, Cambridge, MA.

CTI publishes the New Perspectives, Illustrated, *and* Starts Here *series.*

B

Mastering and Using Microsoft Office Professional

Course Technology maintains a World Wide Web site for easy access to online services and other products for students and professors.

CTI also participates in a World Wide Web site for professors and students who can access the site for additional support, services, and other online products.

In order to provide optimal performance in the competitive information technology book markets, CTI uses Microsoft Office products on a daily basis to enhance productivity by effectively communicating information and ideas throughout the organization.

CTI letters, memos, and reports are prepared quickly and easily using Word 6.0.

Business Simulation: Part One

B

A managing editor easily can review production and sales reports prepared from data analyzed using Excel 5.0.

CTI executives and editorial teams use slide show presentations to anchor meetings where they discuss new ideas and the status of current projects.

B

Mastering and Using Microsoft Office Professional

Simulation Overview

You are employed as an editorial assistant for the MIS Team at CTI. In this simulation, you will be responsible for all the necessary paperwork related to the production of new books by the MIS Team. You report directly to the managing editor of your publishing team, DeVilla Williams. However, because all members of the MIS Team work closely together, you also provide support services for the product manager, Lisa Strite, and the production supervisor assigned to the MIS Team, Donna Whiting.

This simulation will begin with correspondence to an author of a new book requesting data necessary for production estimates.

In Part Two of the simulation, you will create a production budget and

The product manager must communicate clearly and efficiently with authors, other CTI departments, such as publishing operations and sales/marketing, as well as other members of the MIS Team. As a result, preparing effective letters and interoffice correspondence with Word 6.0 is an important daily activity.

Business Simulation: Part One

summary by compiling the data received from the author with additional data provided by the production supervisor on other books currently in production.

In Part Three of the Business Simulation, Lisa, the product manager, will be presenting the production costs budget and summary at a meeting of the MIS Team. You are responsible for creating a slide show presentation for the meeting. Then, you will compose an interoffice memo to members of the MIS Team advising them of the meeting.

Finally, in Part Four of the Business Simulation, you will access the CTI home page on the World Wide Web using the Netscape Web browser, take a brief tour of Web features, save information from a Web page, and then compose a letter to sales and marketing managers, which will include the saved information.

Communicating with authors and other companies often involves sending information by fax (short for facsimile copier).

B

Mastering and Using Microsoft Office Professional

Creating Effective Correspondence with Word 6.0

The MIS Team is preparing to publish a new book called *Mastering and Using Microsoft Office* authored by H. Albert Napier and Philip J. Judd. The product manager, Lisa, has asked you to compose a letter to the author asking for the status of the final manuscript.

Task One

Compose a letter to one of the authors, Dr. H. Albert Napier, asking for the following data, which will be used to estimate production costs:

→ Total number of pages

→ Total number of screen images

→ Number and description of photos

→ Estimated completion date

Business Simulation: Part One

Use the following address for the author:

Dr. H. Albert Napier
Jones Graduate School
Rice University
P. O. Box 1892
Houston, TX 77251

All letters are prepared in block style on the CTI letterhead. Included on the student disk is a SHELL.DOC document containing the letterhead.

1. Use the Arial, 12 point font for the letter text.
2. Send a copy of the letter to Lisa Strite.
3. Spell check the letter.
4. Prepare a Size 10 envelope and save it with the letter.
5. Print the envelope, letter, and letter copy.
6. Save the letter and envelope in the appropriate directory, as specified by your instructor, using the name SIM1.DOC.

Your letter should look similar to Figure Sim-1.

Figure Sim-1
A sample letter to Dr. Napier.

CTI Course Technology, Inc.
One Main Street
Cambridge, MA 02142

January 15, 1996

Dr. H. Albert Napier
Jones Graduate School
Rice University
P. O. Box 1892
Houston, TX 77251

Dear Dr. Napier:

Within the next two weeks, we will be completing the estimated production costs budget and production schedule for your book *Mastering and Using Microsoft Office*.

Please send or fax the following data no later than next Tuesday:

- Total number of pages
- Total number of screen images
- Number and description of photos
- Estimated completion date

Sincerely,

Samantha Smith
Editorial Assistant

cc: Lisa Strite

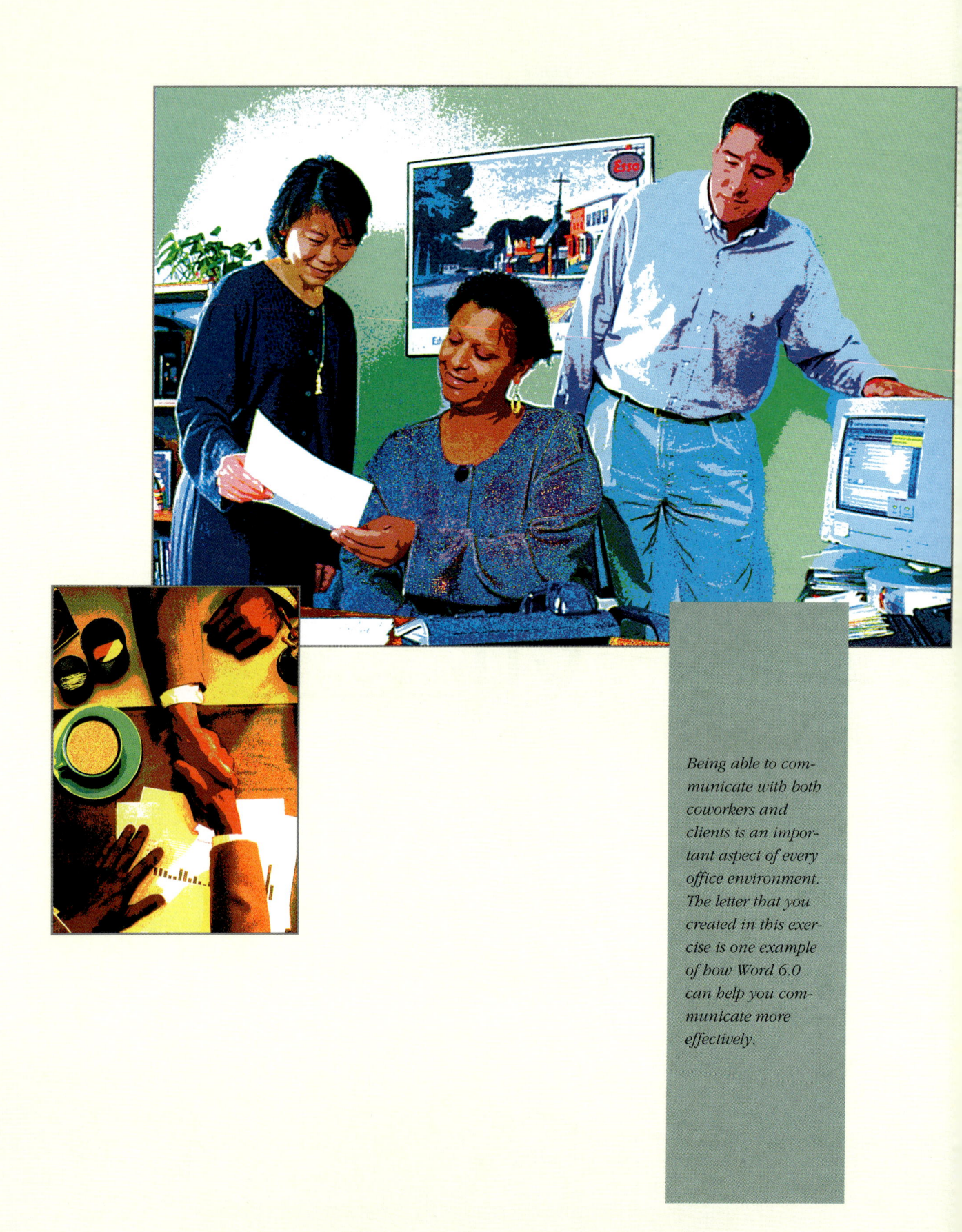

B

Mastering and Using Microsoft Office Professional

Being able to communicate with both coworkers and clients is an important aspect of every office environment. The letter that you created in this exercise is one example of how Word 6.0 can help you communicate more effectively.

Business Simulation: Part Two

Analyzing and Charting Data with Excel 5.0

Lisa Strite, product manager, has asked you to compile the production data from both Dr. Napier and Donna Whiting, production supervisor, into a production budget for the MIS Team.

The production supervisor must monitor the costs involved in producing a new book as well as establish a production schedule. Financial data such as production costs are effectively compiled, analyzed, and reported using Excel 5.0.

Figure Sim-2 illustrates a fax received from Dr. Napier that provides the data you requested on the new Napier & Judd book.

You will create the production cost budget using Excel 5.0. The total production costs for each book then should be linked to a

FAX

		Date	10/19/96
		Number of pages including cover sheet	1
TO:	Samantha Smith CTI	FROM:	Dr. H. Albert Napier Jones Graduate School Rice University P. O. Box 1892 Houston, TX 77251
Phone	(800) 648-7450	Phone	(713) 285-5389
Fax Phone	(617) 225-7976	Fax Phone	(713) 285-5251

CC:

REMARKS: ☐ Urgent ☒ For your review ☐ Reply ASAP ☐ Please Comment

The following is the data you requested in your recent letter.

Mastering and Using Microsoft Office book final manuscript :

Total number of pages	682
Total number of screen images	200
Number and description of photos (See attached descriptive list)	30
Estimated completion date	11/15/96

Figure Sim-2
A sample fax from Dr. Napier with the requested data.

Mastering and Using Microsoft Office Professional

worksheet that summarizes production costs by book. In addition to the production costs budget and summary, Lisa has requested charts showing the relationship of each production cost to total production costs and comparing the total production costs by book.

Task Two

1. Donna Whiting has given you the production department data for current books in progress. This data is in the COSTS.XLS workbook on the student disk. There are two worksheets with data in the workbook: a Summary worksheet and a Production Costs worksheet. You will complete both worksheets.

2. Add the title and number of pages of data for *Mastering and Using Microsoft Office* to row 10 in the Production Costs worksheet. Copy the formulas from row 9 to row 10.

3. Format the Production Costs worksheet titles, data, and column labels. Change the column widths as necessary.

Business Simulation: Part Two

4. Add the following data for the new book to the Summary worksheet:

   Publication Date   1/1/97
   Exact Full Title   Mastering and Using Microsoft Office
   Author(s)   Napier & Judd
   Colors   4
   Editorial Plant$ $20,000

5. Create a formula to link the total production costs for each book in the Production Costs worksheet to the Summary worksheet. Create formulas for the Total Plant$ column by book and summary totals for the Editorial, Prod., and Total Plant$ row.

6. Format the Summary worksheet titles, data, and column headings.

7. Change the column widths as necessary.

8. Edit the header and footer as appropriate.

9. Save the workbook in the appropriate directory as specified by your instructor using the name SIMCOSTS.XLS.

Mastering and Using Microsoft Office Professional

Task Three

1. Create an embedded pie chart on the Summary worksheet that illustrates the relationship of Total Plant$ for each book to the grand Total Plant$.

2. Edit the pie chart title to include a more descriptive multiple-line title.

3. Edit the chart plot area as necessary to accommodate the new chart title.

4. Edit the chart text and data series colors as necessary to make the chart more interesting.

5. Size the chart and place it attractively on the page below the data.

6. Save the workbook.

7. Print the Summary worksheet and embedded chart.

8. Print the Production Costs worksheet.

Business Simulation: Part Two

Figure Sim-3 A sample Summary worksheet.

Pub Date	Exact Full Title	Author(s)	Colors	Editorial Plant$	Prod. Plant$	Total Plant$
10/20/96	Microsoft Windows	Paulson	4	$17,500		
12/15/96	WordPerfect Presentation	Zane	1	$15,600		
12/31/96	Microsoft Word for Windows	Zane	4	$25,000		
12/15/96	Microsoft Excel for Windows	Paulson	4	$39,000		

Figure Sim-4 A sample Budget worksheet.

Production Costs Budget

Title	Number of Pages	Copyediting	Index Compilation	Project Management	Proofreading	Software QA	Production Programming	Video/Audio Production	Multimedia Production	Total Production Costs
Microsoft Windows	475	$950	$713	$2375	$950	$475	$475	$713	$380	$7013
WordPerfect Presentation	680	1360	1020	3400	1360	680	680	1020	544	10064
Microsoft Word for Windows	525	1050	788	2625	1050	525	525	788	420	7771
Microsoft Excel for Windows	535	1070	803	2675	1070	535	535	803	428	7919
Mastering and Using Microsoft Office	682	1364	1023	3410	1364	682	682	1023	546	10094
Total Costs		5794	4347	14485	5794	2897	2897	4347	2318	42879

Task Four

1. Create a combination chart on a separate chart sheet showing all production costs, except Project Management costs, by category in columns. Show the Project Management costs as a line chart on the same chart sheet.

2. Edit the chart text and data series colors as appropriate to make the chart more attractive and interesting.

3. Edit the plot area to make the printed chart easier to read.

4. Save the workbook.

5. Print the chart sheet.

Your printed worksheets and chart sheet should look similar to Figures Sim-3, Sim-4, and Sim-5.

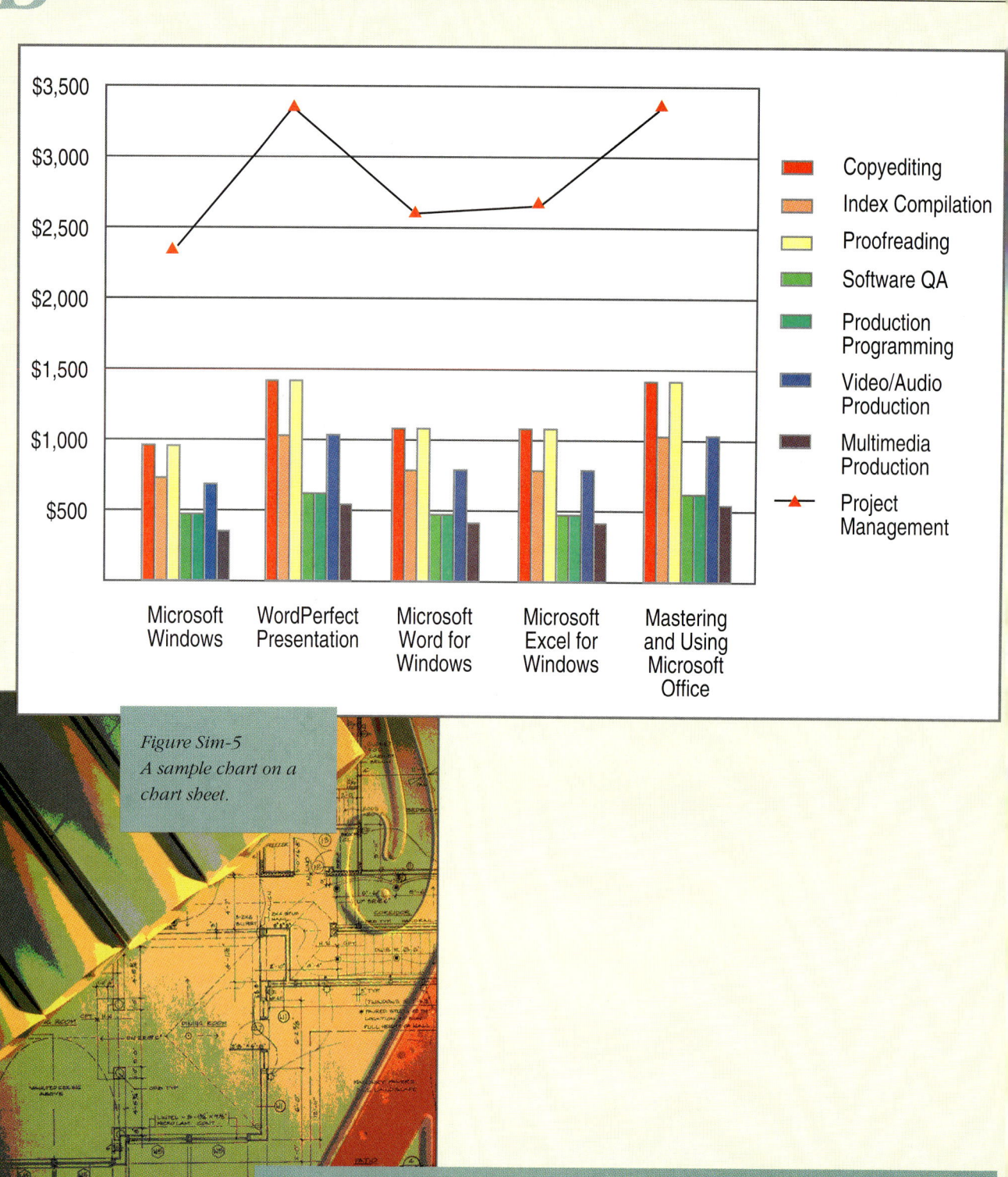

Mastering and Using Microsoft Office Professional

*Figure Sim-5
A sample chart on a chart sheet.*

Microsoft Excel enables you to generate professional-looking graphs quickly and easily.

Business Simulation: Part Two

B

Microsoft Office enables you to compile and integrate large quantities of information in a variety of formats. The ability to move seamlessly among the integrated programs is a powerful aid to communication.

B

Mastering and Using Microsoft Office Professional

The staff at CTI uses the Microsoft Office applications to enhance their overall productivity by improving the effectiveness of internal and external communications. Letters, memos, reports, and presentations are prepared quickly and easily using Word, Excel, PowerPoint, and Access. The Internet and the World Wide Web provide access to information and widespread opportunities for communication for CTI employees and their customers.

Business Simulation: Part Three

Creating Exciting Presentations with PowerPoint

Titles in Production
- Microsoft Windows
- WordPerfect Presentation
- Microsoft Word for Windows
- Microsoft Excel for
- Mastering and Us

MIS Team
- DeVilla Williams
  Managing Editor
- Lisa Strite
  Product Manager
- Richard Keaveny
  Associate Prod. Mgr
- Samantha Smith
  Editorial Assistant

10/30/96

Course Technology, Inc.

MIS Team
Production Meeting

10/30/96

Lisa, the product manager, will present a slide show presentation to the MIS Team that will include an overview of team members and their respective responsibilities, a discussion of the books currently in production, and a review of estimated production costs for these books.

Figure Sim-6
Slide shows are an effective way to communicate information and ideas to a group.

Mastering and Using Microsoft Office Professional

You will create the presentation in PowerPoint. The presentation will include a title slide, a slide with a list of the MIS Team members, a slide with a list of the books in production taken from the Summary worksheet, two slides with the Summary worksheet data and Summary worksheet embedded chart copied from the Excel SIMCOSTS.XLS workbook, and a blank slide at the end of the presentation.

Figure Sim-7 A sample Notes page.

Task Five

1. Create a new, blank presentation.
2. Create a title slide for the presentation.
3. Create a text and clip art slide listing the MIS Team members and including an appropriate clip art picture.
4. Create a bullet slide listing the book titles in production.
5. Copy the Summary worksheet data title, author, and Total Plant$ to a blank slide.
6. Copy the Summary worksheet embedded chart to a blank slide.
7. Apply a template to the presentation.

Business Simulation: Part Three

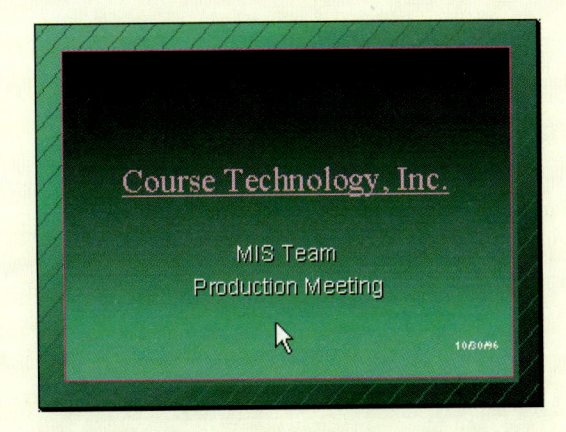

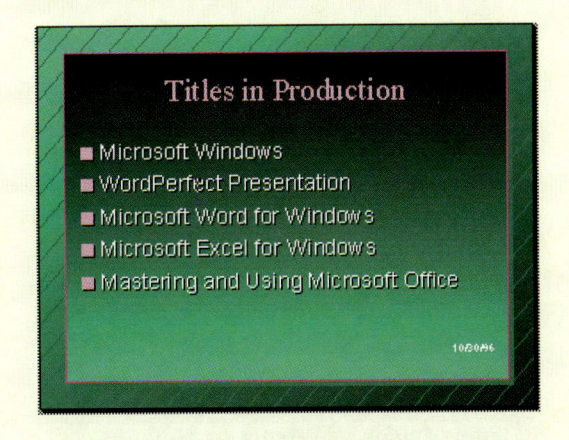

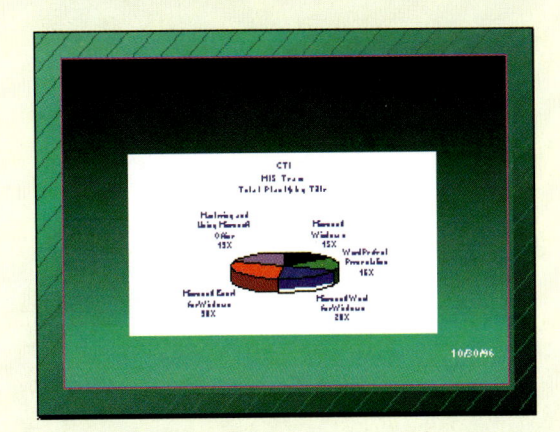

Figure Sim-8 Sample Audience Handout page made from a Slide Presentation. Handouts are a way to remind an audience of the key points that you discussed.

Mastering and Using Microsoft Office Professional

8. Modify the Slide Master to include the date.
9. Apply Build and Transition effects to the slides as appropriate.
10. Create Notes pages and add appropriate notes.
11. Create Audience Handout pages (6 slides per page) for the presentation.
12. Save the presentation using the name SIM.PPT.
13. Print the presentation, Notes pages, and Audience Handout.

Your first three slides should look similar to Figure Sim-6; your Notes pages should look similar to Figure Sim-7; your Audience Handout page should look similar to Figure Sim-8.

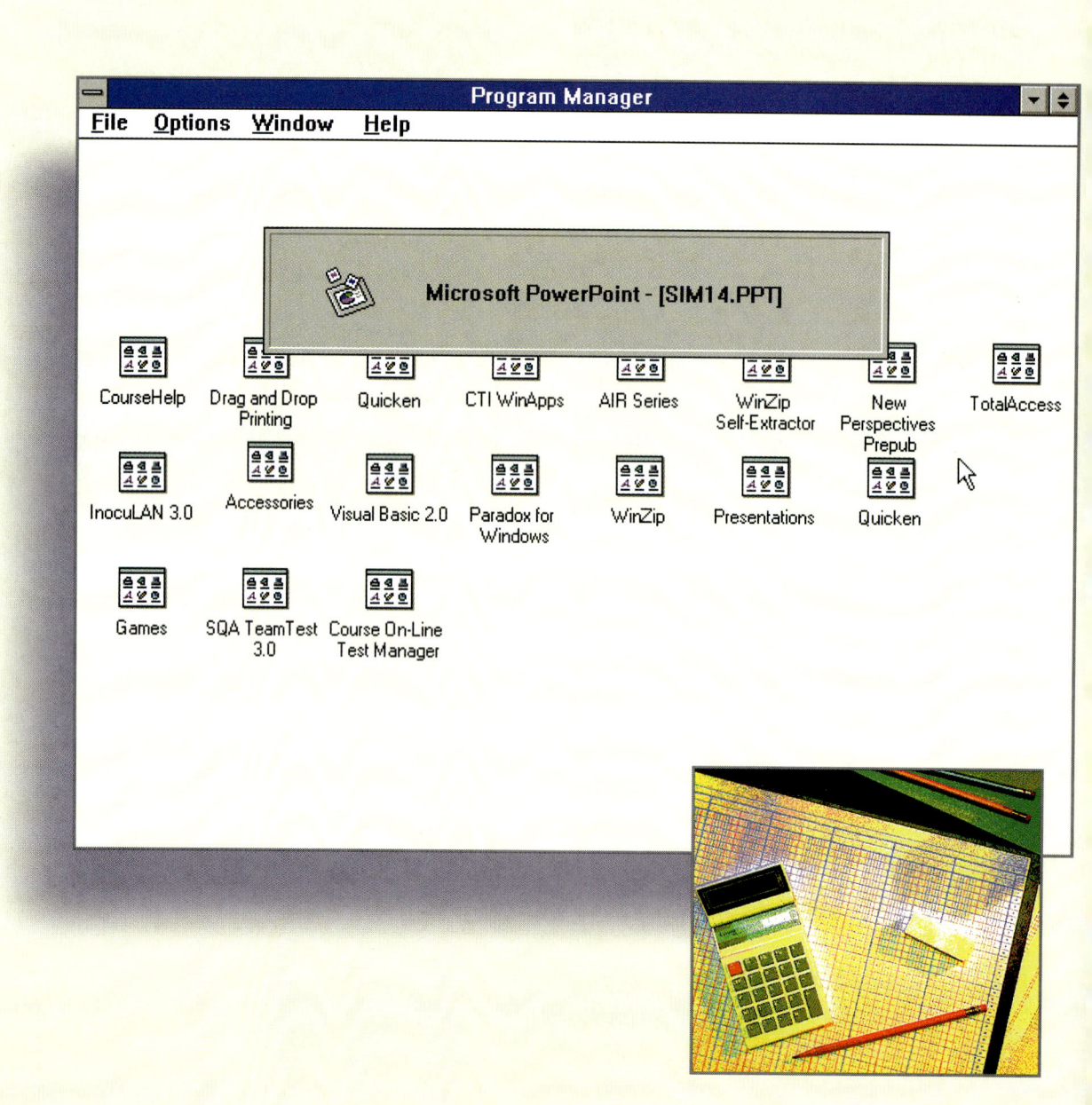

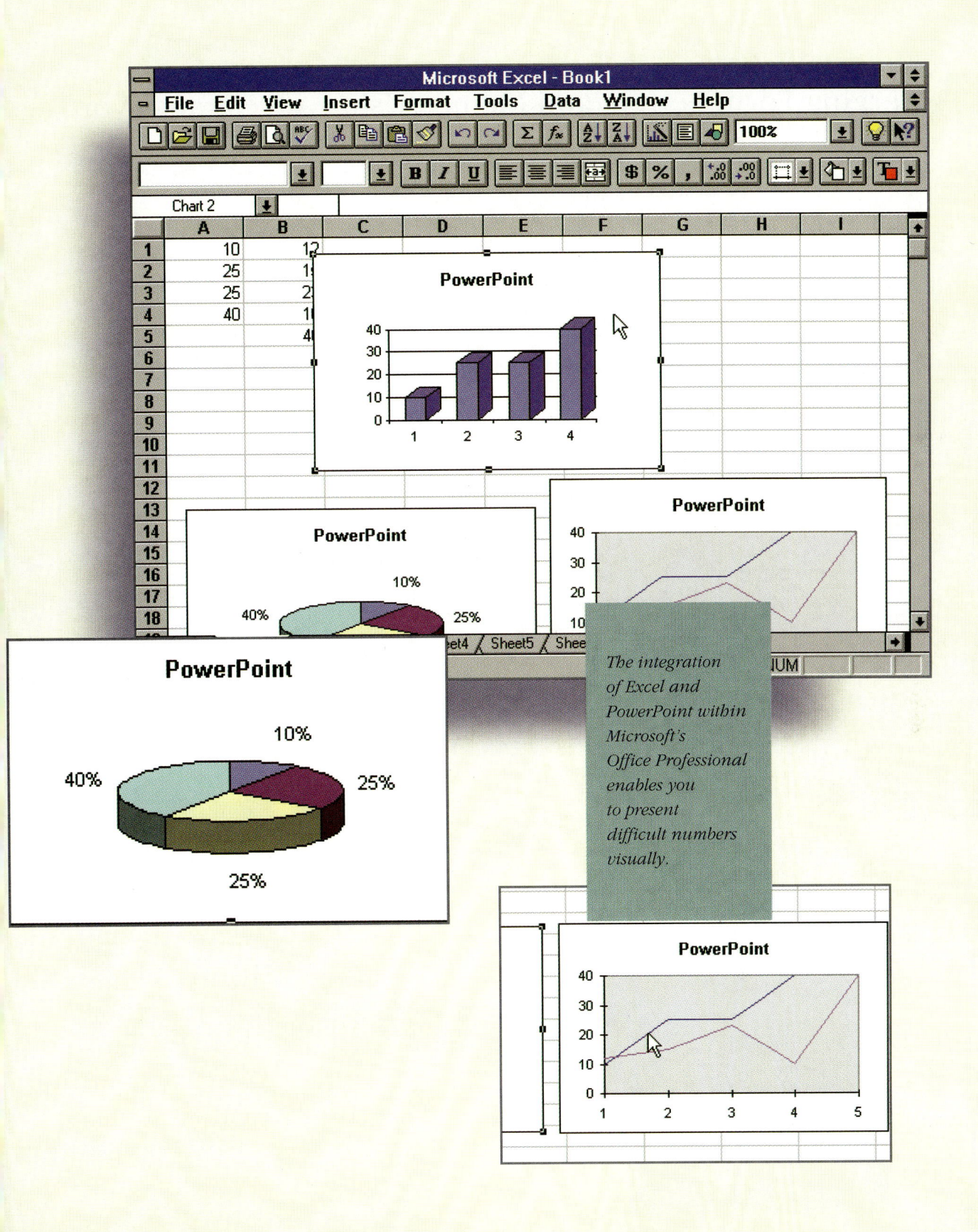

Business Simulation: Part Three

B

The integration of Excel and PowerPoint within Microsoft's Office Professional enables you to present difficult numbers visually.

Mastering and Using Microsoft Office Professional

Merging Form Letters and Memos Using Access and Word

You will send an interoffice memo to all MIS Team members from the product manager advising them of the production meeting that will be held next Tuesday at 9:00 A.M. in the conference room.

MEMORANDUM

DATE: October 30, 1996
TO: [Names]
FROM: [Names]
RE: [Subject]
CC: [Names]

[Type your memo text here]

Figure Sim-9
A fast way to create an interoffice memorandum is to use one of Word's three Memo Templates. You can merge an interoffice memo created with a Memo Template with names and addresses maintained in an Access database.

Business Simulation: Part Three

Task Six

1. Compose a memo using one of Word's Memo Templates advising MIS Team members of the date, time, and content of the Production Meeting.
2. Query the Team Members list in the Access CTI database to list only members of the MIS Team. Do not include Lisa Strite's record in the query. The CTI.MDB database file is located on the student disk.
3. Merge the query with the memo.
4. Save the memo main document using the name SIM2.DOC.
5. Preview the merge.
6. Print the merged memos.

Your memo should look similar to Figure Sim-10.

MEMORANDUM

DATE: January 15, 1996
TO: DeVilla Williams
              Managing Editor
FROM: Lisa Strite
RE: Production Meeting

There will be a meeting next Tuesday, at 9:00 A.M. in the conference room to discuss the alignment of new responsibilities and production costs for books currently in production.

Please contact Samanta Smith if you cannot attend the meeting.

Figure Sim-10 A sample of the merged memo.

B

Mastering and Using Microsoft Office Professional

MEMORANDUM

DATE: October 30, 1996
TO: [Names]
FROM: [Names]
RE: [Subject]
CC: [Names]
          [Type your memo text here]

Business memos (short for memorandums) are a form of communication used within a company or organization to provide information, make a request, or recommend an action. The format of a memo is designed for easy distribution, quick reading, and efficient filing.

MEMORANDUM

DATE: January 15, 1996
TO: DeVilla Williams
          Managing Editor
FROM: Lisa Strite
RE: Production Meeting

There will be a meeting next Tuesday, at 9:00 A.M. in the conference room to discuss the alignment of new responsibilities and production costs for books currently in production.

Please contact Samanta Smith if you cannot attend the meeting.

Business Simulation: Part Four

Accessing the Internet and the World Wide Web

Lisa has asked you to access the CTI home page on the World Wide Web and save to a diskette some information related to the new materials available for Windows 95 products. This information then will be included in a letter to the sales and marketing managers. Because you are unfamiliar with the Internet, Lisa has prepared a brief tutorial on using the Internet and the World Wide Web. You will complete this tutorial before you begin the next task.

Overview

The Internet is a group of interactive computer networks connected with data lines that enable users to transfer information between locations and to communicate with other users around the world. Today millions of people use the Internet to shop for goods and services, listen to music, view artwork, conduct research, get stock quotes, keep up to date with current events, and send electronic mail (e-mail) to other Internet users.

The World Wide Web, also referred to as WWW, W3, or the Web, is a group of interconnected hypertext links on the Internet. A Web site is any computer on the Web that contains hypermedia files accessed by hypertext links. The hypermedia files stored at Web sites are called documents or Web pages. A Web site may have multiple Web pages; however, the first page for a Web site is a specially designed page called the home page. All other pages at a Web site usually are accessed through the home page.

Using Netscape Navigator 1.2 to Access the Web

Netscape Navigator, created by Netscape Communications Corporation, is a graphical browser or interface that makes accessing the World Wide Web easier.

Tutorial Objectives

→ Start Netscape

→ Identify the components of the Netscape window

→ Browse the Web

→ Save information discovered on the Web

→ Print a Web page

→ Identify other Web services and resources

In This Simulation

It is assumed the Netscape home page will appear whenever you double-click the Netscape program icon. Many businesses and universities display their custom home page at this point. If necessary, you can display the Netscape home page by typing

http://www.netscape.com/

in the URL box.

Starting Netscape

First, display the Windows Program Manager and the Netscape group window. Although not required, all other application windows should be closed for this tutorial.

Mastering and Using Microsoft Office Professional

To start Netscape:

Double-click the Netscape program icon in the Netscape group window

The Welcome to Netscape home page appears (URLs are discussed in more detail in the next section of this tutorial).

Maximize the Netscape window, if necessary. You now are connected to Netscape Communication Corporation's Web site. Your screen should look similar to Figure Sim-11.

Identifying the Components of the Netscape Window

Figure Sim-11 shows the components of the Netscape window.

Title Bar
The title bar contains the Control-menu box, the name of the application, the Welcome to Netscape message, and the Minimize and Maximize or Restore buttons.

Menu Bar
The menu bar contains the commands you use to access Netscape features, such as saving Web pages, sending e-mail, managing bookmarks, selecting Netscape options, and accessing Internet services.

Toolbar
The toolbar is located under the menu bar and contains buttons that represent commonly used commands. The toolbar buttons are shortcuts to performing menu commands.

Figure Sim-11

URL
The Universal Resource Locator (URL) is the unique address of a Web site. A URL consists of the protocol, the domain name, and the path of the Web site. A protocol is a set of rules or a standard for communications, the domain name is the host computer, and the path specifies where to find the host computer.

Directory Buttons
The directory buttons are located under the URL text box. Use the directory buttons to display links of new or popular Web sites, to display Netscape documentation, to search the Web, to display a directory of Web resources, and to contact newsgroups.

Status Indicator
The status indicator is the Netscape Communications Corporation logo and is animated while a Web page is being retrieved.

Content Area
The content area is the portion of the Netscape window where the Web page is displayed.

Status Message Area
The status message area displays the URL that will be used to retrieve a Web page and other messages indicating the status of the retrieval process.

Business Simulation: Part Four

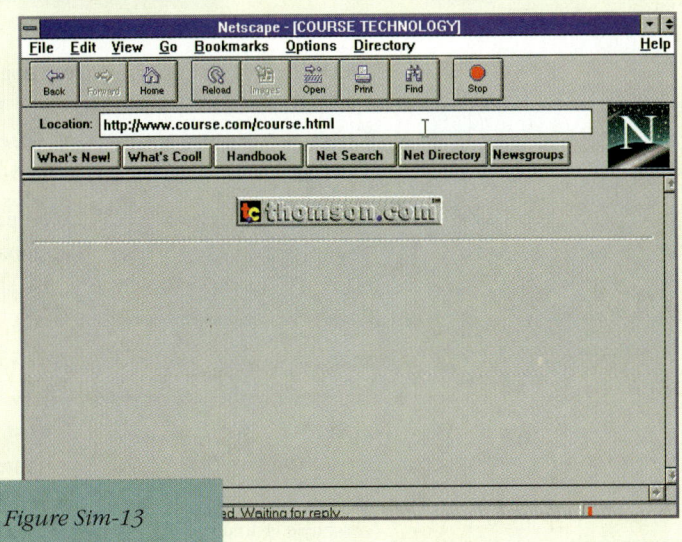

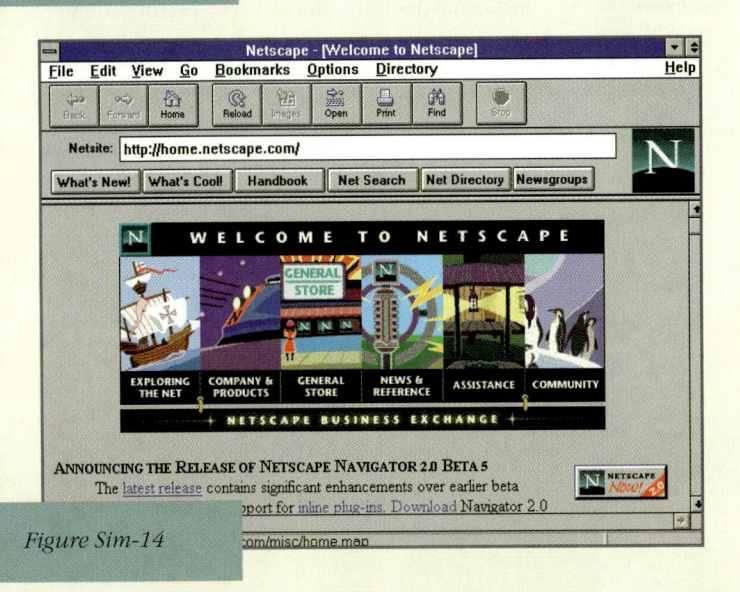

Figure Sim-12

Figure Sim-13

Figure Sim-14

Progress Bar

The progress bar provides information about the Web page retrieval progress.

Scroll Bars

The vertical and horizontal scroll bars enable you to view more of a retrieved Web page.

Browsing the Web

You can begin browsing the Web at the Netscape home page. You can use the What's New! and What's Cool! directory buttons to display some of the newer and more popular Web page links. These links are updated frequently by Netscape Communications Corporation and may change daily.

One method of accessing a Web page is to type the URL of a Web page in the URL text box. To access the CTI home page:

Select   the contents of the URL text box

Type   http://www.course.com/course.html

You must follow the syntax and punctuation of the URL exactly. Notice the colon, slashes, and periods are required punctuation. Your screen should look similar to Figure Sim-12.

To continue:

Press   the ENTER key

Netscape begins retrieving the CTI home page. The Stop button on the toolbar changes to red, the Status Indicator is animated, a message appears in the Status Message Area, and the progress of the retrieval is displayed in the Progress Bar. Your screen should look similar to Figure Sim-13.

After the CTI home page is retrieved, a message appears in the Status Message Area stating that the retrieval is complete. The Stop button on the toolbar returns to gray, and the Status Indicator activity stops. Your screen should look similar to Figure Sim-14.

You can use the vertical scroll bar to view the entire CTI home page. Scroll to view the Microsoft Windows 95 picture.

Using Hypertext Links on a Web Page

Hypertext links can be words or pictures. The colored and underlined text, Netscape, in Figure Sim-14 is a hypertext link to the Netscape home page. The Microsoft Windows 95 picture is a hypertext link to the CTI Microsoft Windows 95 Web page.

User Tip

Occasionally, you may experience difficulty retrieving a Web page. For example, you may retrieve the text but not the graphics. Web pages may be deleted or moved resulting in an error message when you try to retrieve them. If the page does not retrieve properly with all text and graphics, click the Reload button on the toolbar to repeat the process.

In This Simulation

One important advantage of using the Internet and the Web is that Web pages are constantly being updated with new information and improved graphics. However, because Web pages are dynamic, you may find it necessary to modify the following instructions on using Hypertext links and saving information found on a Web page. If the links used in the next sections are not available, substitute other links found on the CTI home page.

To go to the Microsoft Windows 95 page:

Move   the mouse pointer to the Microsoft Windows 95 picture

The mouse pointer's shape changes and becomes a pointing hand indicating a hypertext link. The status message area displays the URL of the linked page.

Click   the Microsoft Windows 95 picture

The Microsoft Windows 95 page begins to display. After the retrieval of the Web page is complete, your screen should look similar to Figure Sim-15.

You can stop the retrieval of a Web page by choosing the Stop Loading command on the Go menu or by clicking the Stop button (when it is red) on the toolbar.

While you are displaying different Web pages, Netscape maintains a History list of the Web sites you visit. This History list is empty each time you start Netscape. As you retrieve a Web page, Netscape adds the URL to the list and maintains the list in the order you retrieved the pages. You can use the Back and Forward buttons on the toolbar to move through a short History list and to redisplay Web pages. To display the entire History list, choose the Go command on the menu bar. The Web page titles in the History list are displayed at the bottom of the Go menu. A check mark is displayed beside the name of the currently displayed page. To return to a previously viewed Web page, click the page title in the History list.

To return to the CTI home page:

Choose   Go

Click   COURSE TECHNOLOGY

The CTI home page redisplays. Scroll to the top of the page.

Figure Sim-15

Business Simulation: Part Four

Using the Bookmarks Feature to Save the URL of a Favorite Web Page

Suppose you want to save the URL of a favorite Web page so you do not have to type the URL each time you want to access the page. You can create a bookmark consisting of the title and URL of the page. You can easily maintain bookmarks by adding or deleting them with the Bookmarks command on the menu bar.

To create a bookmark for the CTI home page:

Choose   Bookmarks

Choose   Add Bookmark

The Bookmarks menu closes and the title of the CTI home page is added to the end of the Bookmark List. If the Bookmark List is long, you may have to choose More Bookmarks. This will display the Bookmark List as a series of files in a folder. You then can scroll to the end of the Bookmark List to see the added bookmark. You can also display the Bookmark List dialog box with the View Bookmarks command on the Bookmarks menu.

To view the Bookmark List:

Choose   Bookmarks

Choose   View Bookmarks

The Bookmark List appears. You can add a bookmark, visit the Web page selected in the Bookmark List, search for a string of characters, delete a bookmark, and show the properties of the selected Web page. You can also view the Bookmark List in the Browser. The Bookmarks become hypertext links to those pages.

Scroll to the bottom of the list of bookmarks. Notice the CTI home page title, COURSE TECHNOLOGY, is now added to the end of the list. Your screen should look similar to Figure Sim-16.

After viewing the Bookmark List, close the Bookmark List dialog box.

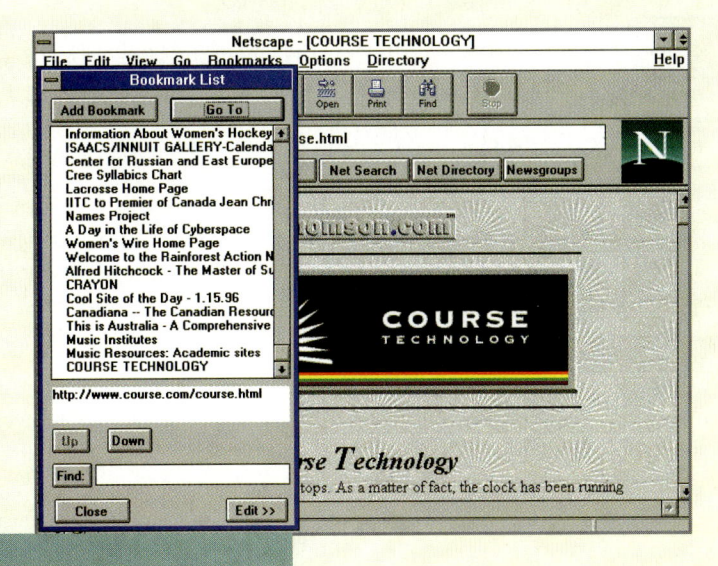

Figure Sim-16

To return to the Netscape home page:

Click   the Netscape icon in the upper-right corner

The Netscape home page redisplays.

Mastering and Using Microsoft Office Professional

To access the CTI home page using a bookmark:

Choose	Bookmarks
Click	COURSE TECHNOLOGY
	or
Choose	Bookmarks
Choose	View Bookmarks
Scroll	to the end of the Bookmark List
Double-click	COURSE TECHNOLOGY
Click	the Close command button

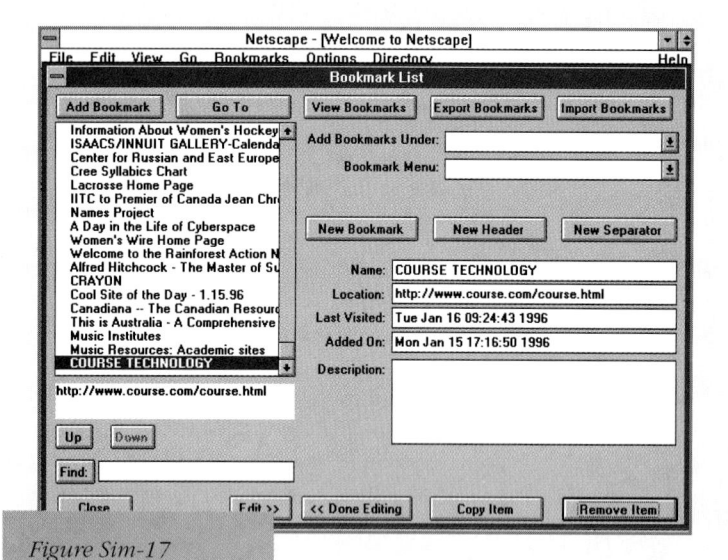

The CTI home page redisplays.

To display properties:

Choose	Bookmarks
Choose	View Bookmarks
Scroll	to view the end of the Bookmark List
Choose	Item
Click	the Edit >> command button
Choose	Properties

The Bookmark List dialog box expands to display additional editing features and information about the CTI home page. It also lists when the site was last visited and when the bookmark was added. Your screen should look similar to Figure Sim-17.

Figure Sim-17

Because Web sites change daily, you may want to delete a bookmark. You can delete bookmarks with the View Bookmarks command on the Bookmarks menu.

To delete the CTI bookmark and close the Bookmark List dialog box:

Verify	the CTI home page is selected in the bookmark list
Choose	Edit
Choose	Delete

The CTI bookmark is removed from the list of bookmarks. You can display the Bookmarks menu to verify the CTI bookmark is deleted.

User Tip

It is a good idea to save your Bookmark List to a diskette. You can then take your personal Bookmark List to any computer running Netscape and use your bookmarks by restoring your list from diskette.

Saving Web Pages

You can save information from Web pages, or save entire Web pages, for future reference. You also can save just a picture from a Web page. Suppose you want to save the Microsoft Windows 95 picture from the CTI home page so you can use it in a letter to the sales and marketing managers.

> **User Tip**
>
> *You also can copy and paste text from a Web page to a Windows application by first selecting the text on the Web page and then choosing the Copy command on the Edit menu. The text is placed on the Clipboard. Then switch to the Windows application, such as Word, and choose the Paste command on the Edit menu or click the Paste button on the Standard toolbar.*

To save the Microsoft Windows 95 picture:

Scroll	to view the Microsoft Windows 95 picture
Move	the mouse pointer to the Microsoft Windows 95 picture
Click	the right mouse button to display a shortcut menu
Choose	Save this Image as....
Type	CTIPICT.TIF in the File Name dialog box. Switch to the appropriate disk drive and directory.
Click	the OK command button

The picture is saved and can be displayed in documents created with a program such as Word.

Printing a Web Page

You can print both the text and graphics associated with a Web page by choosing the Print command on the File menu or by clicking the Print button on the toolbar. Suppose you want to print the CTI home page. To print the CTI home page:

Scroll	to the top of the page
Click	the Print button on the toolbar

The Print dialog box appears. Your screen should look like Figure Sim-18.

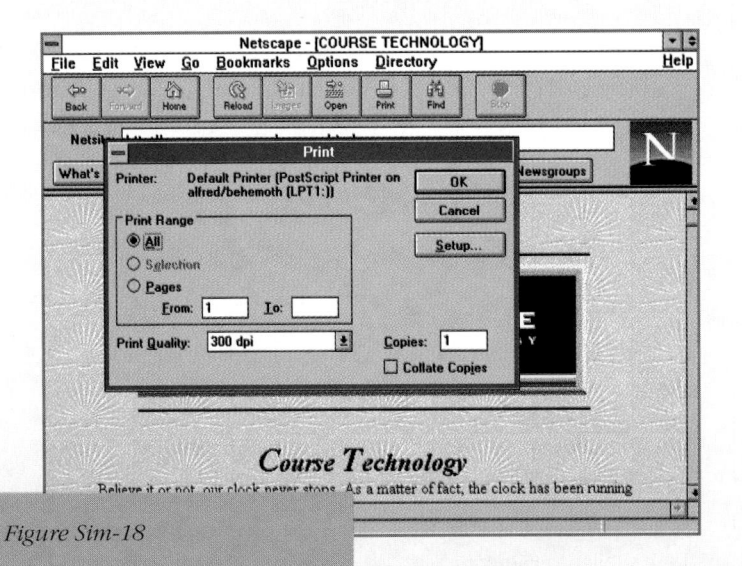

By default Netscape will print the entire Web page document. You can also choose to print a portion of the page, or selected multiple pages. You also specify the number of copies to print and change the printer setup in this dialog box.

Return to the Netscape home page. Exit Netscape.

Figure Sim-18

Sending Electronic Mail

You can send and receive electronic mail (e-mail) using Netscape. Before you can send an e-mail message to someone, you must first know their e-mail address. An e-mail address consists of a username followed by the @ sign, and the Internet address or hostname of the computer where the person's e-mail account is located. For example, in the e-mail address, ryxzt@aol.com, the username is ryxzt and the hostname is aol.com. You must also set up your own e-mail address in the Netscape Preferences dialog box before you can send any e-mail.

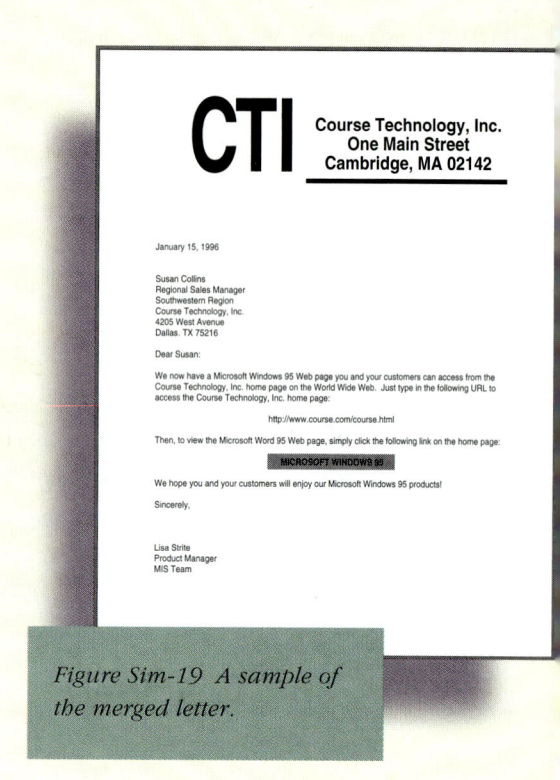

Figure Sim-19 A sample of the merged letter.

Using Internet Information

Now that you have completed the Netscape tutorial, you are ready to use the information that you saved from the CTI home page.

Task Seven

1. Compose a letter to the national and regional sales managers advising them that the CTI home page now contains a link to a Microsoft Windows 95 page.
2. Use the SHELL.DOC document on the student disk for the letterhead.
3. Insert the Windows 95 picture saved from the CTI home page.
4. Query the Sales and Marketing table in the Access CTI database for names and addresses of the national and regional sales managers.
5. Merge the query with the letter.
6. Save the letter main document using the name SIM3.DOC.
7. Preview the merge.
8. Print the merged letters.
9. Merge the query with a new document to create 5160-Address mailing labels for the letters.
10. Preview the merge.
11. Print the labels on plain paper.

Your letter should look similar to Figure Sim-19. Your labels should look similar to Figure Sim-20.

Figure Sim-20 A sample of the merged labels.

Index

A

Absolute cell references E53-E55

Access, definition O4

Active cell E5, E6

Advanced Filter E125

Assumptions E31, E33, E57

AutoFill E28-E29

AutoFilter E118-E124

AutoSum feature E41

C

Cell, definition E5

Chart
    creating a chart on a chart sheet E78-E81
    creating an embedded chart E81-E83
    formatting charts E85-E96
    identifying parts of a chart E76-E78
    toolbar E80

ChartWizard E76

Closing a workbook E12-E13

Column headings E5

Column widths E31-E32

Control-menu box
    application O12
    document O12

Copy O4
    absolute cell references E53
    drag-and-drop E50, E160
    Excel formulas E36
    Excel worksheet to PowerPoint O26
    Excel worksheet to Word O22, E150
    formats E52

Cut O24
    drag-and-drop E50, E160

D

Database, Excel list E109

Destination or client E154, E161

Dialog box, definition O20

E

Embed O4
    Excel worksheet into Word document E154-E161

Excel, definition O4
    assumptions E31, E33, E57
    charts E76-E96
    closing a workbook E12
    column widths E31-E32
    creating a workbook E8
    designing a workbook and worksheets E18-E23
    editing worksheet data E10
    formatting worksheets E41-E44, E46-E50, E51-E52
    grouping worksheets E100-E101

1

inserting new worksheets E103
linking workbooks E106
new workbook E13
opening an existing workbook E14
Personal Macro Workbook E140-E144
printing E12, E64-E71
range names E72
saving a workbook E11-E12
using multiple worksheets E101-E103
window E4-E6

Exiting Excel E15

F

Filename O21, E11-E12

Footers E67

Format Painter E52

Formatting Excel E33, E41-E44, E46-E53

Formula bar E5

Formulas
   3-D references E104
   copying E36
   entering E33-E36
   order of precedence E35
   relative cell location E35
   shortcut menu E40

Functions E39

Function Wizard E40

H

Hardware O8

Headers E67

Help feature O28-O29

K

Keyboard, using O8
   Excel E7

L

Link, definition O4
   Excel chart to Word E163
   Excel worksheet to Word E161, E163
   workbooks E106-E107

Lists, definition E109
   adding records E116
   creating subtotals E128
   Data Form E111, E117
   editing records E116
   filtering E118-E127
   finding records E117-E118
   sorting E114-E116
   subtotals E128

M

Macro, Excel, definition E133
   assigning to Tools menu E145
   creating E134
   editing E138-E140
   executing E137
   Personal Macro Workbook E140-E144
   shortcut keys E144

Mail, definition O4

Margins, Excel E64, E66

Maximize button O12

Menu bar O12

Menu method O19

Index

Microsoft Office Manager menu O34-O35, O39

Microsoft Office Professional, definition O4

Minimize button O12

Module sheet E134

MOM toolbar O9-O10, O34-O35, O37-O39

Mouse, using O8
   Excel E6-E7

N

Name box E5

O

Object E163-E164

Office, definition O4

Opening a workbook E13-E14

P

Page breaks E70

Paste O4, E36

Personal Macro Workbook E140

PowerPoint, definition O4

Printing
   embedded chart E83-E84
   embedded chart and worksheet E84-E85
   multiple worksheets E105
   previewing a worksheet E64
   worksheet E12, E64-E67, E69-E70

R

Range O23, E29-E30, E72

Restore button O12

Rounding errors E44-E46

Row headings E5

S

Saving a workbook E11-E12

Scroll bars O13, E6

Scrolling buttons E5

Select All button E30

Selecting cells E7, E29-E30

Sheet tabs E5, E22

Shortcut menu E40

Sizing handles O24, E155

Sorting Excel lists E114

Source or server E154, E161

Spelling feature, Excel E57

Split box E6

Spreadsheets (see worksheets)

Status bar E6

Subtotals E128

Summary Info dialog box O25

Supplies O8

Switching to another Office application O9-O10, E154, E160

T

Tip of the Day O11

Title bar O11

Toolbar O12
   Excel E4, E80

Toolbar method O19

ToolTip O13

U

Undo feature E10

W

Wildcard characters E124

Window
   common elements O11
   Excel E4, E76-E78
   splitting into panes E55

Word, definition O4

Word processing O4

Workbook
   closing E12
   design E18-E23
   linking E106
   new E13
   opening E14
   Personal Macro E140-E144
   saving E11-E12

Worksheets, definition O4
   assumptions E31, E33, E57
   charts E76-E96
   column widths E31-E32
   creating E8
   editing E10
   formatting E41-E44, E46-E50, E51-E52
   grouping E100-E101
   inserting E103
   layout E18-E23
   printing E12, E64-E71
   range names E72
   rounding errors E44-E46
   titles E26-E30
   using multiple E101-E103